SHORT PLAYS OF
THEATRE CLASSICS

Selected and Edited by

AURAND HARRIS

ANCHORAGE PRESS
Post Office Box 8067
New Orleans, Louisiana 70182

DEDICATED
to
MY GOOD SAMARITANS:

George Eells
Nancy Swortzell
Lowell Swortzell

SHORT PLAYS OF
THEATRE
CLASSICS

Selected and Edited by
AURAND HARRIS

Forewords

A high percentage of the one thousand plays produced annually in the Texas One-Act Play Contest are adaptations of theatre classics. Quality adaptations — forty minutes — are in heavy demand for both junior high and high school.

Good directors seek good scripts and most find classics, adapted for classroom and contest use, such as these in SHORT PLAYS OF THEATRE CLASSICS, excellent material for secondary school theatre programs.

LYNN MURRAY Director
Texas State Drama
Austin, Texas

My group of Senior Citizens enjoy reading aloud and performing in great plays of the past; but, for many reasons, we can use only mini versions. Our last success was FASHION from SHORT PLAYS OF THEATRE CLASSICS.

BETTY BOBP Director
Harwich, Massachusetts

With the growing interest in quality theatre in this community and elsewhere, public library users are requesting more play titles to read and produce. Teachers and university professors are especially interested in condensed versions of outstanding plays. I am sure SHORT PLAYS OF THEATRE CLASSICS will have a wide circulation.

JUDY MILLER
Central Library
Public Library
Indianapolis, Indiana

Here is a complete repertory of world drama from the Middle Ages to the present century, selected and edited to introduce readers and players to twelve of our most beloved plays. From Shakespeare to Shaw, from Molière to Edmund Rostand and from Oliver Goldsmith to Oscar Wilde, the plays in these special acting editions now are accessible for classroom use, for school and community productions and for the sheer pleasure of understanding how a great play speaks anew to each age. They have been given expert attention by an editor who is himself both a distinguished playwright and experienced director. Because this volume will make readers want to see these plays performed, our theatres and their audiences will be all the richer when they come to life. Meantime, they are here to be treasured on every page.

Lowell Swortzell
Professor of Educational Theatre
New York University

Introduction

Here is an anthology of twelve theatre classics — plays from different countries, different periods, reflecting different cultures, written in different styles. All of these plays have been critically acclaimed popular successes, and remain of interest to both modern readers and modern audiences.

This volume is assembled to serve librarians, teachers, play directors, actors and students with short versions of theatre classics. Librarians whose budgets have been cut can offer a larger sampling of important literature of world drama. Teachers can use this anthology to introduce and stimulate interest in a wide range of classic drama in abridged form. Actors who need scenes for classes, auditions, and performances will find these famous characters and dramatic moments highlighted in mini versions. Directors who do not have the facilities to give full and elaborate productions can easily produce condensed versions of plays of quality. Students can be introduced to these stage classics, whetting their interest to read more full length historical plays.

One of the big demands for short plays in America lies in high school one-act play contests. Most of the fifty states conduct such contests. In Texas alone, for instance, one thousand high schools enter the state meet each year. A number of these abridged plays have been popular winners in these contests.

Each of these plays is introduced by a brief summary about the playwright, the period, and the dramatic style of the script. Several of these short versions have been included in literature collections, including the MacMillan new Literature Series, and the Scott Foresman new Eighth Grade Reader. One, A TOBY SHOW, was created with the assistance of a playwrighting grant from the National Endowment for the Arts.

Contents

The Second Shepherd's Play
Adapted by Aurand Harris

Introduction

The Second Shepherd's Play, original title: the *Secunda Pastorum*, is generally considered to be the best example of comedy in early religious drama. The plot is from the Bible, the second chapter of the Gospel according to Luke, verses 6–16, with a side-plot of Mak stealing a sheep, a humorous scene which introduces an element of realistic low comedy (perhaps a daring innovation at the time) but one which the fifteenth century English audiences were beginning to demand.

To understand medieval drama, a look at the preceding years is necessary. European theatre was weakened by the invasion of the barbarians and then exterminated by the churchmen. By the middle of the sixth century, theatre as such was extinct. Then, ironically enough, dramatic activities were reborn in the church itself. By the ninth century, the Mass was embellished with antiphonal singing. Later, words (dialogue) were added, with priests impersonating biblical characters. As episodes increased in number, the drama moved from the choir down through the nave of the church with temporary "multiple settings." The performers moved from one setting to the next.

By the thirteenth century the drama included passages of the vernacular and was being performed outside the church. As more and more elaborate scenes were added, more performers were needed and expenses accelerated. This resulted in the local workmen's guilds producing the cycles of playlets, from the Creation to the Judgment, as the annual "miracle play." The system of "multiple settings" was used in some towns. In others, the plays were performed on a procession of wagons (stages). Each one stopped at a designated place, that playlet was performed, and then moved on to the next stop. *The Second Shepherd's Play* was probably performed on a wagon with three areas – the fields, Mak's house, and the manger.

Little is known about the author of any of the thirty-two plays believed to have been performed by the guilds in the town of Wakefield about 1450. These scripts are known as "The Towneley plays" because the Towneley family preserved the manuscripts. There are two plays dramatizing the visit of the shepherds to the manger. The second one, far superior, and included here, gets its title because it was the second of the shepherd's plays. The original play is written in a peculiar form of a nine-line stanza with internal rhymes as well as rhymes at the end of lines. For modern audiences, the verse form has been modified for this short version.

The miracle play helped to give drama a re-birth in England. It accustomed audiences to plays spoken in verse. It freed drama of the unities of time, place and action. All of these helped to prepare the way and to influence the next century, the Golden Age of Shakespeare.

CAST

FIRST SHEPHERD, *Coll*
SECOND SHEPHERD, *Gib*
THIRD SHEPHERD, *Daw*
MAK, *a sheep-stealer*
GILL, *his wife*
ANGEL
MARY

The Second Shepherd's Play

(*A field. FIRST SHEPHERD enters.*)

FIRST SHEPHERD: Lord, but these weathers are cold; And I am ill wrapped.
I am near numb, so long have I napped;
My legs they fold, my fingers are chapped.
The rich land-owners on us they thrive.
It were a great wonder that we stay alive.

It does me good, as I walk thus by mine own,
Of this world for to talk in manner of moan.
To my sheep will I stalk, and sit on a stone
For I trust, full soon,
We get more company ere it be noon.

SECOND SHEPHERD: (*Enters. He does not see FIRST SHEPHERD.*)
Blessings upon us, such days I seldom have seen.
Lord, these weathers are spiteous, and the winds full keen.
And the frost so hideous they water mine eyes.
It is not all easy. I speak no lies.

But as far as I've been, or yet as I go,
We men who are wed suffer a great woe.
Some men will have two wives,
And some men three.
Some are grieved that have any.
Woe to him that has many.

But, know what you wrought young men of wooing,
Be well ware of wedding, and think what you're doing.
"Had I known" is a thing that serves nought.
Much grief and mourning has wedding home brought.
Alas, for I have one for my wife,
Rough as a burr; tongue sharp as a knife.
She's great as a whale, full of gall that does foster.

I would I had run till I had lost her.

FIRST SHEPHERD: Look about. Full deafly ye stand there. Saw thou young Daw?

SECOND SHEPHERD: He comes.

FIRST SHEPHERD: Where?

SECOND SHEPHERD: He will tell us a lie. Best we beware.

THIRD SHEPHERD: (*Enters. He is a boy. He does not see the other shepherds.*)
Was never since Noah's flood such floods seen,
Winds and rains so rude and storms so keen —
We that walk in the nights, our cattle to keep,
We see sudden sights when other men sleep.
   (*FIRST and SECOND SHEPHERD move. He is frightened.*)
Yet — methinks — two giants! — my heart skips a beat!
Two rogues — two giants! — I meet.
Back to my sheep I will slip and go,
   (*Tip-toes away.*)
And pray I do not trip my toe.

FIRST SHEPHERD: Daw! Why and whence trot ye?

THIRD SHEPHERD: Tis my master! I knew not ye.

SECOND SHEPHERD: Where are our sheep? Blow ye the horn.

THIRD SHEPHERD: Safe they are left in the corn.
They have pasture good, they can not go wrong.

FIRST SHEPHERD: That is right. By the rood, these nights are long!
Ere we went, how I would that one gave me a song.

SECOND SHEPHERD: Let me pitch the tenory.

FIRST SHEPHERD: And the treble I bring.

THIRD SHEPHERD: Then the mean falls to me.

FIRST SHEPHERD: Together we sing.

   (*They sing. MAK enters, wearing a cape.*)

MAK: Oh, Lord, maker of the stars and all,
And of more than I can recall,
Were I in heaven where no children stirred,
Nor ranting of a wife was heard!

FIRST SHEPHERD: Who is that who pipes off tone?

MAK: A man who has no life of his own.

SECOND SHEPHERD: Mak, where hast thou gone? What tidings bring?

THIRD SHEPHERD: Mak? Then each one take heed to his thing!

FIRST SHEPHERD: What means this so late thou goes,
A rogue in the night, taking a peep,
Men will suppose thou has a good nose.
For stealing a sheep.

MAK: I am true as steel, all men wot;
But a sickness I feel, that holds me full hot;
My belly fares not well; it is out of estate.

THIRD SHEPHERD: Seldom lies the devil dead by the gate.

MAK: I am ill, fullsore;
May I stand stone-still,
If I have eat meat
This month or more.

FIRST SHEPHERD: How fares thy wife? By the hood, how fares she?

MAK: Lies lolling a-bed, calling for brew
Each year a baby she brings anew,
And some years bringeth two.

SECOND SHEPHERD: I am weary of watching sheep in the night.

THIRD SHEPHERD: I am cold. I would be near a fire burning bright.

FIRST SHEPHERD: I am tired and would sleep. Stay awake thou?

SECOND SHEPHERD: Nay, I be with you and sleep now.

(*They lie down.*)

THIRD SHEPHERD: As good a man's son am I as any of you.
But, Mak, come hither. Rest between us two.

(*Lies down.*)

MAK: I'll hear secrets ye whisper, but I'll do.
  (*Sits between them.*)
A prayer I say, on bended knee.
From my top to my toe,
Manus tuas commendo,   ("Into thy hands I commend,
Poncio Pilato;   Pontius Pilate.")
May Christ's cross cover me.
  (*He lies down. THREE SHEPHERDS snore. MAK rises.*)
Now's the time for a man that lacks what he would
To privily take from the fold what he could.
  (*Makes a magic spell around Shepherds.*)
Here about you a circle I make, as round as a moon,
Till I have done what I will; sleep ye till noon.
May ye lie stone-still till I be done.
  (*Waves hand over their heads.*)
Over your heads, my hand I run.
Out go your light. Fordo your sight!
  (*SHEPHERDS snore louder.*)
Lord, how they sleep hard, and buzz like a fly.
Was I never a shepherd, but now will I try.
Though the flock be scattered, I'll catch one.
  (*Cautiously catches a stuffed sheep.*)
Nab — grab — a prize I've won!
A fat sheep, I dare say,
A good fleece, dare I lay,
Repay when I may,
So ends my sorrow,
For this will I borrow.
  (*He takes sheep, hidden under his cape; to his house.*)
How, Gill, art thou in? Get us some light.

GILL: Who makes such a din this time of night?

MAK: Good wife, open. I bring meat to eat.

GILL: (*Opens door.*) Ah, come, my husband, my sweet.

MAK: See. In a pinch — and in my way —
I get more than they that sweat all day. (*Shows sheep.*)
I would it were slain; I would well eat.
This twelvemonth I taste not one sheep-meat.

GILL: Come they before it be slain, and hear the sheep fret —

MAK: Then might I be taken. That were a cold sweat!

GILL: A good trick have I spied, since thou can none;
Here shall we him hide till they be done —
In the cradle abide. Let me alone.
And I shall beside the sheep lie, and groan.

MAK: And I shall say thou was light
Of a male-child this night.

GILL: This is a good guise and a fair cast;
A woman's advice helps at the last.
But I fear they awake; return, go thou fast.

MAK: I'll go ere they rise, or they'll blow a cold blast.
    (*MAK returns to Shepherds.*)
Yet still sleep, these three.
In I shall creep, and be
As though I had not been he
Who stole their sheep.

    (*MAK lies down in place. FIRST SHEPHERD and SECOND SHEP-
HERD awake.*)

FIRST SHEPHERD:
Resurrex a mortunus.   ("Resurrection from the dead)
Have hold my hand.
Judas carnas dominus!   ("Judas, lord of the flesh.")
I can not well stand.

SECOND SHEPHERD: Lord, what I have slept well!
And thus I feel
As fresh as an eel;
As light, ah, ye,

As a leaf on a tree.

THIRD SHEPHERD: (*Awakes.*)
Blessing be herein! My body does quake;
My heart out of skin, thus does shake.
See you ought of Mak now?

FIRST SHEPHERD: We were up ere thou.

SECOND SHEPHERD: Man, I give God a vow
That he did not stir.
He sleeps as a kitten doth purr.

THIRD SHEPHERD: Methought, when we napped, he, in a wolf-skin
trapped a fat sheep, but made no din.

SECOND SHEPHERD: Be still! Thy dream makes thee mad.
It is but a phantom, my lad.
    (*They awaken Mak.*)
Rise, Mak, for shame! Thou liest right long.

MAK: What is this? Ah, my neck has lain wrong.
I trust I be the same.
Alack! My leg is lame.
    (*Others help him.*)
Many thanks. since yester-even,
Now by Saint Steven,
A bad dream did my head fill
That did stop my heart still!
I thought my wife, Gill, croaked full sad,
And gave birth to another child-lad!
Too many ere before she has had,
Now another she doth add!
Oh, my head!
Woe for him what numbers grow,
And there be little bread!

I must home, by your leave, to Gill, as I thought.
I pray look in my sleeve, that I steal nought.
I am loath you to grieve, or from you take ought.

    (*He leaves.*)

THIRD SHEPHERD: Go forth. Best we sought
If a sheep be naught.

FIRST SHEPHERD: We'll meet before the morn.

SECOND SHEPHERD: Where?

THIRD SHEPHERD: At the crooked thorn.

   (*They depart.*)

MAK: (*At his door.*)
Undo the door! How long shall I stand?

GILL: Who is there?

MAK: I, Mak, your husband.

GILL: Ah, Sir Guile! Let him cool his toes.
Let him attend, so he knows
Who brews, who bakes, who makes us our hose?

MAK: (*Aside.*) Day and dark thus her mouth goes.

GILL: Full woeful is a man's life
What lacks a helpful wife.
   (*Opens door.*)
What end has thou made with the shepherds, Mak?

MAK: The last word they said when I turned my back
They would look that they had their sheep, all the pack.
I think there will be trouble when they their sheep lack.
Here they will hie and peep.
"Thief!" they'll cry. "Where be the sheep?"
Quick! Thou must do as thou said.

GILL: I shall swaddle the sheep in the cradle bed.
   (*Gill puts sheep in cradle.*)
Twere better, if I helped still.
I will lie down. Come wrap me.

MAK: I will. (*Covers her.*)

GILL: Behind! Watch. Give a sign full straight
When Coll comes and his mate.
Harken well. Thou sing alone.
Thou sing "lullay" for I must groan.

(*Practices crying loudly.*)

(*Three Shepherds meet.*)

THIRD SHEPHERD: Ah, Coll, why lookest thou so bobbed?

FIRST SHEPHERD: Alas, of one sheep we have been robbed!

SECOND SHEPHERD: The devil you say!

THIRD SHEPHERD: A sheep astray!

SECOND SHEPHERD: Who should do us this foul play?

FIRST SHEPHERD: I have sought with my dogs
All Horbury bogs,
Of the fifteen we keep
Found all but one sheep.

THIRD SHEPHERD: Now believe me, if you will, iwis,
Either Mak or Gill hath done this.

FIRST SHEPHERD: Peace man, be still.
I saw when he went.
Thou slanderest him ill;
Thou ought to repent.

SECOND SHEPHERD: I will stake my life if need,
It were he, what did the deed.

THIRD SHEPHERD: Go we thither. Search about.
I shall never eat bread, till the truth is out.

SECOND SHEPHERD: Brother. Let us swear in our plight,
Until we see him in sight,
Shall we never sleep one night
Where we do another.

(*SHEPHERDS approach Mak's house. GILL begins to groan. MAK sings loudly.*)

THIRD SHEPHERD: Will ye hear how they hack? Our sire can croon.

FIRST SHEPHERD: Heard I never none sing so clear out of tune.
Call on him.

SECOND SHEPHERD: Mak, undo your door soon!

MAK: Who is that spake, as it were noon?

THIRD SHEPHERD: Good fellows what ye know and see oft.

(*SHEPHERDS enter the house.*)

MAK: I beg, sirs, speak soft.
A sick woman, in bed, lies distressed.
I had rather be dead than give her unrest.

GILL: Come not by my bed! My breath wheezes.
Each step that ye tread, my nose sneezes.

MAK: Ye have run in the mire, and are wet yet!
I shall make you a fire, if ye will sit.
I have sons, if ye knew,
Well more than a few!
Yet another is born to add to the brood.
    (*Points to cradle.*)
Ere ye go ye must take drink and some food.

SECOND SHEPHERD: Nay, meat nor drink mends not our mood.

MAK: Why, sir, tell me, is ought not good?

THIRD SHEPHERD: Our sheep were stolen as they stood.

MAK: Sirs, drink! Had I been near
Some should have felt it full dear!

FIRST SHEPHERD: Some men hold that ye were there.
And so think I, I swear.

SECOND SHEPHERD: Mak, some men propose that it were ye.

THIRD SHEPHERD: Either ye or your spouse, so say we.

MAK: If ye suppose it of Gill or of me —
Search our house, and ye will see
If I have a sheep or half,
Or if I have a cow or a calf.
And Gill, my wife, less live than dead,
Rose not, from her child-bearing bed.
I swear tis true what I say,
Or this be the first meal I eat today.

(*Points to cradle.*)

(*SHEPHERDS begin to search.*)

GILL: Out thieves, away from me go!
Ye come to rob us, that I know.

MAK: Hear ye not how she groans?

GILL: I swelt!

MAK: Hark! Do ye hearts not melt?

GILL: Off, thieves. Away from the son I bore!

MAK: Ah, the pain she is in, be ye hearts not sore?

GILL: Oh, my middle! I pray to God so mild,
If ever I you beguiled.
That I will eat this child!

MAK: Please, woman, for God's pain, cry not so.
Thou spill your brain, and make me great woe.

SECOND SHEPHERD: What find ye two? I think our sheep be slain.

THIRD SHEPHERD: We may as well go. No sheep is here, tis plain.

FIRST SHEPHERD: As the wind blows, I know by my nose.
Of all animals, boy or beast that dwells,
   (*Points to cradle.*)
None do as loud as he smells!

GILL: Nay, to a mother tis a sweet smelling child.

FIRST SHEPHERD: We have marked amiss; I hold us beguiled.
(*To Mak.*) Friends we be for we are one.

MAK: Nay. No one helps me.

SECOND SHEPHERD: We are done.

MAK: (*Aside.*) Go then and be about.
Farewell all three.

THIRD SHEPHERD: Fair words they be, but love is left out.

   (*SHEPHERDS leave the house.*)

FIRST SHEPHERD: Gave ye the child anything?

SECOND SHEPHERD: I swear not one farthing.

THIRD SHEPHERD: Fast again will I run.
Abide here.
   (*Runs to house.*)
I bring, Mak, a gift for your son.

MAK: Nay, to me foul hast thou done!

THIRD SHEPHERD: By your leave, let me give him but sixpence.

MAK: Nay, I pray you go hence. He sleeps.

   (*Other SHEPHERDS enter. Sheep "Baa's."*)

THIRD SHEPHERD: Methinks he peeps.

MAK: When he wakens he weeps.

THIRD SHEPHERD: Give me leave him to kiss, and lift up the clout.
   (*Lifts cover.*)
What the devil is this? He has a long snout!

   (*Others look.*)

FIRST SHEPHERD: He is marked amiss. We wait not about.

SECOND SHEPHERD: Look! He is like to our sheep!

THIRD SHEPHERD: How, Gib, may I peep?

SECOND SHEPHERD: This is a prank, a trick, a false riddle!

THIRD SHEPHERD: See how the four feet they tied in the middle.
Two horns saw I on many a cow,

But never two horns on a boy ere now!

MAK: Peace bid I! Leave off your care.
I be the father, yond woman him bear.

GILL: A pretty child as ere a mother had.
A dillydown, sweet little baby lad.

THIRD SHEPHERD: Tis our sheep! His ear-mark proves a good token.

MAK: I tell you sire. His nose was broken.
Twas told he was bewitched one night.

FIRST SHEPHERD: This is false work. We will make it a-right!
Get weapons!

GILL: He was taken with an elf.
At the stroke of midnight. I saw it myself.

SECOND SHEPHERD: Ye two are clever, but we are not misled.

FIRST SHEPHERD: They repent not their stealing. Let's see them both dead.

MAK: If again I trespass, cut off my head.
Give mercy, I beg you.

FIRST SHEPHERD: Listen and dread.
We will neither curse nor fight,
Chide nor smite,
Hang nor beat,
But cast him in a sheet.

(*They toss Mak in a sheet. Then they return to the field.*)

FIRST SHEPHERD: Lord, what I am sore. My strength put to a test.
Faith, I may do no more; therefore will I rest.

SECOND SHEPHERD: I vow, Mak weighed more than seven score.
For to sleep anywhere me think that I best.

THIRD SHEPHERD: Now I pray you lie on the grass yonder.

FIRST SHEPHERD: On these thieves I still ponder.

SECOND SHEPHERD: Peace. Silent keep and sleep.

(*SHEPHERDS lie down and sleep.*)

ANGEL: (*Enters and sings "Gloria in excelsis."*)
Rise herdsmen kind, for now he is born,
The Savior who can the devil destroy.
God is made your friend now at this morn.
He requests, to Bethlehem go ye and see the boy.
In a rude crib he lies, waxen and wealed.
Ye will find him there betwixed two beasts of the field.

(*ANGEL withdraws. SHEPHERDS rise.*)

FIRST SHEPHERD: This was a sweet voice that ever yet I heard.
It is a marvel to hear, thus to be stirred.

SECOND SHEPHERD: As I woke, of God's son of heaven he spoke.
Like a wonderous light, methought the sky be bright.

THIRD SHEPHERD: In Bethlehem born,
He spoke of a child fair.

FIRST SHEPHERD: That betokens yon star. (*Points.*)
Let us seek him there.

SECOND SHEPHERD: Say, what was his song? Heard ye not
How fine he split a note?

THIRD SHEPHERD: Yea, marry, twas a sweet trill, I wot.

FIRST SHEPHERD: I'll try the song among us, by rote.

SECOND SHEPHERD: Let see how ye croon.
Can ye bark at the moon?

FIRST SHEPHERD: Hold your tongue. Be ye still — and I will.

(*He sings.*)

SECOND SHEPHERD: To Bethlehem he bade that we be gone;
I am full 'fraid that we tarry too long.

FIRST SHEPHERD: Hie we thither therefore,
Though we be weary with woe.
To that child and that lady;

We have it in haste to go.

THIRD SHEPHERD: The angel said of that child
In a crib he lay meek and mild.

FIRST SHEPHERD: We shall see him this morn, I feel.
And know it be true as steel
All that the prophets spoke clear,
To so poor as we he would appear.

SECOND SHEPHERD: Go we now. The place is near.

THIRD SHEPHERD: I am ready and with you; go we with cheer.
Lord, if they will it be—
We are humble all three—
Now grant us the joy
To comfort thy boy.

(*The stable is revealed.*)

FIRST SHEPHERD: (*Kneels.*)
Hail, comely and clean! Hail, young child!
Hail, maker, as I mean, of a maiden so mild.
Thou has beaten, I ween, the devil so wild.
Lo, he laughs, my sweeting!
A welcome meeting.
I here have a gift and do—
Give a bob of cherries—to you.

SECOND SHEPHERD: (*Kneels.*)
Hail, sovereign savior, for thou have we sought!
Hail, noble child, that all things has wrought.
Hail! I kneel. A bird have I brought
To you from afar. Hail, a little day-star.

THIRD SHEPHERD: (*Kneels.*)
Hail, darling dear. Hail, sweet is thy cheer.
I pray thee be near when I have need.
Wrapped thee so poor, makes my heart bleed.
Pray put forth thy tiny fist,
That I may in it put, I wist,
The gift from me I bring to thee.
Tis all I have—and it be small,

I bring thee but a ball.

MARY: The Father of Heaven, God Omnipotent,
That made all things, his son has he sent.
I fulfilled God's intention, as he meant;
And now is he born.
He keep you from woe.
I shall pray him so.
Tell forth as ye go,
And remember ye this morn.

FIRST SHEPHERD: Farewell, lady, so fair to behold,
With child on thy knee.

SECOND SHEPHERD: But he lies full cold.
Lord, well is me. Now we go, thus behold.

THIRD SHEPHERD: Forsooth, full oft this night will be told.

FIRST SHEPHERD: What grace we have found.

SECOND SHEPHERD: Come forth. Glad tidings we sound.

THIRD SHEPHERD: Let voices abound!
Cries of joy let ring!
Lift ye aloft your voice and sing!

(*They sing, and go out.*)

Ralph Roister Doister

by Nicholas Udall
Adapted by Aurand Harris

Introduction

Generally accepted as the first "regular" English comedy, *Ralph Roister Doister* is a robust, earthy play, using a back-ground of middle-class England of its time.

The comedy was written by Nicholas Udall, probably between 1550 and 1553. Udall was a headmaster at Eton, a Latin School for boys. Being a scholar, he was familiar with Roman comedies. So it seems natural for him to have modeled *Ralph Roister Doister* after the scripts of the Roman playwrights, Plautus and Terence. Udall adapted for his own use such stock characters as the fool, the braggart and the parasitic rogue. Further, he borrowed the plot for his play from the Roman comedies, utilizes the always serviceable mistaken identity ploy with the resultant complications and misunderstandings.

The play was no doubt written for and acted at Eton as an exercise for the school boys to perform. Since the script lends itself to vigorous action and satire bordering on burlesque, it is easy to imagine what a spirited performance the all-male cast must have given. The custom of men playing women's parts was a tradition that continued in the theatre through Shakespeare's time.

Although the play is rooted in Roman drama, the characters and broad humor are uniquely English. The title character, Ralph Roister Doister, is based on the Latin *Miles Glorious*, the boastful warrior, but in Udall's play he speaks and acts in the distinct accents and mannerisms of an Englishman of his time. The same is true of the other characters.

The entertainments popular at Court at the time were spectacles, revels, pastoral plays and fantasies. *Ralph Roister Doister*, with its middle-class characters, high spirits, bustling action and doggerel couplets, did not appeal to those of aristocratic tastes. However, those very qualities later caused it to be cited as part of the dawn of Elizabethan drama. Shakespeare, with his genius, incorporated this folk humor into his bumpkin characters—his rogues, clowns, and comic policemen.

Many critics point to *Ralph Roister Doister*, only a footnote in dramatic literature and written by a scholarly but amateur playwright, as the first English comedy of the Renaissance.

CAST

Ralph Roister Doister, *a vain-glorious gull*
Matthew Merrygreek, *a scamp*
Gawyn Goodluck, *affianced to Dame Custance*
Tristram Trustie, *his friend*
Dobinet Doughtie } *servants to Roister Doister*
Harpax

Tom Truepenny, *servant to Dame Custance*
Sym Sureby, *servant to Goodluck*
Dame Christian Custance, *a young lady*
Margerie Mumblecrust, *her old nurse*
Tibet Talkapace } *her maids*
Annot Alyface
Other servants and musicians

SCENE: *England, 1560, a street near Dame Custance's house.*

Ralph Roister Doister

(The scene is a street in an English town, 1560. There is an entrance Down Right and Down Left. Dame Custance's house is at Center Upstage.

MERRYGREEK enters at Left. He is a lively scamp who lives by his wits)

MERRYGREEK: The merry man liveth as long, they say,
As doth the sorry man, and longer by a day.
But know ye, for all this merry note of mine,
I sometimes want for a place to dine.
Yet with my wit I can find a seat,
Today at Ralph Roister Doister's I will eat.

All day he boasts of bravery, but when put to proof
Roister Doister runs away, fast of hoof.
And if any woman smiles or cast on him an eye,
Up is he to his ears in love with a sigh.
And in haste decides she must be his wife,
Else farewell good days, farewell his life!
But for my council he provides me a fair living,
So why should I not take what he is giving? *(Looks off)*
But lo! he cometh with melancholy sound.
He is in love again, I'll wager a pound!

(DOISTER enters Right. He is a comic vain-glorious gull. He is fashionably overdressed and speaks at the moment with exaggerated melancholy)

DOISTER: Come death when thou wilt. I am weary of my life.

MERRYGREEK: *(Aside)*
I told you, he's ready to woo another wife.

DOISTER: Why was I made such a handsome and goodly person?

MERRYGREEK: (*Aside*)
Up to the ears in love! We'll have sport anon.

DOISTER: Ah, Mathew Merrygreek; yon is he;
Ho! Merrygreek, my friend, a word with thee.

MERRYGREEK: Of love, he will speak.

DOISTER. Ah! Of love . . . I am weak.

MERRYGREEK: Who is the lady who causes such complaint?

DOISTER: A woman . . .

MERRYGREEK: I warrant.

DOISTER: She is a saint.

MERRYGREEK: Who?

DOISTER: A woman yond . . . (*Points to house*)

MERRYGREEK: Her name?

DOISTER: Mistress . . . Mistress . . . Ah-h-h-h.

MERRYGREEK: Fie, for shame!
Love ye, and know not who?
How can we get such a wife for you?

DOISTER: I know . . . I know she dwelleth in that house.

(*Points to house*)

MERRYGREEK: Here! I know her well, a fair young spouse.
'Tis Christian Custance. But I tell you this as a brother,
She hath made a promise to marry another.

DOISTER: (*Loudly, as the bragging captain*)
No matter! With *me* in church she shall stand.

MERRYGREEK: 'Tis to Gawyn Goodluck she hath promised her hand.

DOISTER: Who is that Gawyn Goodluck?

MERRYGREEK: A merchant man.

DOISTER: Shall he speak afore me? Nay, by Saint Anne!

(*Draws sword and fences fiercely*)

MERRYGREEK: (*Aside*)
The sport doth begin to go round and round! (*To him*)
Yet a fitter wife for you might be found.

DOISTER: (*Preening with flattery*)
'Tis true. It is a burden daily I bear.
That I am so courtly, so comely, so fair,
That all women are enamoured of me and stare.

MERRYGREEK: (*Aside*)
And, I warrant, laugh if they dare. (*Plays up to him*)
To her, then! Speak and sing from the heart:
Wooers never speed well that have a slow start.
I'll call your musicians. Time doth waste.

DOISTER: Faith, I'll serenade her. Speed in haste.

MERRYGREEK: I run! (*Aside*)
And will return for the fun! (*Exits Left*)

(*DOISTER looks and points at house, as NURSE MUMBLECRUST, an old crone, comes out of the house, followed by TIBET TALKA-PACE, a talkative young maid*)

DOISTER: But who cometh forth from my sweetheart's house?
My matter frameth well; tread I a-foot like a mouse.

(*He tip-toes to Right and listens*)

NURSE: Sit down to your work, Tibet.
   (*TIBET starts to speak*)
And I'll do the same.
   (*TIBET starts to speak*)
Your work may stop, but never your tongue be lame.
Ye were not for nought named Tib Talkapace.

TIBET: Doth my talk grieve you? Beg pardon, your grace!

DOISTER: (*Aside*)
See what servants she keepeth that will be my wife!

Shall not I, when I have her, lead a merry life?

NURSE: (*Sees DOISTER*)
Psst! Look with young eyes I can trust —

TIBET: Look and see what, Madge Mumblecrust?

NURSE: Yond stands a man. Why doth he come this way?

DOISTER: (*Aside*)
Now might I speak, if I wish what to say.

NURSE: Follow. We will together see what he is.

DOISTER: (*Gallantly*)
One that hath heard and liked your talk I-wis.
For the love I bear your mistress, you I will kiss.

(*NURSE pleased and anxious, wipes her mouth, puckers her lips and closes her eyes*)

NURSE: I come anon.

DOISTER: (*Crosses to TIBET*)
'Tis you I would kiss, if I might.

TIBET: (*Flirting*)
What should that need?

DOISTER: To honor your comely sight.
A kiss I give to all I love, I vow.

TIBET: Then pray, sir, when did ye last kiss your cow?

ANNOT: (*Enters quickly from house*)
Tidings, ho! Dame Custance greeth you well!

DOISTER: Greeth me well?

ANNOT: You sir? No, sir. 'Tis her I tell.

TIBET: Tell me what?

ANNOT: Tibet Talkapace,
Our mistress will speak with your grace.

TIBET: With me?

ANNOT: Ye must come. Make haste, out of all doubts.

(ANNOT exits into house)

TIBET: And my work half done! Oh, a mischief take all louts!

DOISTER: How doth Mistress Custance? Tell me plain.

NURSE: Very well.

DOISTER: Your words maketh me alive again. I promise thee, Nurse, I have vowed to woo her.

NURSE: E'en so sir.

DOISTER: I would your help as I pursue her.

NURSE: E'en so, sir.

DOISTER: If so, your hand will not go without pay.

NURSE: E'en so, sir.

DOISTER: Come, I will in thine ear tell you what to say.

NURSE: E'en so, sir.

(DOISTER whispers romantically to NURSE, who giggles. MERRY-GREEK enters followed by DOBINET, HARPAX, and Musicians who play bells, flute, etc. as they march in. They stop — a comic group)

MERRYGREEK: Come, sirs, and quit yourselves like men. Your pains shall be rewarded.

DOBINET. *(A young comic servant)* But I wot not when.

MERRYGREEK: Harpax, look that thou the leader be.

HARPAX: (*A robust servant, slow in speech, action and thought*)
By my fist I warrant they'll follow me!

(*All servants react in fear*)

MERRYGREEK: Your master is in love again. Help him with speed.

DOBINET: Oft is he a wooer, but never the doer of the deed.

(*MERRYGREEK points to Right where DOISTER and NURSE stand talking. All look*)

MERRYGREEK: But with whom is he now talking steady?
(*He crosses to DOISTER*)
Wife and husband! Ye've done the deed already!

DOISTER: Wife! No, fool. Thou art deceived.

MERRYGREEK: Welcome my good lady, ye shall be well received.
(*To musicians*)
Up with a tune to homeward bring the bride!

(*He leads the Musicians who start playing loudly*)

DOISTER: (*Stopping them*)
Art thou mad! Of the mark thou art wide!
This is not she! Tut a whistle!

MERRYGREEK: No is? Then who be this thistle?

DOISTER: This same is my lady's nurse, know ye not?

MERRYGREEK: She is but a nurse? Hence home, old trot!

DOISTER: She will help in my suit, my letters convey.

MERRYGREEK: Then teach her rightly what words to say.

NURSE: I am taught already.

MERRYGREEK: Then go, make no delay.
(*To Musicians*)
Sirs, pipe a merry note as she goes within.

This wooing with sweet music will begin!

(*Musicians play comically. A piano score may be used with the Musicians sounding out the beat. The song may be sung or omitted, and DOISTER, MERRYGREEK, NURSE do a boisterous dance*)

SONG:

WHOSO TO MARRY A DAINTY WIFE
HATH HAD GOOD CHANCE AND HAP,
MUST LOVE HER AND CHERISH HER ALL HIS LIFE,
AND DALLY HER ON HIS LAP.

ABOUT WHAT AFFAIRS SO-EVER HE GO
HE MUST SHOW HER ALL HIS MIND;
NONE OF HIS COUNSEL SHE MAY BE KEPT FRO,
ELSE IS HE A MAN UNKIND.

(*NURSE exits into house, with a wave of the letter and a wiggle and a giggle*)

DOISTER: Ah, it is done! Custance is won!!

MERRYGREEK: Now pipe up homeward, sirs, with a hungry beat.
Love battles better after ye've a meal to eat!

(*Musicians play vigorously. DOISTER marches off proudly, followed by Musicians. MERRYGREEK is last. He dances off, full of mischief, and winks at audience. Music is heard off. CHRISTIAN CUSTANCE, a beautiful young woman, enters from the house. She looks to Right and to Left, puzzled; holds up Doister's letter, becomes annoyed; tears the letter in two; throws it away; and angrily goes back into the house. Music dims out. DOBINET enters, comically confused*)

DOBINET: Where is the house I go to? Before? Behind?
I know not where nor when nor how to find.
Now my Master Doister is new set on wooing,
And me he sends ahead for his doing.
To Dame Custance I am sent out.
I bring her a ring—
   (*Points to house. NURSE enters from it*)

— Ah, 'tis her house out of doubt.
Yond is the nurse who helped us yesterday.

NURSE: I was never so shook up afore, since I was born!
The way my mistress did chide me yester-morn.

DOBINET: Good day, good nurse. (*Aside*)
And I hope it will be good for me.

NURSE: Fir, sir! In trouble am I because of thee.

DOBINET: Of me? Why so?

NURSE: Were not thou one of them, say,
That sang here with the gentlemen yester-day?

DOBINET: Yea, and he would know if you have for him spoken,
And prays you to deliver this ring and token.

NURSE: Now, by the token that ye tokened, brother,
I will deliver no token, one nor other!

DOBINET: He will thank you, woman.

NURSE: I will none of him — no more!

   (*NURSE exits into house*)

DOBINET: Here stand I, with letter undelivered, as before
Home again without answer I dare not tread.
It would better I walk to Rome on my head!
   (*TRUEPENNY enters from house*)
But lo — yond cometh from the house a lad.
A fairer sight my eyes have never had!

TRUEPENNY: (*A young servant, quick in action and in wit*)
Where would thou go, that thou lookest so about?

DOBINET: Yea; but whether ye can help, or no, I doubt.
I seek Mistress Custance's house, her dwelling.

TRUEPENNY: It is my mistress ye seek, by your telling!

DOBINET: She is engaged for a husband?

TRUEPENNY: Yea, so think we.

DOBINET: (*Triumphant*)
And *I* dwell with her husband that trusteth to be.
To your mistress this ring I deliver now,
But by what way I know not how.

TRUEPENNY: (*Grabs box*)
Marry, I will be the messenger with speed,
And be rewarded by her for the deed.
Well met we were, and hope we meet again.

DOBINET: 'Tis well for *me* we met.

TRUEPENNY: I go within.

(*Exits into house*)

DOBINET: So my hands are rid of it, I care no more.
And homeward go, where I dared not go afore.

(*DOBINET exits Right. CUSTANCE enters from house in an angry state. TRUEPENNY follows*)

CUSTANCE: Stand forth! Why should you take such things in hand?

(*Holds out ring*)

TRUEPENNY: It came from him that is to be your husband.

CUSTANCE: How do ye know?

TRUEPENNY: Forsooth, the boy said so.

CUSTANCE: What was his name?

TRUEPENNY: I did not ask.

CUSTANCE: Ye should.
A fool he be, in all likelihood.
Now listen well. If ever I perceive

That henceforth you do letters or tokens receive,
To bring unto me from any person or place,
Ye must first show me the person face to face!

TRUEPENNY: Forgive me this one fault, and lay on for the next.

CUSTANCE: Then in at doors, and let me no more be vexed.
    (*TRUEPENNY exits into house*)
How this foolishness began I cannot comprehend.
But I'll search a way to put it to an end!

MERRYGREEK: (*Enters Right*)
I am sent in all haste to espy what's achieved,
How our letter and token are received.
Good morrow, Dame Custance, your health I heed.

CUSTANCE: Welcome, friend Merrygreek, and a friend I need.

MERRYGREEK: And you have one — willing, waiting to marry ye.
    (*Points off, romantically*)
A gentleman ye know; and that ye love, saith he.

CUSTANCE: A gentleman I know of? A gentleman I love?

MERRYGREEK: Yea, he swearth it by the galaxies above!

CUSTANCE: All this knavery must cease — be done!
No man hath my faith and troth but for one,
That is Gawyn Goodluck; and if, it be not he,
He hath no title this way, whoever he be.

MERRYGREEK: The gallant gentleman is — (*Poses like DOISTER*)

CUSTANCE: I'll guess and speak out!
It is Ralph Roister Doister without a doubt.

    (*MERRYGREEK nods. She laughs*)

MERRYGREEK: He biddeth you send word by me.
That ye his wife will be,
And on Sunday next, will be wed.

CUSTANCE: Doth he bid so?

MERRYGREEK: 'Tis what he said.

CUSTANCE: Go say that I bid him to keep warm at home.
For if he comes here— (*Raises her fist*)
—with pain he will moan!
And add whatsoever more thou want to say.

MERRYGREEK: 'Twill be done. And laugh we will today!

CUSTANCE: Fare ye well. I will in and prepare most foul
To meet my wooer—with a growl! (*She exits into house*)

MERRYGREEK: Now that the whole answer in my devise doth rest,
I shall appoint our wooer in colors of the best.
But could cometh Doister now ready for romance.

   (*MERRYGREEK stands at side as DOISTER enters from other side. He is followed by servants who carry flowers, bells, etc., a comic assembly of men*)

DOISTER: (*Poses romantically*)
Juno send me this day good luck and good chance.
   (*He motions and servants waves flowers, ring bells, etc.*)
Hast thou with my love spoken?

MERRYGREEK: I have done that.

DOISTER: Gave her my token?

MERRYGREEK: She threw it to her cat!
She called you a fool, an ass, a block,
A lilburn, a hoball, a lobcock.
"Ye are happy," said I, "that ye are a woman;
This would cost you your life in case ye were a man."

DOISTER: (*Draws his sword and slashes it dangerously. Servants cringe*)
Yea, an hundred thousand pounds should not save her life!

MERRYGREEK: Only—that ye would have her be your wife.

DOISTER: (*Suddenly sad*)
Heigh ho, 'tis true. What will I do? Alas?

MERRYGREEK: Be of good cheer, man, and let the world pass.

DOISTER: (*Dramatic and tragic*)
Nay, all is lost. The end draweth nigh.

Naught is left, but to take me home and die.

MERRYGREEK: Yet tarry and hear what I shall say.
Ye may still win Dame Custance today.

DOISTER: I still will win my love?

MERRYGREEK: By the stars above!
But first — ye must stay alive for an hour or two.
  (*DOISTER nods*)
Continue your wooing, but attack with a different hue!
Speak not with faint heart, no tokens send by hand;
But face her. Show her she must answer to a man!

DOISTER: (*Again his vain self*)
Ah, I can do that as well as any can.

MERRYGREEK: Nay, first homeward let us set our feet —
My stomach doth say 'tis the hour to eat.
There we will compose a song of battle — as we dine;
Return here, comfort her — and she is thine!

DOISTER: Homeward, ho, rhyming sonnets we will learn,
And woo and win my lady when I return!

(*DOISTER, MERRYGREEK and servants sing — solos and in
chorus — with marching steps and finally a fast comic dance*)

SONG:

I MUST BE MARRIED A SUNDAY;
I MUST BE MARRIED A SUNDAY;
WHO-SO-EVER SHALL COME THAT WAY,
  I MUST BE MARRIED A SUNDAY.

ROISTER DOISTER IS MY NAME;
ROISTER DOISTER IS MY NAME;
A LUSTY BRUTE, I AM THE SAME.
  I MUST BE MARRIED A SUNDAY.

WHEN WE SHALL MAKE OUR WEDDING-FEAST;
WHEN WE SHALL MAKE OUR WEDDING-FEAST;
THERE SHALL BE CHEER FOR MAN AND BEAST;
  I MUST BE MARRIED A SUNDAY.

(*They exit*)

(*Enter SYM SUREBY, faithful servant of GAWYN GOODLUCK*)

SUREBY: Is there any man but I, Sym Sureby, who
Would have taken such an enterprise to do?
To weather such an outrageous tempest as I did,
Cross such a dangerous sea to do as my master bid?
But safely I have set foot on solid shore,
Preceding my master Gawyn Goodluck a day before.
First, I must salute Dame Custance, his wife to be.
If all is well or wrong with her I'll see.
Now will I go knock that I may despatch with speed —
  (*CUSTANCE enters from house*)
But lo, forth cometh herself, happily indeed.

CUSTANCE: What friend Sym Sureby? Forsooth, right welcome are ye!
How doth mine own Gawyn Goodluck be?

SUREBY: When he knoweth of your health, he will be perfect well.

CUSTANCE: When will he be home, I pray thee tell?

SUREBY: His heart is here e'en now, his body cometh by noon.

CUSTANCE: Faith would I see him soon.

SUREBY: (*Looks off*)
But who are these who cometh to your door?

(*DOISTER and MERRYGREEK enter*)

CUSTANCE: (*Aside*)
For me, they be double trouble and more.
If they speak, he will think I am in league,
And shall suspect me involved with intrigue.

SUREBY: What is their business?

CUSTANCE: (*Aside*)
I have naught to do of them.
I am innocent, but I must be rid of them.

SUREBY: (*Aside*)
I will harken them; somewhat is here, I fear it.

DOISTER: (*Aside*)
I will speak out aloud, so best she may hear it.
   (*Shouts and crosses to her*)
Well found, sweet wife, I trust, for all your sour look.

CUSTANCE: Wife? Why call me ye wife?

SUREBY: (*Aside*)
Wife! This matter goeth acrook.

CUSTANCE: Come in with me, Sym Sureby.

DOISTER: Received you my ring and token?

CUSTANCE: Heed not the foolish words he's spoken.
Come, take some repast.

SUREBY: Thank you, no.
In haste I on a new matter now must go.

CUSTANCE: Take to your master my message on your way.

SUREBY: No message I take this time. I say — goodday.

   (*Bows curtly and exits*)

CUSTANCE: Surely this fellow misdeemeth some ill in me.
But I am innocent.

DOISTER: (*Calls after SUREBY*)
Yea, farewell to thee,
And I pray, tell thy master Goodluck
That he cometh too late for this blossom to pluck!

CUSTANCE: Oh! I will be even with thee, thou beast, thou lout!

DOISTER: Will ye have me, then?

CUSTANCE: Never, with my senses about!
Go to, you goose!

MERRYGREEK: Well, sir, ye preceive
For all your kind offer, she will not you receive.

DOISTER: (*Suddenly wild with revenge*)
I'll fire thee out of thy house if ye be not mine!
I will destroy thee and all of thine!

CUSTANCE: What! Away! Get gone! Go! (*Calls*)
Come forth, Truepenny! What ho!
    (*Truepenny runs out of house*)
Fetch Tristram Trustie, my honest friend.
Bring him quickly, that he may me defend.

TRUEPENNY: It quickly shall be done, by your grace,
So on return ye shall say I went —
    (*Exits running and calling*)
— apace!

CUSTANCE: Come not near me. Stand yond, there!
Or I shall clout thee on thy head. Beware!

MERRYGREEK: (*Between them, pleading*)
Ah, good dame Custance, take a better way.

CUSTANCE: Prithee, *he* may away if he is afraid to stay.

DOISTER: Afraid? Forsooth! I am renowned for my bravery.

CUSTANCE: Nay, for your doltish devilish knavery.

MERRYGREEK: Peace!

CUSTANCE: Let him do his worst!

DOISTER: We will see who for help cries first!

    (*DOISTER and CUSTANCE circle, sparring, DOISTER guarding himself. Suddenly CUSTANCE slaps him. He yells and holds his cheek.*

She turns away triumphant. He, angrily, grabs her around the wrist, lifts her and circles with her feet kicking in the air and with her screaming. He drops her and turns away triumphant. She grabs him by the ear. He yells and grabs her hand. She pulls his hand to her mouth and bites it. He releases her and yells. She kicks him on the shins. He hops and yells, turns around and bends over to rub his leg. She then kicks him squarely in the seat, sending him sprawling toward MERRYGREEK)

MERRYGREEK: Yield in time! Retreat is part of defence.

DOISTER: (*Weak and moaning*)
Yea — homeward! Follow thence. With my men I shall return.
A lesson in war she shall learn.

    (*DOISTER exits, hobbling. MERRYGREEK follows, imitating him and laughing at the fun of it*)

CUSTANCE: Now my folks I will call, before a minute lapse,
If he returns, we'll give him more knocks and raps.
Meg Mumblecrust, come forth! And Tibet Talkapace!
And come forth, too, Mistress Annot Alyface.

    (*The three servants enter from house*)

ANNOT: I come.

TIBET: And I am here.

NURSE: And I am here, too, at length.

CUSTANCE: Like warriors if need be, ye must show your strength!
Ralph Roister Doister comes here with men to fight,
I charge you, if he come, *on him* with all your might!

NURSE: I with my distaff will reach him a rap!

TIBET: And I with my new broom will sweep him a swap!

ANNOT: And I with our skimmer will fling him one flap!

TIBET: Then Truepenny with the firefork will after him fray,
And you with the roasting spit can drive him away!

CUSTANCE: Go! Make ready, that it may be even so!

(*The three servants march into the house, already waving their fists in excited anticipation*)

NURSE: Rap!

TIBET: Tap!

ANNOT: Fray and away!

(*They exit as TRUEPENNY, pushing TRISTRAM TRUSTIE, enters at side. TRUSTIE is a rich and old gentleman, comically weak in speech and step*)

TRUEPENNY: Faster! Ye are a slow goer. Hurry for shame,
My mistress, if we tarry, will on me lay the blame.

CUSTANCE: Grammercies, Truepenny, for your speed I thank you.

TRUEPENNY: Forsooth, since I went no grass hath grown on my shoe!
But Master Tristram Trustie here maketh no speed.

CUSTANCE: That he come at all, I thank him indeed.
Truepenny, get thee in, I trow,
For soon, a kitchen war begins!

TRUEPENNY: A fight? I go!

(*Exits into house*)

CUSTANCE: (*TRUSTIE has finally arrived beside CUSTANCE. She occasionally speaks loudly in his ear*)
Now, Tristram Trustie, I thank you indeed
For coming so — quickly — to help in my need.

TRUSTIE: (*Comically weak and shaking*)
Ah, Dame Custance, while my life shall last
For my friend Goodluck's sake I hurried fast.

CUSTANCE: But, alack, I fear he will find displeasure and blame.

TRUSTIE: Wherefore?

CUSTANCE: For a foolish matter.

TRUSTIE: Repeat the same.

CUSTANCE: (*Crying*)
I am ill used by a couple of fools, 'tis true.

TRUSTIE: Nay, weep not, woman, but tell what they do.

CUSTANCE: Here stood Sym Sureby and Merrygreek,
While Ralph Roister Doister for promise of marriage did seek.
And because I will not his wife be,
He sweareth to kill all my kin and me.
Yea, will beat and burn my house flat.
Therefore I pray your aid.

TRUSTIE: (*Tottering with bravery*)
I promise you that.

CUSTANCE: (*Looks off*)
Yond cometh Merrygreek. (*MERRYGREEK enters*)
Sir, ye have used me well!

TRUSTIE: Yes, Merrygreek, why join ye with Doister, pray tell?

MERRYGREEK: Please forgive, I pray, I beg no scorn.

CUSTANCE: I was never more vexed since the first day I was born.

MERRYGREEK: But I thought ye would take it up at first bound.
And enjoy and laugh at the sport we had found.
Come! 'Tis still time. We'll end the fun today,
And Gawyn Goodluck will laugh with us, I dare say.

CUSTANCE: (*To TRUSTIE, in his good ear*)
Advise me. What shall I do? Enter the row?

TRUSTIE: Whatever ye do, it can be no worse than 'tis now.

CUSTANCE: I should like to put Doister in his proper place,
Make him suffer as I in my disgrace.

MERRYGREEK: He brags he will return and make ye yield.

CUSTANCE: (*To TRUSTIE, loudly and slowly*)
If ye bid me, we will with him pitch a field,
I and my maids together!

TRUSTIE: Go to it. Be bold!

CUSTANCE: (*Declares war*)
Ye shall see a woman's war!

TRUSTIE: This fight will I behold!

MERRYGREEK: I will go fetch him!

TRUSTEE: Begone!

CUSTANCE: Ye shall find us ready!

MERRYGREEK: For victory anon! (*Exits*)

CUSTANCE: Come, good friend, within we make our preparation!

(*She exits into house*)

TRUSTIE: Yes, 'twill be a jolly recreation! (*He totters after her into the house*)

(*GAWYN GOODLUCK, followed by SUREBY, enters. They stand at side and talk. GOODLUCK is a stalwart handsome hero*)

GOODLUCK: Sym Sureby, my trusty man, I advise thee well,
See that you no false surmise tell.
The ado about Custance my heart has struck,
I will know the truth or my name is not Gawyn Goodluck.

SUREBY: To report what I heard and saw did seem best,
Now thou, my master, can discharge the rest.

GOODLUCK: I shall do what is right, and as I see cause why.
Now seek we Custance and shall know all by and by.

(*GOODLUCK and SUREBY exit. Marching music is heard as DOIS-TER and his servants march in from the other side. The servants are armed for battle. HARPOX beats a drum. MERRYGREEK follows*)

DOISTER: Now, sirs, keep your ray. Hearts be stout!
But where be the women? Me thinks they dare not rout!
(*Boldly waves his sword*)

Yea, they knowest a stomach for a weapon have I!

MERRYGREEK: (*Aside*)
Ten men can scarce match him with a spoon in a pie.

DOISTER: Let the bugle sound. Forward march! And around!

(*DOISTER leads the march. Servants and MERRYGREEK follow. It is a loud and funny procession with drum beating and servants shouting. TIBET and ANNOT appear from the house, see the military formation, and scream. Men stop, turn and see the maids. Maids scream again and rush off*)

DOISTER: Didst thou see how they fled out of sight?
With a wag of a feather I'll win this fight!
Forward! Forth! Onward! All!

(*Men take one step when CUSTANCE enters from house. Men stop. She shouts at them*)

CUSTANCE: What caitiffs are those that so shake my house-wall?
(*Calls loudly*)
Maidens! Come forth armed with your tools!
We fight a war with an army of fools!

(*All of CUSTANCE's servants march out from the house, armed with kitchen utensils, which they wave and bang. There can be many girls against the several men*)

DOISTER: (*Shaking with fear, on one side with his men*)
They come — so many.

CUSTANCE: (*Commanding her army, on the other side*)
Women, a-ray!

MERRYGREEK: 'Twill be writ in history, this battle today!

CUSTANCE: Forward! Strike, my kin. Let the battle begin!

(*Drums and pans beat, as the women attack the men. It is a loud and comic fight. TIBET chases DOBINET. NURSE beats a pan with a long spoon, also hitting anyone on the head who passes by. MERRYGREEK and CUSTANCE urge their fighters on. DOISTER tries to hide. The women, kicking, hitting and biting are more savage than the men. When the comic battle reaches a climax, CUSTANCE stands at Center and points toward DOISTER)*

CUSTANCE: I myself will the brave captain undertake!

(CUSTANCE starts after him. DOISTER tries to hide behind MER-RYGREEK. Others quiet down. DOISTER's men having been beaten away, and CUSTANCE's maids tired but happy in the background)

DOISTER: They win ground!

MERRYGREEK: Save yourself, sir, for your sake!

(Pushes DOISTER towards CUSTANCE who hits him on the head with her kitchen weapon)

DOISTER: Out! Alas, I am slain!

MERRYGREEK: *(Grabs DOISTER's short sword and waves it)*
At her — again!

(He swings at CUSTANCE but circles around and hits DOISTER)

DOISTER: Thou hittest me!

MERRYGREEK: I will strike her — certainly.

(Swings again and again hits DOISTER)

DOISTER: Thou hittest me still!

MERRYGREEK: At her — so I will!

(Again hits DOISTER who staggers)

DOISTER: I am done!

(Sinks in MERRYGREEK's arms)

MERRYGREEK: *(Lifting him up)*
Save yourself — run!

DOISTER: Help! Cease! I am slain!

MERRYGREEK: Truce! Truce between the twain.
How say you, Custance? For the saving of your life,

Will ye now yield and be this gentleman's wife?

(*CUSTANCE raises her weapon*)

DOISTER: Nay, nay, she shall be none of mine!

MERRYGREEK: Why so?

DOISTER: She is no woman. She is a *man*-kind.

CUSTANCE: To it again, my kin! Down they shall fall!

(*Her maids give a battle cry, beat the pans, and start to advance*)

DOISTER: Away! Away! Away, else she kills us all!

MERRYGREEK: Nay, stick to it like a hardy man and tall.

DOISTER: Retreat! Retreat! All men on their feet!
The order is — follow me. The order is — flee!

(*He runs off, followed by MERRYGREEK, waving his white hand-kerchief of peace. Men servants follow*)

CUSTANCE: Away, lout and lubber! We have driven them all away!

NURSE: Ah, good mistress, we have won a glorious day!

(*Beats on her pan and all cheer. NURSE leads the march, beating her pan. All servants follow, marching victoriously, shouting, 'Rap . . . Tap . . . Fray . . . And away!" and exit into house*)

CUSTANCE: Friend Tristram, I pray you, now be witness for me.

TRUSTIE: Dame Custance, I shall uphold your honesty!

CUSTANCE: One fool I have defeated, but my problem is not broken.
Gawyn Goodluck must know to him I am spoken.
And lo, yond I see him, the only hope of my life.
    (*GOODLUCK and SUREBY enter*)
Welcome home, speakest your true and intended wife!

GOODLUCK: Nay, I hear doings of yours that are very strange.

CUSTANCE: What fear ye, that my faith towards you should change?

GOODLUCK: I hear a promise of marriage to another you have made.

CUSTANCE: This report is false I will you persuade.
Tristram Trustie here for me will testify.

GOODLUCK: I will believe and credit all that he shall verify. What, good friend, of this matter do ye report?

TRUSTIE: 'Twas a joke. Done in fun. A lively sport!

(*Comically, weakly imitates the fight, "Rap . . . tap . . . fray and away"*)

CUSTANCE: Now knowing the truth, I trust all shall be well.

GOODLUCK: Sweet Custance, neither heart can thank nor tongue can tell
What joy I have in your constant fidelity.
You are indeed the pearl of perfect honesty!

MERRYGREEK: (*Enters from side*)
I return — to speak for a defeated man.

GOODLUCK: Who?

MERRYGREEK: Roister Doister, forgive him if you can.

TRUSTIE: We ne'er had better sport.

(*Mumbles and totters, "Rap . . . tap . . . fray and away"*)

GOODLUCK: I forgive him. Let him to us report.

MERRYGREEK: Come, Doister, the sun shines bright.
All wrongs are now right.

DOISTER: (*Enters quickly*)
They are not angry?

MERRYGREEK: They know 'twas a harmless wrong.

DOISTER: (*Again the bragging captain*)
Ah, 'tis true. No man, woman, nor child can hate me long.

GOODLUCK: All are friends again. No quarrel or fuss.
I beseech you, come sup with us.

DOISTER: I will do thus and honor you.

MERRYGREEK: And I will happily come, too! (*Aside*)
O see, by using my wit I find a seat,
Today under Gawyn Goodluck's table I'll put my feet!
Musicians, come; lead with a merry beat!
We'll end the day with a song—before we eat!

(*The entire cast, on stage, sings a rousing finale, ending with a merry dance*)

THE END

A Midsummer Night's Dream

by William Shakespeare
Adapted by Aurand Harris

Introduction

A Midsummer Night's Dream, Shakepeare's lyrical gift to theatre, has been called that "little drama born of a smile." Combining fantasy, slapstick farce, folklore and romantic comedy with lyrical poetry, he raised one entertainment form of dramatic art to perfection.

Shakespeare lived in the "Golden Age" of England. It was a time of zestful creativity and exploration. Thomas Kyd wrote his "mighty line"; Christopher Marlowe brought blank verse to dramatic plots; Robert Greene wrote idyllic romances; then came Shakespeare, an "upstart crow" from Stratford.

In 1576 the first permanent theatre was built in England. Modeled after the open bear-baiting pits and the semi-circular courtyards with several galleries, it was called The Theatre. Other theatres followed, including The Curtain, The Rose, The Swan. After a fire, The Theatre was rebuilt and renamed. It became the most famous playhouse in English theatrical history — The Globe, home of England's greatest playwright, William Shakespeare. Here he was busy as an actor and playwright. His life was contained in the theatre where his "friends and fellows" called him "our Shakespeare."

Shakespeare is generally believed to have written *A Midsummer Night's Dream* in 1595–96. Some critics think the plot of the four lovers (omitted in this short version) was written earlier and later combined with the poetic fairy scenes. All agree the play, as we know it, was first performed at a great wedding of some nobleman — then performed at The Globe. It was first published, from the prompt book used at The Globe, in 1600 and is known as *The Fisher Quarto*.

There has been much speculation as to the sources of the three threads of the plot. The Court of Theseus and the four lovers may have been inspired by Chaucer's *Knight's Tale* and North's Plutarch's *Life of Theseus*. The comic adventures of Bottom and his fellows may come from Ovid's 4th Book of *Metamorphoses*, which includes the story of *Pyramus and Thisbe*. The fairy element may have sprung from Shakespeare's memory of the fairy and nursery legends he heard as a boy in Warwickshire.

There is no doubt that by the time Shakespeare wrote *A Midsummer Night's Dream* he had become master of his craft. Max Beerbohm wrote of a later production of *A Midsummer Night's Dream*, "Here we have the Master, confident in his art, at ease with it as a man in his dressing gown, kicking up a loose slipper and catching it on his toe."

Since its first performance, the play has been performed continuously. It has been cut, re-shaped, made into operas, ballets, etc., and an all-star motion picture.

In a magical world of a moonlit forest, mixed with the world of reality and reason, the play sings with poetry. The plot and characters delightfully demonstrate, in Puck's words, "What fools these mortals be."

CAST

PETER QUINCE, *a carpenter*
NICK BOTTOM, *a weaver*
FRANCIS FLUTE, *a bellows-mender*
TOM SNOUT, *a tinker*
ROBIN STARVELING, *a tailor*
SNUG, *a joiner*
OBERON, *King of the Fairies*
TITANIA, *Queen of the Fairies*
ROBIN GOODFELLOW, *the Puck*
FAIRIES
DUKE
DUCHESS
ATTENDANTS OF THE COURT

SCENE: *A wood near Athens.*

A Midsummer Night's Dream

(*In front of the curtain. Comic music. The Tradesmen of Athens enter. They are an assorted and comical looking group of laborers. QUINCE enters first. He is the temperamental "director" of the group. FLUTE follows him. Flute is young, nervous and eager to please. Next BOTTOM enters. He swaggers with importance, knowing he is the "star." STARVELING follows, a happy soul who has a toothless grin. Close behind him is SNUG, shy, not-too-bright, and has a bumpkin laugh. Last is SNOUT, feeble, with a beard and a cane. They stand facing the audience — a picture of low comedians.*)

QUINCE: Is all our company here?

BOTTOM: You were best to call them generally, man by man, according to the script.

QUINCE: Here is the scroll of every man's name which is thought fit through all Athens to play our interlude before the Duke and Duchess.

BOTTOM: First, good Peter Quince, say what the play treats on, then read the names of the actors, and so grow to a point.

QUINCE: Marry! Our play is — The most lamentable comedy, and most cruel death of Pyramus and Thisby.

BOTTOM: A very good piece of work, I assure you, and a merry one. Now, good Peter Quince, call forth your actors by the scroll. Masters, spread yourselves.

QUINCE: Answer as I call you. Nick Bottom, the weaver.

BOTTOM: (*Steps forward.*) Ready. Name the part I am for, and proceed.

QUINCE: You, Nick Bottom, are set down for Pyramus.

BOTTOM: What is Pyramus? A lover — or a tyrant?

QUINCE: A lover, that kills himself most gallant for love.

BOTTOM: That will ask some tears in the true performing of it; if I do it, let the ladies look to their eyes; I will move storms. I could play Ercles rarely!
   (*Dramatically.*)
The raging rocks
And shivering shocks
Shall break the locks
   Of prison gates;
And Phibbus' car
Shall shine from far
And make and mar
   The foolish Fates.
This was lofty! Now name the rest of the players.

QUINCE: Francis Flute, the bellows-mender.

FLUTE: (*Eagerly and anxiously steps forward.*) Here, Peter Quince.

QUINCE: Flute, you must take Thisby on you.

FLUTE: What is Thisby? A wandering knight?

QUINCE: It is the lady that Pyramus must love.

FLUTE: Nay, faith let not me play a woman; I have a beard — coming.

QUINCE: That's all one. You may speak as small as you will.

BOTTOM: Let me play Thisby, too. I'll speak in a monstrous little voice —

QUINCE: No, no, you must play Pyramus. And Flute, you Thisby.

BOTTOM: Well, proceed.

QUINCE: Robin Starveling, the tailor.

STARVELING: (*Steps forward and grins.*) Here, Peter Quince.

QUINCE: Robin Starveling, you must play Thisby's mother.
  (*Starveling grins and steps back.*)
Tom Snout, the tinker.
  (*Goes to Snout who is standing and asleep.*)
Tom Snout!

SNOUT: (*Wakes with a start. Speaks in a feeble voice.*)
Here, Peter Quince.

QUINCE: You, Pyramus's father; myself Thisby's father.
Snug, the joiner —
  (*Snug shakes with sudden fear.*)
you, the lion's part; and I hope here's a play well fitted.

SNUG: Have you the lion's part written? Pray you, if it be, give it to
me, for I am slow of study.

QUINCE: You may do it extempore — for it is nothing but roaring.

  (*SNUG roars.*)

BOTTOM: Let me play the lion, too. I will roar, that I will do any
man's heart good to hear me. I will roar, that I will make the ladies say
"Let him roar again, let him roar again."

QUINCE: And you should do it too terribly, you would fright the
Duchess and the ladies, that they would shriek, and that were enough to
hang us all.

BOTTOM: I grant you, friends, if that you should fright the ladies out
of their wits, they would have no more wit but to hang us; but I will
aggravate my voice so that I will roar as gently as any sucking dove — I
will roar as 'twere any nightingale.

QUINCE: You can play no part but Pyramus! For Pyramus is a sweet-
faced man; a proper man, as one shall see in a summer's day; a most
lovely gentleman-like man; therefore you must needs play Pyramus.

BOTTOM: Well, I will undertake it.

QUINCE: (*QUINCE takes small scrolls from inside his hat.*)
Masters, here are your parts;
  (*Gives scroll to FLUTE.*)

and I entreat you,
  (*Gives scroll to STARVELING.*)
request you,
  (*Gives scroll to SNUG.*)
and desire you,
  (*Gives scroll to SNOUT.*)
to con them by tomorrow night —

SNOUT: (*Cups hand to ear.*) Aye?

QUINCE: To con them by tomorrow night! And meet me in the palace wood, a mile without the town, by moonlight; there we will rehearse, for if we meet in the city, we shall be dogged with company, and our devices known. In the meantime I will draw a bill of properties, such as our play wants. I pray you, fail me not.

BOTTOM: (*Taking the lead; all follow.*)
We will meet; and there we may rehearse most obscenely and courageously. Take pains. Be perfect. Adieu.

  (*He exits. Others follow.*)

QUINCE: (*Last.*) At the Duke's oak we meet!

  (*He exits. Fairy music. Curtains open. Scene is the woods. FAIRIES enter and dance. NOTE: As many Fairies as desired may be used, or only two. The dialogue has been broken up for several, but can be alternated between two. Fairies' names are Peaseblossom, Cobweb, Moth, Mustardseed.*)

FAIRIES: Over hill,
Over dale,
Through bush,
Through brier,
Over parks,
Over pale,
Through flood, through fire.
We do wander everywhere
Swifter than the moon's sphere;
And we serve the Fairy Queen,
To dew her orbs upon the green.

PUCK: (*Enters.*) How now, spirits! Whither wander you?

FAIRIES: I must go seek some dewdrops here
And hang a pearl in every cowslip's ear.
Farewell, thou lob of spirits. Be gone!
Our queen and all her elves come here anon.

PUCK: The king doth keep his revels here tonight;
Take heed that queen come not within his sight;
For Oberon is passing full of wrath
Because that she as her attendant hath
A lovely boy stolen from an Indian King,
And jealous Oberon would have the child;
And now never Oberon and she meet in grove or green,
By fountain clear, or spangled starlight sheen,
But they do square, that all her elves for fear
Creep into acorn-cups and hide them there!

FAIRY: (*All FAIRIES exit, except one.*)
Either I mistake your shape and making quite,
Or else you are that shrewd and knavish sprite
Called Robin Goodfellow: are not you he?

PUCK: Thou speak'st aright.
I am that merry wanderer of the night.
I jest to Oberon and make him smile
When I a fat and bean-fed horse beguile,
Neighing in likeness of a filly foal:
And sometimes lurk I in a gossip's bowl,
In very likeness of a roasted crab,
And when she drinks, against her lips I bob
And on her wither'd dewlap pour the ale.
The wisest lady, telling the saddest tale,
Sometimes for the three-foot stool mistaketh me;
Then slip I from her bum, down topples she,
And "tailor" cries, and falls into a cough;
And then the whole quire hold their hips and laugh,
And waxen in their mirth and sneeze and swear
A merrier hour was never wasted there.

FAIRY: Sh! My fairy Queen.

PUCK: Sh! My fairy King!

(*Fairy music as TITANIA enters from L. If many fairies are used it
can be a beautiful procession, with fairy musicians, train-bearers, royal*

leaf-umbrella holder, etc. QUEEN and FAIRIES circle and stand at L.
PUCK, with great to-do, bows, and with sweeping gesture points R.
OBERON enters R. Music stops.)

OBERON: Ill met by moonlight, proud Titania.

TITANIA: What, jealous Oberon! Fairies, skip hence:
I have forsworn his bed and company.

OBERON: Tarry, rash wanton: am not I thy lord?

TITANIA: (*Curtsies in playful mockery.*)
Then I must be thy lady.

OBERON: Why should Titania cross her Oberon?

TITANIA: Never since the middle summer's spring,
Met we on hill, in dale, forest or mead,
To dance our ringlets to the whistling wind,
But with thy brawls thou hast disturb'd our sport.

OBERON: I do but beg a little changeling boy
To be my page.

TITANIA: Set your heart at rest!
The fairy kingdom buys not the child from me!

OBERON: How long within this wood intend you stay?

TITANIA: If you join in our dance in our round,
And see our moonlight revels, go with us:
If not, shun me, and I will spare your haunts.

OBERON: Give me the boy and I will go with thee.

TITANIA: Not for thy fairy kingdom! Fairies away!
We shall chide downright, if I longer stay.

(*Music as TITANIA and FAIRIES exit.*)

OBERON: Go thy way: thou shalt not from this grove
Till I torment thee for this injury.
My gentle Puck, come hither. Thou remembrest

Since once I sat upon a promontory
And heard a mermaid on a dolphin's back
Uttering such dulcet and harmonious breath
That the rude sea grew civil at her song
And certain stars shot madly from their spheres,
To hear the sea-maid's music.

PUCK: I remember.

OBERON: That very time I saw, but thou couldst not,
Flying between the cold moon and the earth,
Cupid all arm'd: a certain aim he took,
And loosed his love-shaft smartly from his bow,
As it should pierce a hundred thousand hearts;
Ah, I might see young Cupid's fiery shaft
Quench'd in the chaste heart of my fairy queen.
Yet mark'd I where the bolt of Cupid fell:
It fell upon a little western flower,
Before milk-white, now purple with love's wound,
And maidens call it Love-in-idleness.
Fetch me that flower; the herb I show'd thee once:
The juice of it on sleeping eyelids laid
Will make or man or woman madly dote
Upon the next live creature that it sees.
Fetch me this herb; and be thou here again
Ere the leviathan can swim a league.

PUCK: I'll put a girdle round about the earth
In forty minutes. (*Exits.*)

OBERON: Having once this juice,
I'll watch Titania when she is asleep,
And drop the liquor of it in her eyes.
The next thing then she waking looks upon,
Be it on lion, bear, or wolf, or bull,
Or meddling monkey, or on busy ape,
She shall pursue it with the soul of love!
And ere I take this charm from off her sight,
I'll make her render up the child to me.
My page he will be!
  (*PUCK enters.*)
Welcome, wanderer. Hast thou the flower there?

PUCK: Ay, there it is.

OBERON: I pray thee, give it me.
I know a bank where the wild thyme blows,
Where oxlips and the nodding violet grows,
There sleeps Titania sometime of the night,
Lull'd in these flowers with dances and delight;
And with the juice of this I'll streak her eyes,
And make her full of hateful fantasies.
Meet me ere the first cock crow!

(*OBERON exits.*)

PUCK: Fear not, your servant shall do so!

(*Exits.*)

TITANIA: (*Fairy music. TITANIA and her FAIRIES enter.*)
Come, on this bank we will rest our flight,
And sleep until again it be night.
Sweet sleep—over-canopied with lush woodbine,
With sweet musk-roses and with eglantine.
Sleep, and keep this night of dreams.

(*One by one she dismisses the Fairies. One FAIRY GUARD remains. He lifts the golden cobweb at center back. Behind is a green bank. TITANIA sits and gracefully lies on it—asleep. GUARD lets web down, and standing at attention, goes to sleep.*

PUCK enters. Motions to OBERON, who enters. PUCK lifts the web. OBERON moves the flower over her eyes, then comes downstage and says the magic words.)

OBERON: What thou seest when thou dost wake,
Do it for thy true-love take.
Love and languish for his sake;
Be it ounce, or cat, or bear,
Pard, or boar with bristled hair,
In thy eye that shall appear
When thou wakest, it is thy dear;
Wake when some vile thing is near.

(*OBERON exits. PUCK lets web down and exits. GUARD exits. Dream music dims out. Lights come up bright. Comic music, as the tradesmen enter.*)

BOTTOM: Are we all met?

QUINCE: Pat, pat; and here's a marvelous convenient place for our rehearsal. This green plot shall be our stage, this hawthorn-brake our tiring-house; and we will do it in action as we will do it before the Duke.

BOTTOM: Peter Quince.

QUINCE: What sayest thou, bully Bottom?

BOTTOM: There are things in this comedy of Pyramus and Thisby that will never please. First, Pyramus must draw a sword to kill himself; which the ladies cannot abide. How answer you that?

SNOUT: By'r lakin, a parlous fear.

STARVELING: I believe we must leave the killing out, when all is done. (*Grins happily.*)

BOTTOM: Not a whit. I have a device to make all well. Write me a prologue; and let the prologue seem to say, we will do no harm with our swords and that Pyramus is not killed; that I Pyramus am not Pyramus, but Bottom the weaver; this will put them out of fear.

QUINCE: Well, we will have such a prologue.

SNOUT: Will not the ladies be afeard of the lion?

STARVELING: I fear it, I promise you. (*Grins.*)

BOTTOM: Masters, you ought to consider with yourselves: to bring in—God shield us!—a lion among ladies is a most dreadful thing; for there is not a more fearful wild-fowl than your lion living.

(*SNUG roars.*)

SNOUT: Therefore another prologue must tell he is not a lion.

BOTTOM: Nay, you must name his name, and half his face must be seen through the lion's neck: and he himself must speak, saying, "Ladies, I would wish you not to fear, I come not as a lion—
(*SNUG roars.*)

I am a man, Snug the joiner — not a lion.
(*SNUG roars.*)

QUINCE: Well, it shall be so. But there is two hard things yet: to bring in moonlight by the wall; for, you know, Pyramus and Thisby meet by moonlight.

BOTTOM: Someone must come in with a bush or lantern, and say he comes to disfigure, or to present, the person of Moonshine.

QUINCE: Then, there is another thing: we must have a wall, for Pyramus and Thisby, says the story, did talk through the chink of a wall.

SNOUT: You can never bring in a wall. What say you, Bottom?

BOTTOM: Some man or other must present Wall; and let him hold his fingers thus, and through that cranny shall Pyramus and Thisby whisper.

QUINCE: If that may be, then all is well. Come, every mother's son, and rehearse your parts. Pyramus, you begin; when you have spoken your speech, enter into that brake, and so every one according to his cue.

(*STARVELING, SNOUT and QUINCE exit talking. SNUG, realizing he should follow, roars and exits. BOTTOM is left alone and starts pantomiming his part. PUCK enters, puzzled by Bottom's strange actions. He makes a circle of inspection.*)

PUCK: What hempen home-spuns have we swaggering here,
So near the cradle of the Fairy queen?
What a play! Ah! I'll be an auditor;
An actor too perhaps, if I see cause.

QUINCE: (*Enters.*) Speak, Pyramus. Thisby stand forth.

(*FLUTE enters, stands frightened. BOTTOM kneels to him.*)

BOTTOM: Thisby, the flower of odious savours sweet —

QUINCE: Odorous, odorous!

BOTTOM: — odours savours sweet;
So hath thy breath, my dearest Thisby dear.
But hark, a voice! Stay, I pray, but a while,
And by and by I will come to thee here.

(*Exits.*)

PUCK: And he will be a stranger Pyramus when he reappears!

(*Exits after Bottom.*)

FLUTE: Must I speak now?

QUINCE: Ay, merry, must you; for you must understand he goes but to see a noise that he heard, and is to come again.

FLUTE: Most radiant Pyramus, most lily-white of hue,
Of colour like the red rose on triumphant brier,
Most briskly juvenal and eke most lovely Jew,
As true as truest horse, that yet would never tire.
I'll meet thee, Pyramus, at Ninny's tomb.

QUINCE: "Ninus' tomb," man: why you must not speak that yet, that you answer to Pyramus. You speak all your part at once, cues and all. Pyramus enter: your cue is past: it is "never tire."

FLUTE: As true as truest horse, that yet would never tire.

BOTTOM: (*Enters with ass's head covering his own head.*)
If I were fair, Thisby, I were only thine.

QUINCE: O monstrous! O strange! We are haunted. Pray, master! Fly, master!

FLUTE: Help!

(*Exits.*)

QUINCE: Save us!

(*Exits.*)

PUCK: (*Enters and teases Bottom.*)
I'll follow you, I'll lead you about a round,
Through bog, through bush, through brake, through brier;
Sometimes a horse I'll be, sometimes a hound,
A hog, a headless bear, sometimes a fire!
And neigh, and bark and grunt and roar and burn,

Like horse, hound, hog, bear, fire at every turn.

(*Exits.*)

BOTTOM: Why do they run away? This is a knavery of them to make me afeard.

SNOUT: (*Enters.*)
O Bottom, thou art changed! What do I see on thee?

BOTTOM. What do you see? You see an ass-head of your own, do you?

(*BOTTOM starts toward SNOUT. SNOUT exits. QUINCE enters.*)

QUINCE: Bless, thee, Bottom! Bless thee! Thou art translated!

(*Exits.*)

BOTTOM: I see their knavery: this is to make an ass of me; to fright me, if they could. But I will not stir from this place, do what they can; I will walk up and down here, and I will sing, that they shall hear I am not afraid.
    (*Sings off-key.*)
The ousel cock so black of hue,
With orange-tawny bill,
The throstle with his note so true,
The wren with little quill.

(*He holds the last note, as TITANIA enters from behind web.*)

TITANIA: What angel wakes me from my flowery bed?

BOTTOM: (*Sings.*)
The finch, the sparrow and the lark,
The plain-song cuckoo gray,
Whose note full many a man doth mark,
And dares not answer nay.

TITANIA: I pray, thee, gentle mortal, sing again;
Mine ear is much enamour'd of thy note;
So is mine eye entralled to thy shape;
And thy fair virtue's force perforce doth move me
On the first view to say, to swear, I love thee.

BOTTOM: Methinks, mistress, you should have little reason for that; and yet, to say the truth, reason and love keep little company now-a-days.

TITANIA: Thou art as wise as thou art beautiful!

BOTTOM: Not so, neither, for if I had wit enough to get out of this wood, I would.

TITANIA: Out of the wood do not desire to go;
Thou shalt remain here, whether thou wilt or no.
I am a spirit of no common rate;
The summer still doth tend upon my state;
And I do love thee: therefore, go with me;
I'll give thee fairies to attend on thee.
And they shall fetch thee jewels from the deep.
And sing while thou on pressed flowers dost sleep.
Oh, I will purge thy mortal grossness so
That thou shalt like an airy spirit go.
    (*Motions, and FAIRIES enter.*)
Be kind and courteous to this gentleman.
Nod to him and do him courtesies.
Music for his wonderous ear to hear!
Cushions of moss and flit so that he may softly sit.
O, hop in his walk and gambol in his eye;
Behold his grace; his voice a musical sigh.
Bring him apricots and dewberries,
With purple grapes, green figs and mulberries;
The honey bags steal from the humble bees.
And for night tapers crop their waxen thighs,
And light them with the glow of the glow worm's eyes.
And pluck the wings from painted butterflies
To fan the moonbeams from his sleeping eyes.

    (*BOTTOM sits proudly surrounded by the serving FAIRIES.
TITANIA stands beside him stroking his long ears.
PUCK enters, motions for Oberon. OBERON enters.*)

OBERON: How now, mad spirit? What news, my messenger?

PUCK: My mistress with a monster is in love.
While she was in her dull and sleeping hour
A crew of comic tradesmen met to rehearse

A play intended for the Duke and Duchess.
One fool left and enter'd in a brake;
When I did him at this advantage take,
An ass's noll I fixed on his head;
When in that moment, so it came to pass,
Titania waked and straightway loved an ass.

OBERON: Oh, sprite, Oh, my clever impish elf,
'Tis better than I could devise myself!

    (*BOTTOM "brays" a sigh.*)

PUCK: Oh, master, see — what fools these mortals be!

TITANIA: Oh, sit thee still upon this flowery bed,
While I thy amiable cheeks do coy,
And stick musk-roses in thy sleek smooth head,
And kiss thy fair large ears, my gentle joy.

BOTTOM: Where is Peaseblossom?

FIRST FAIRY: What do you command?

BOTTOM: Scratch my head.
    (*FAIRY tickles left ear. BOTTOM sighs.*)
Ah. Where is Mustardseed?

SECOND FAIRY: What is your wish?

BOTTOM: Pray you, also — scratch!
    (*FAIRY tickles right ear. BOTTOM sighs, then motions FAIRIES away.*)
I must to the barbers, for methinks I am marvelous hairy about the face; and I am sure a tender ass, if my hair do but tickle me, I must scratch.
    (*Kicks his legs and yawns.*)
I pray you, let none of your people stir me. I have an exposition of sleep come upon me.

TITANIA: (*Motions FAIRIES away. They exit. BOTTOM drops his head in sleep.*)
Oh, sleep thou wilt, and I will wind thee in my arms
As doth the woodbine the sweet honeysuckle

Gentle entwist; the female ivy so
Enrings the barky fingers of the elm.
Oh, how I love thee. How I dote on thee!

(*Closes her eyes in sleep.*)

OBERON: Good Robin. Look you at this sweet sight! (*Laughs.*)
I will undo this hateful imperfection.
And gentle Puck, take this transformed scalp
From off the head of this Athenian swain;
That when he awakes he will think no more
Of this night than of a dream.
But first I will release my Fairy Queen.
    (*Mysteriously waves his hand over the sleeping Titania.*)
Be as thou wast want to be;
See as thou wast want to see.
Dian's bud o'er Cupid's flower
Hath such force and blessed power.
Now, my Titania! Wake you, my sweet queen.

TITANIA: (*Opens eyes.*)
My Oberon, what visions have I seen!
Methought I was enamour'd of an ass.

OBERON: There lies your love.

TITANIA: How came these things to pass?

PUCK: (*Over Bottom's head, in magic tones.*)
Now when thou wak'st from your sleep,
With thine own eyes you will peep!

(*Lifts ass's head from Bottom's head.*)

BOTTOM: I have had a dream. Methought I was—
    (*Feels where his long ears were.*)
Methought I was . . . and Methought I had—
    (*Feels where his long nose was.*)
Oh, Peter Quince, Masters Flute, Snout, Starveling!
Where are you?

(*Exits.*)

OBERON: Titania, your fairies call. Your music sound.
(*Fairy music. FAIRIES enter.*)
Come, my queen, take hands with me.
Again your king I will be.

TITANIA: I come, tell me, and in our flight
Tell me how it came this night
That I sleeping here was found
With this mortal on the ground.

(*She, OBERON, PUCK and the FAIRIES dance and exit. Music dims out.*
Lights up bright. BOTTOM enters. QUINCE enters. They rush to each other. FLUTE, STARVELING, SNUG and SNOUT follow Quince, each carrying his properties for the play.)

QUINCE: Oh, Bottom. Bully Bottom!

BOTTOM: Oh, Quince!

QUINCE: Oh most courageous day!

BOTTOM: Oh most happy hour! Masters, I have experienced wonders.

FLUTE: Let us hear, sweet Bottom. Let us hear!

BOTTOM: When you stole hence, and left me asleep, I — I had a most rare vision. I had a dream past the wit of man to say what dream it was. Methought I was —
(*Feels where his long ears were, and suddenly brays like an ass. Royal trumpets sound, off.*)
It is the trumpet! It is the Duke and the Duchess. Quick into your apparel. Everyman look his part; for the short and the long is, our play is ready to begin! Who — who smells of onions and garlic? Oh, we did want to utter nothing but sweet breath, so the ladies would say it was a sweet comedy. Away! Away! They come!

(*All hide behind the web or scenery. SNUG is next to last and roars as he exits. QUINCE is last, peeking to be sure the Duke is coming, then ducks out of sight. DUKE and DUCHESS and ATTENDANTS enter. There may be one Attendant or many. If many, the dialogue can be divided among them.*)

DUKE: What masques, what revels have we for this night?

ATTENDANT: A play there is my lord, some ten words long,
Which is as brief as I have known a play;
But by ten words, your grace, it is too long.

DUCHESS: (*Reads scroll.*)
"A tedious brief scene of young Pyramus
And his love Thisby; very tragical mirth."
Merry and tragical! Tedious and brief!
What are they that do play it?

ATTENDANT: Hard-handed men that work in Athens here,
Which never labour'd in their minds till now.

DUKE: And we will hear it.

ATTENDANT: No, my noble lord,
It is not for you; I have heard it over,
And it is nothing.

DUKE: I will hear this play;
For never anything can be amiss,
When simpleness and duty tender it.
Go bring them in; and let the play begin.

(*ATTENDANT goes to back curtain.*)

DUCHESS: He says they can do nothing in this kind of acting.

DUKE: Then the kinder we, to give them thanks for nothing.

ATTENDANT: So please your grace, the Prologue is address'd.

QUINCE: (*Peeks from web or curtain, then enters, bows, takes a deep breath and begins.*)
If we offend, it is with our good will,
That you should think, we come not to offend,
But with good will. To show our simple skill,
That is the true beginning of our end.
Consider then we come but in despite,
Our true intent is for your delight.
The actors are at hand and by their show

You shall know all that you are like to know.

(*Bows. Retreats to back.*)

DUKE: This fellow doth not stand upon points.

DUCHESS: He hath rid his prologue like a rough colt; he knows not the stop.

ATTENDANT: A good moral, my lady, it is not enough to speak, but to speak true.

QUINCE: (*Motions and actors enter, each in "costume."*)
Gentles, perchance you wonder at this show;
This man is Pyramus, if you would know;
This man doth present Wall,
Vile Wall which did these lovers sunder.
This man with lantern presenteth Moonshine,
For if you will know, by Moonshine
Did these lovers think to meet
At Ninus' tomb, there to woo.
This grisly beast, which Lion hight by name,
   (*SNUG roars.*)
The trusty Thisby, coming first by night,
Did scare away, or rather did affright;
And, as she fled, her mantle she did fall,
Which Lion,
   (*SNUG roars.*) vile with bloody mouth did stain.
Anon comes Pyramus, sweet youth and tall,
And finds his trusty Thisby's mantle slain;
Whereat, with blade, with bloody blameful blade,
He bravely broach'd his boiling bloody breast;
And Thisby, tarrying in mulberry shade,
His dagger drew, and died. For all the rest,
Let Lion,
   (*SNUG roars.*) Moonshine, Wall, and lovers twain
At large discourse, while here they do remain.

(*QUINCE bows. DUKE applauds. QUINCE pushes Bottom, Flute, Snug and Starveling off. SNOUT stands alone.*)

DUCHESS: I wonder if the lion be to speak?

DUKE: Surely one lion may when so many asses do.

SNOUT: In this same interlude it doth befall
That I, one Snout by name, present a wall:
And such a wall, as I would have you think,
That had in it a crannied hole or chink,
Through which the lovers, Pyramus and Thisby,
Did whisper often very secretly.

(*He turns his back, showing the painted wall placard he wears, and stands, back to audience.*)

DUCHESS: Would you desire lime and hair to speak better?

ATTENDANT: It is the wittiest partition that ever I heard discourse, my lady.

(*BOTTOM enters from back.*)

DUKE: Sh! Pyramus draws near the wall.

BOTTOM: Oh grim-look's night! O night with hue so black!
O night, which ever art when day is not!
O night, O night! Alack, alack, alack,
I fear my Thisby's promise is forgot!
And thou, O wall, O sweet, O lovely wall
That stand'st between her father's ground and mine!
Thou wall, O wall, O sweet and lovely wall,
Show me thy chink, to blink through with mine eyes!
    (*SNOUT extends his arm backwards making a "wall"
and opens two fingers for the "chink."*)
Thanks, courteous wall:
    (*SNOUT turns his head and nods.*)
Jove shield thee, wall, for this!
    (*BOTTOM peers through "chink."*)
But what see I? No Thisby do I see.
O wicked wall, through whom I see no bliss!
Curst be thy stones for thus deceiving me!

ATTENDANT: The wall, methinks, being sensible, should curse again.

BOTTOM: No, in truth, lady, he should not. "Deceiving me" is Thisby's cue; she is to enter now, and I am to spy her through the wall. You shall see. Yonder she comes.

FLUTE: (*Enters comically imitating female voice.*)
O wall, full often hast thou heard my moans
For parting my fair Pyramus and me!
My cherry lips have often kiss'd thy stones,
Thy stones with lime and hair knit up in thee.

BOTTOM: I see a voice: now will I to the chink
To spy as I can hear my Thisby's face.
   (*Whispers loudly through "chink."*)
Thisby!

FLUTE: My love thou art, my love, I think.

BOTTOM: Think what thou wilt, I am thy lover's grace;
And, like Lisander, am I trusty still.

FLUTE: And I like Helen, till the Fates me kill.

BOTTOM: Not Shafalus to Procrus was so true.

FLUTE: As Shafalus to Procrus, I to you.

BOTTOM: O, kiss me through the hole of this vile wall!

   (*They kiss.*)

FLUTE: I kiss the wall's hole, not your lips at all.

BOTTOM: Wilt thou at Ninny's tomb meet me straightway?

FLUTE: 'Tide life, 'tide death, I come without delay.

   (*FLUTE exits. BOTTOM exits.*)

SNOUT: (*Turns and faces front.*)
Thus have I, Wall, my part discharged so;
And, being done, thus Wall away doth go.

   (*SNOUT bows and exits. DUKE and DUCHESS applaud. STARVE-LING enters from back, followed by SNUG whose face is covered with the lion's mane.*)

DUCHESS: Here come two noble beasts — a man and a lion.

   (*STARVELING stands silently. SNUG bows, speaks timidly.*)

SNUG: You ladies, you, whose gentle hearts do fear
The smallest monstrous mouse that creeps on floor,
May now perchance both quake and tremble here,
When lion rough in wildest rage doth roar.
   (*He roars.*)
Then know that I, one Snug the joiner am;
No lion fell, nor lion's dam'
For, if I should as lion come in strife
Into this place, 'twere pity on my life.

STARVELING: This lantern doth the horned moon present;
Myself the man i' the moon do seem to be.

   (*Grins happily.*)

DUCHESS: This is the greatest error of all the rest; the man should be put into the lantern. How is it else the man in the moon?

DUKE: Ah, here comes Thisby.

FLUTE: (*Enters from back.*)
This is old Ninny's tomb. Where is my love?

SNUG: (*Roars.*)
R-r-r-r-roar!

FLUTE: Oh! A lion!

   (*SNUG roars and chases FLUTE. Finally SNUG stops, exhausted. FLUTE takes off scarf, lays it on floor, and exits at back.*)

DUCHESS: Well roared, Lion.

ATTENDANT: Well run, Thisby.

DUKE: Well shone, Moon.

   (*SNUG roars, creeps upon scarf, mouths it savagely and throws it down, exits at back. QUINCE enters, streaks scarf with red paint and exits.*)

DUCHESS: Well moused, Lion.

ATTENDANT: And so the Lion vanished.

DUKE: And then comes — Pyramus.

BOTTOM: (*Enters.*)
Sweet, Moon, I thank thee for thy sunny beams;
I thank thee, Moon, for shining now so bright;
For, by thy gracious, golden, glittering gleam,
I trust to take of truest Thisby sight.
    (*STARVELING shakes his head and grins. BOTTOM sees scarf.*)
But stay, O spite!
But mark, poor Knight,
What dreadful dole is here!
Eyes, do you see?
How can it be?
O Dainty duck! O dead!
Thy mantle good.
What, stain'd with blood!
Approach, ye Furies fell!
O fates, come, come,
Cut thread and thrum;
Quail, crush, conclude, and quell!
O wherefore, Nature, didst thou lions frame?
Since lion vile hath here deflower'd my dear:
Which is — no, no — which was the fairest dame
That lived, that loved, that liked, that look'd with cheer.
Come, tears, confound;
Out, sword, and wound
The pap of Pyramus:
Aye that left pap,
Where heart doth hop;
    (*Dramatically stabs himself between chest and arm. STARVELING becomes interested and walks around so he can better see the stabbing, holding the lantern high.*)
Thus die I, thus, thus, thus.
Now am I dead.
Now am I fled;
My soul is in the sky;
Tongue lose thy light;
Moon, take thy flight,
    (*STARVELING nods, grins, and exits.*)
Now die, die, die, die, dead!

(Expires on floor.)

DUCHESS: How chance Moonshine is gone before Thisby comes back and finds her lover?

ATTENDANT: Oh she will find him by starlight. Here she comes; and her passion ends the play.
　(FLUTE enters.)
She hath spied him already with those sweet eyes.

FLUTE: Asleep, my love?
What, dead, my dove?
O Pyramus, arise!
Speak, speak.
Quite dumb!
Dead, dead? A tomb
Must cover thy sweet eyes.
These lily lips,
This cherry nose,
These yellow cowslip cheeks,
Are gone — are gone!
Lovers, make moan:
His eyes were green as leeks.
O Sisters Three,
Come, come to me,
With hands as pale as milk;
Lay them in gore,
Since you have shore
With shears his thread of silk.
Tongue, not a word:
Come, trusy sword;
Come, blade, my breast imbrue;
And farewell, friends;
Thus Thisby ends:
　(Stabs himself with Bottom's sword.)
Adieu, adieu, adieu, adieu — adieu.

(Falls dead.)

DUCHESS: Moonshine and Lion are left only to bury the dead.

ATTENDANT: Ay, and Wall, too.

BOTTOM: (*Sits up.*)
No, the wall is down that parted their fathers.

(*Lies down "dead" again.*)

QUINCE: (*Enters from back.*)
Will it please you to see the Epilogue, or to hear a dance?

DUKE: No epilogue, I pray you; for your play needs no excuse. It was a fine tragedy; and notably discharged. A dance, please, and let your Epilogue alone.

(*The actors do a comic dance and exit.*)

DUKE: The iron tongue of midnight hath told twelve:
(*Lights dim to moonlight.*)
'Tis almost fairy time. Come, we will leave
This wood enchanted to spirit, elf, and sprite
That they may dance and enjoy this midsummer night.

(*DUKE, DUCHESS, and ATTENDANT exit.
Fairy music, as FAIRIES dance in, followed by
OBERON, TITANIA and PUCK.*)

OBERON: Now, until the break of day,
Through this wood each fairy stray.
And hand in hand, with fairy grace
Will we sing, and bless this place.

TITANIA: Dance, attend the mark,
Before we hear the morning lark.

OBERON: The globe we will compass soon,
Swifter than the wandering moon.
Trip away: make no stray;
Meet me all by break of day.

(*FAIRIES dance, and all exit, except PUCK.*)

PUCK: If we shadows have offended,
Think but this, and all is mended,
That you have but slumber'd here
While these visions did appear,

And this weak and idle theme,
No more yielding but a dream.
If we be friends, with your hands tell,
And we will know all has ended well.

(*He bows. Curtains close.*)

A Doctor in Spite of Himself

by Molière
Adapted by Aurand Harris

Introduction

Jean Baptiste Poquelin took the name of "Molière" at the age of twenty-one when he became a founder of a theatre group called *Illustre Théâtre*. Molière, the playwright, became a name known in France and throughout the theatre world as the master of modern comedy.

Molière was born January 15, 1622. He studied Latin and Greek and received a law degree in 1642. Forsaking law, he turned to the theatre and became an actor, director, administrator, and one of the great playwrights of France. In 1659 his play, *The Precious Maidens Ridiculed*, established him as the most popular comic playwright of his day. Following that he wrote a succession of acclaimed satiric comedies, including *A Doctor in Spite of Himself* and *Scapin*. He died at the age of fifty-five. Seven years later, the King, uniting Molière's theatre company with a rival company, formed a French National Theatre, The *Comédie Française*, which became known as the House of Molière.

French drama, which led the world in the seventeenth century, was dominated by the formal neoclassical tragedies of Corneille and Racine. Molière introduced social satire, which gave comedy respectability equal to tragedy. This was comedy which appealed to the intellect rather than to the emotions. The characters are less real than the situations, as in *A Doctor in Spite of Himself*, where Sganarelle, a realistic woodcutter, becomes an improbable doctor. Molière's plays evoke, as George Meredith observed, "thoughtful laughter."

Molière's plays have elements of *commedia dell' arte*. He was undoubtedly influenced by an Italian *commedia* troupe, directed by Tiberio Fiorelli, which at one time shared the *Théâtre du Petit Bourbon* with Molière's company. Molière's plays took the form of Roman comedies which he made into great theatrical farces. As Shakespeare did, Molière used other people's plots to which he gave his own unique touch. He endowed stock types with contemporary characterizations, developing a genre often called "character comedy."

Molière's plays were usually written in the formal Alexandrine couplets and adhered to the unities of time, place and action. Plays written in such graceful poetry are often difficult to translate into English prose.

A Doctor in Spite of Himself was first performed August 6, 1666. The idea for it was suggested by a medieval painting, *The Rascally Apothecary*. The script evolved from an earlier Molière farce, *The Shuttlecock Doctor*. The play, an immediate success, is a joyous comedy, with only an occasional satirical thrust at the medical profession.

In *Scapin*, Molière returned to pure farce. It was first performed in Paris at the *Théâtre du Palais-Royal*, May 24, 1671. Molière himself played the title role, where "on his own stage he was one of the marvels of his time."

CAST

SGANARELLE, *a woodcutter*
MARTINE, *his wife*
ROBERT, *a neighbor*
VALERE, *a servant of Geronte*
LUCAS, *another servant*
JACQUELINE, *wife of Lucas*
GERONTE, *a rich gentleman*
LUCINDE, *his daughter*
LEANDRE, *a young gentleman*

SCENE: *France, 1600*

A Doctor in Spite of Himself

(The curtain opens. There is a painted cut-out tree standing at R, large enough for an actor to be concealed behind. SGANARELLE, followed by MARTINE enter L. They walk angrily to C, and stop.)

SGANARELLE: Be quiet, quiet, quiet woman. I am the master.

MARTINE: I will not be quiet, quiet, quiet. I will be heard.

SGANARELLE: *(Aside.)* Oh, the misery of married life.

MARTINE: *(Aside.)* Oh, the misery to be married to a stupid husband.

SGANARELLE: How right the great Aristotle was when he said: a wife is the devil in disguise.

MARTINE: What does a woodcutter know about Aristotle?

SGANARELLE: My little wife, I am a husband to be proud of. Six years I served a famous doctor. I learned by heart his Latin grammar.
(Poses and speaks loudly and proudly.)
Cabricius arci thuram, catalamus, singulariter, numerum et casus.

MARTINE: Yes doctor woodcutter . . . doctor blockhead! A curse on the day and on the hour when I went to church with you and said, "I will."

SGANARELLE: And a curse on the Magistrate who made me swear away my freedom.

MARTINE: You should thank heaven every minute of your life that you have me for your wife.

SGANARELLE: Thank you? You were the lucky one when you got me.

MARTINE: Lucky! To marry a man who only works his mouth, a scoundrel who eats me out of house and home.

SGANARELLE: (*Aside.*) Not true. I drink as well as eat.

MARTINE: Who has sold every stick of furniture in the house.

SGANARELLE: That is living on one's means.

MARTINE: Do you think things will go on like this forever and ever and ever?

SGANARELLE: Now little wife, calm yourself —

MARTINE: Do you think I am going to put up with this forever and ever and ever?

SGANARELLE: (*Aside.*) She is slightly annoyed.

MARTINE: Do you think I don't know how to bring you to your senses?

SGANARELLE: I know, my little wife, that you know that I have a strong right arm! (*Holds it up.*)

MARTINE: And so do I! (*Holds it up.*)

SGANARELLE: You are asking for a beating.

MARTINE: Beat me. Beat me! If you dare!

SGANARELLE: Ah, so you force me —

MARTINE: Scoundrel! Beggar! Villain!

SGANARELLE: A switch! (*He goes to side of tree. From behind the tree a green hand is extended and hands him a slap-stick. They shake hands.*)

MARTINE: Rascal! Thief! Doctor Blockhead!

(*He beats her with the slap-stick. It is a fast and funny scene. She jumps and yells. He looks at the audience between the whacks and grins. She stands and rubs her hip.*)

SGANARELLE: (*Aside.*) That is the way to quiet a wife.

ROBERT: (*Enters from L, an old man.*) Hello . . . Hello? What is all this. Sganarelle beating his wife.
  (*Crosses to Sganarelle, stands between husband and wife.*)
Disgraceful behavior. Come. Enough. You are a scoundrel, monsieur, to beat your wife.

MARTINE: What did you call him?

ROBERT: He is a scoundrel, a villain, a rascal —

MARTINE: (*Slaps Robert.*) Don't you call my husband names.

ROBERT: But he beat you — like a rascal — (*She slaps him.*) like a villain — (*She slaps him.*) like a — (*He hides on the other side of Sganarelle.*)

MARTINE: Suppose I want him to beat me?

ROBERT: Ah, then it is his pleasure.

MARTINE: Is it any of your business? (*Aside.*) Imagine if everyone went around stopping husbands from beating wives.

ROBERT: I apologize.

MARTINE: What right have you for butting in?

ROBERT: I won't say another word.

MARTINE: I like being beaten.

ROBERT: (*To Sganarelle.*) I beg your pardon, my friend. Carry on. Hit her! I'll be happy to give you a hand.

SGANARELLE: No. I don't want to now.

ROBERT: Ah, a pity.

SGANARELLE: (*Suddenly angry.*) She's my wife, not yours.

ROBERT: Happily, yes!

SGANARELLE: (*Ready to strike him.*) And I don't need your help.

ROBERT: I was being neighborly.

SGANARELLE: Good neighbors do not interfere in other neighbor's business. Remember what Cicero said: do not put the bark of a tree between the trunk and your finger. (*Starts hitting Robert with slap-stick, as ROBERT runs off L, crying for help.*) Remember! Remember! Remember! (*He gives slap-stick back to "Tree." They touch hands. He smiles at wife.*) Our quarrel is over.

MARTINE: (*Smiles.*) Over.

MARTINE: Say you are sorry.

SGANARELLE: I'm sorry!

MARTINE: I forgive you. (*They hold hands. She aside.*) But I'll pay him back for hitting me — (*Rubs hip*) so hard.

SGANARELLE: (*Aside.*) A few blows between husband and wife — now and then — prove that it is a happy marriage. (*To wife.*) Now, little wife, I'm off to bundle firewood, and I promise you I shall return with a hundred sticks and more. (*Sings, as he exits L.*)

See me lift my little bottle
Hear the gurgle in my throttle . . .

MARTINE: (*Looks after him.*) Be off with you. And I'm not forgetting — no matter what happy face I wear — how I feel. (*Aside.*) Oh, if I could find some means of paying him back for the beating he gave me, I'd do it! Now what could I do to make him know I — (*Savagely.*) Truly — (*Tenderly.*) love him (*Sits and thinks.*)

(*VALERE and LUCAS enter from L. Both are servants. Valere affects a grand manner and Lucas is a country bumpkin.*)

VALERE: We will rest here and catch our breath.

LUCAS: It's a fool's errand we're sent on. What are you and I going to get out of it? Nothing . . . nothing . . . nothing.

VALERE: We must obey the master. He has sent us. And I am deeply concerned for the health of the master's daughter.

LUCAS: Now there's a strange sickness.

VALERE: But don't you see—if her sickness can be cured, she will marry Horace— and Horace is very rich—so if you and I can fetch a doctor who can cure the master's daughter— Our errand will be worth a great deal to us.

LUCAS: That's just what I said! We'll get something out of it. Something . . . something . . . something.

MARTINE: (*To herself.*) Think . . . think how he beat you. Think how to get even with him.

VALERE: Of course the master's daughter has a fancy to marry another—young Leandre.

LUCAS: And if she marries him, we'll get nothing . . . nothing . . . nothing.

VALERE: The master will never consent for her to marry young— poor—Leandre.

LUCAS: Ah, how wise is our good master.

VALERE: So now we will find a wondrous doctor who can cure the master's daughter.

LUCAS: So she can marry Horace.

VALERE: And they will live richly ever after.

LUCAS: And so will we!

MARTINE: (*Rises. To herself.*) There must be some way I can make him feel a good whack. (*Curtsies to her imaginary husband, while VALERE and LUCAS bow to each other.*) To show my dear husband my tender love. (*She and VALERE, bowing, back into each other.*) Oh, I beg your pardon, gentlemen. I was thinking—how I could find— what I'm looking for.

VALERE: (*Bowing grandly to her.*) Ah, madame, we too are looking— for what we are trying to find.

MARTINE: If I can be of help, gentlemen, in your search—

LUCAS: We are looking for a doctor.

MARTINE: A doctor?

VALERE: A most clever doctor who can cure our master's daughter. She has been affected with a strange malady which has suddenly made her speechless. All the doctors nearby have tried — and failed.

LUCAS: They've run out of physic and rhubarb. They've even run out of Latin.

MARTINE: (*Looks off L.*) Latin . . .

VALERE: One hears sometimes of an obscure doctor who has his own remarkable secrets —

MARTINE: (*Nods.*) A doctor . . . Who speaks Latin . . . Gentlemen, your search is over! (*Aside.*) I have thought of a way that my husband will feel the sting of a stick!

VALERE: Where shall we find him!

MARTINE: He is there — (*Points R. They look.*) cutting wood.

LUCAS: A doctor — cutting wood?

MARTINE: Oh, I must warn you, he is a very extraordinary man. In fact, he will tell you he is *not* a doctor.

VALERE: Odd. But often the greater the man the more fool he is with little quirks.

MARTINE: Oh, he is a great fool all right. As great as he is a doctor.

VALERE: We shall find him. (*They nod and start.*)

MARTINE: (*Stops them.*) First, I must tell you there is only one way in which you can make him say he is a doctor. He will not admit he is a doctor — unless —

VALERE: Unless —

LUCAS: Unless —

MARTINE: Unless you take a stick — and whack him! (*Goes to tree.*) Beat him — beat him until he admits in the end what he denied in the beginning. (*"Tree" hands her a slap-stick.*)

VALERE: Beat him?

MARTINE: With a stick. (*Holds up slap-stick.*)

LUCAS: (*Takes stick and swings it.*) I can do that!

VALERE: (*Takes second slap-stick which "Tree" has given to MAR-TINE and which she gives to Valere.*) And I — if he will cure the master's daughter.

MARTINE: Cure? Ah, miracles he has performed! Six months ago there was a woman — dead the doctors said — dead. And just as they were going to bury her, this doctor was made — by beating — to attend the body. He looked at the dead woman, put something in her mouth, and lo and behold — up she rose from the dead — and started dusting the room.

VALERE: Ah.

LUCAS: Ah.

MARTINE: Ah-ha! And — just three months ago a boy fell from the top of the bell tower — down — down — (*She looks away to avoid seeing him crash.*) His head was smashed, his arms, his hands, his chest, his legs, his toes. The people made this doctor — by beating him — cure the boy.

LUCAS: Ah.

VALERE: Ah.

MARTINE: Ha-ha!

VALERE: What is his name?

MARTINE: He is called Sganarelle.

VALERE: And what is his appearance?

MARTINE: He has a stupid face, but do not let that stop you. He wears a green and yellow coat. His talk is loud — sprinkled well with Latin words, and he swings his arms with a painful whack.

VALERE: He will not escape us. Thank you madame. You have found for us what we were wishing for.

MARTINE: Thank you, monsieur. You are going to do what I was wishing to be done. (*Aside.*) We will soon see if he is a doctor hard to beat! (*She exits L.*)

VALERE: Come. We will find the doctor. (*They nod and start "walking" facing R. They walk in the same spot, looking about, as the "Tree" moves toward L. There is music. They stop, "Tree" stops, Music stops.*) Surely this doctor will cure the silent tongue of the master's daughter. (*They nod. Music starts. They walk. "Tree" moves. All stop.*) Surely then he will reward us generously for fetching such a remarkable doctor.

LUCAS: And all we have to do is whack him. (*Swings stick. They nod. Music starts. They walk. "Tree" moves. All stop.*)

VALERE: Listen. Someone is chopping wood.

LUCAS: A woodchopper!

VALERE: He comes this way. Quick . . . hide . . . we will see. (*They look about, see tree, hurry toward it, each circles around a different side and hide behind it. SGANARELLE enters R.*)

SGANARELLE: Two big bundles of sticks deserve one little refreshing drink. (*Holds up small bottle. Sings.*)

See me lift my little bottle,
Hear the gurgle in my throttle.
Ah! how folk would envy me,
Think how happy I should be
If every time I took a pull
I still found my bottle full —

(*Starts to take a drink, but discovers the bottle is empty. Shakes it, upside down.*) Empty. A little wine before a meal, which I don't have, or a little wine after a meal — which I don't have, would improve the enjoyment of that meal — which I don't have.

VALERE: (*Peeks from one side of tree.*) He wears a green and yellow coat.

LUCAS: (*Peeks from other side of tree.*) He wears a stupid look.

Ah, how happy I should be
Alas, why can't it really be?

(*Shakes bottle angrily and vigorously.*)

VALERE: He whacks his arms about.

SGANARELLE: Cabricius arci thuram, catalamus, singulariter, numerum et casus!

VALERE: (*He and LUCAS come around from each side of tree.*) He speaks in Latin!

LUCAS: In Latin! (*They embrace wildly.*)

VALERE: It is the doctor!

SGANARELLE: What two long legged birds do I see? And — they are looking at me.

VALERE: Come. We must introduce ourselves.

LUCAS: You do the talking. I'll do the whacking.

VALERE: (*He bows on one side of Sganarelle, LUCAS bows on the other side.*) Bonjour, monsieur. (*SGANARELLE looks from one to the other and puts bottle in pocket.*) Your name is — you are — Sganarelle?

SGANARELLE: Yes — (*Looks at Lucas.*) and no. It depends on what you want with him.

VALERE: We want to pay him our humble respect.

SGANARELLE: In that case — I am Sganarelle.

VALERE: Oh, monsieur, we are delighted to meet you!

(*Embraces him.*)

LUCAS: (*SGANARELLE backs away and LUCAS embraces him.*) Delighted!

VALERE: You have been recommended to us for something — we are seeking. We have come to ask you — to beg you — to help us.

SGANARELLE: (*Takes off hat.*) Gentlemen, I am entirely at your service.

VALERE: Great men are always sought after. And — we know — how great you are.

SGANARELLE: Well, it is true, I am the best woodcutter in France.

VALERE: (*Playfully.*) More than that, monsieur.

SGANARELLE: And my price is one hundred and ten sous a bundle.

VALERE: Let us stop this kind of talk.

SGANARELLE: You may get wood chopped for less from some others. There is wood — and — wood. But mine is the best. One hundred sous is my final price!

VALERE: Monsieur, you cannot fool us with all this talk of wood cutting. We know you want to keep — who you are — a secret. But one as great, as famous, as renowned as you, can never conceal his true identity.

SGANARELLE: (*Looks at VALERE who shakes his head, looks at LUCAS who shakes his head. Aside.*) They're crazy!

VALERE: Let us have no more attempts at deceiving us.

LUCAS: We know who you are.

SGANARELLE: You do?

VALERE: We do.

SGANARELLE: Who am I?

VALERE: You are — Doctor Sganarelle. (*Bows.*)

SGANARELLE: Doctor! (*Goes to one and then the other.*)
I am a woodcutter. A woodcutter! A woodcutter! I am not a doctor!

VALERE: (*Aside, elated.*) He *is* a doctor because he says he is not! Oh, monsieur, do not make us force you. (*Holds up stick.*)

SGANARELLE: Force me?

LUCAS: (*Holds up stick.*) Say you are a doctor!

SGANARELLE: I will say — I am not a doctor!

VALERE: (*Aside.*) We will have to use the sticks.
(*To Sganarelle.*) Once again, I implore, admit you are a doctor.

LUCAS: (*Waving stick.*) Better nod your head — or get knocked on the head!

SGANARELLE: (*Aside.*) They are mad — raving mad!

VALERE: Say the word.

LUCAS: Say it.

SGANARELLE: I am — *not* a doctor!

VALERE: Lay on, Lucas. Give him the treatment! We will *make* him a doctor! (*They beat him. SGANARELLE jumps, yells, and runs in a circle as the sticks slap about him. It is not a realistic scene of torture, but one of slap-stick comedy. Finally between them, SGANARELLE raises both hands and begs them to stop.*)

SGANARELLE: (*Between them, on his knees.*) Help! Stop! I am dying. Enough! I'll be anything — anything you say. I am a doctor — a bone breaker — a knifer — a cutter — a bleeder — but let me be a *live* one.

VALERE: (*Aside.*) He has admitted it.

LUCAS: (*Aside.*) A curious way to become a doctor.

VALERE: (*SGANARELLE rises.*) I am pleased to find that at last you know yourself. (*He and LUCAS give the sticks back to "Tree."*)

SGANARELLE: (*Aside.*) They are sure I am a doctor. Can it be I have changed without noticing it?

VALERE: Ah, monsieur, the happiness you will bring to our master's daughter when with your miraculous cure you heal her strange sickness.

SGANARELLE: (*Frightened.*) I — I am going to have to cure — a patient? You are certain I am a doctor? (*Looks at VALERE who nods, at LUCAS who nods, then smiles.*) And I never knew it!

VALERE: Our master will pay you bags of money.

SGANARELLE: Money? Bags of money? Gentlemen—I *am* a doctor. As Cicero said: Hail, Caesar! We who are about to try, salute you. What is the sickness and when do we start?

VALERE: Our young lady has lost her tongue.

SGANARELLE: I haven't got it.

VALERE: His little jokes. (*They all laugh.*)

SGANARELLE: Let us go! The money is—the patient is waiting for me.

LUCAS: You will need your doctor's robe.

VALERE: I will get you one.

SGANARELLE: Come. Lead the way. That is—the doctor's orders!

(*Sings.*)

When I wear my doctor's hat
Giving pills for this and that.
Ah, how folks will envy me.
Think how happy I will be
Every day a patient's worse
Means more money in my purse.
Ah, how happy hangs my goose,
I'm a doctor on the loose.

(*They dance, and exit L.*)

(*Curtains close.*)

(*Curtains open. Scene: a room in Geronte's house.*)

GERONTE: (*Enters R. He is a comic old man, he is followed by JAC-QUELINE.*) Where is he? Where is he? Where is the new doctor?

VALERE: (*VALERE and LUCAS enter L.*) Monsieur Geronte. Bonjour.

(*They bow.*)

GERONTE: Bonjour . . . bonjour. Where — where is he? Where is the doctor?

VALERE: He awaits your pleasure. Oh, monsieur, he is the greatest doctor in France. He has performed miraculous miracles.

GERONTE: Can he make a silent tongue — talk?

LUCAS: He can make the dead come to life.

GERONTE: My daughter is not dead — just dumb. Call him. Bring him in at once.

VALERE: Yes, monsieur, at once. (*He bows and exits L.*)

GERONTE: Tell me . . . what is he like? His voice? His demeanor?

LUCAS: He — he — he is — a — a — (*Pantomimes a description.*) Well, he — he — (*More pantomimes.*) He likes to cut wood.

GERONTE: Cut wood?

LUCAS: Oh, he is full of all kinds of humours — little jokes. Sometimes he acts as if he was a — a bit touched in the head — but other times, he talks like a book filled with Latin.

JACQUELINE: He sounds like all the rest. He will dose her with rhubarb and physic and Latin. The right cure for her is a right husband.

GERONTE: What husband would take a wife who cannot talk?

LUCAS: Better to have a wife who never talks than one who talks too much. Hold your tongue, wife!

GERONTE: I did offer her a husband — Horace, a fine rich gentleman. But she turned her back on him and then the illness struck, and she has not spoken a word since.

JACQUELINE: Horace . . . Horace . . . Horace. He's not the man she loves. If you'd offer her to Monsieur Leandre, she'd obey quick enough.

GERONTE: Monsieur Leandre is not a suitable husband. He has no money.

JACQUELINE: He has a rich uncle, and he is the only heir.

GERONTE: Never count your relatives' money until you have it in your hand. Death does not always listen to the prayers of the living.

VALERE: (*Rushes in at L.*) He comes, monsieur. The doctor — the doctor comes!

GERONTE: The doctor! He is coming! Everyone bow!
(*All stand ready. SGANARELLE enters L, comical in a doctor's bright robe and hat.*) Bonjour, monsieur. I am delighted to see you — delighted. (*All bow to doctor who grandly bows to them.*) We are in great need of your great help.

SGANARELLE: (*All wait for his first wise word. After suitable suspense, he strikes a pose and speaks loudly.*) Hippocrates says: — that we should both keep on our hats.

GERONTE: Hippocrates says so?

SGANARELLE: Yes.

GERONTE: In what chapter, please?

SGANARELLE: In his chapter — on hats.

GERONTE: Then we must both do so. (*Each touches his hat and bows to the other.*)

SGANARELLE: My dear doctor —

GERONTE: Whom are you addressing as doctor?

SGANARELLE: You. My dear doctor —

GERONTE: Me?

SGANARELLE: My most learned doctor —

GERONTE: But I am not a doctor.

SGANARELLE: You are not a doctor?

GERONTE: No.

SGANARELLE: Then I will make you one. (*He walks to table as all watch, picks up a slap-stick, looks at it, at Geronte, and smiles.*) I will make you a doctor. (*He suddenly starts after Geronte, slapping the stick about him, smiling at the audience after each whack.*)

GERONTE: (*Runs about wildly, hiding behind Valere.*) Help! Help! What are you doing?

SGANARELLE: (*Proudly holds up stick.*) I have made you a doctor. (*Aside.*) That is all the qualification I have.

GERONTE: What madman have you brought into my house?

VALERE: I told you he was full of humours.

GERONTE: I'll send him packing—with his humours! (*Starts toward SGANARELLE who lifts the stick threateningly. GERONTE quickly retreats and hides, shaking, beside Valere.*)

VALERE: (*Also shaking.*) Take no notice of it, master. He is having his little joke. (*Laughs weakly.*)

GERONTE: Let's see how you feel when the joke is on you? (*Angrily grabs the stick from Sganarelle and whacks at VALERE who yells and runs off L.*)

SGANARELLE: Monsieur, I beg your pardon for the liberty I have taken.

GERONTE: (*Composing himself.*) Don't mention it.

SGANARELLE: Forgive me—

GERONTE: 'Twas nothing.

SGANARELLE: For the whacking—

GERONTE: No harm is done.

SGANARELLE: Which I had the honour of giving you.

GERONTE: We'll say no more about it. (*They bow to each other. GERONTE puts stick on table.*) I sent for you because I have a daughter who has fallen victim to a strange malady.

SGANARELLE: I am delighted, monsieur, that your daughter is in need of my service. I only wish you were sick, too, that your whole family were ill, so that I could show how anxious I am to be of service to all of you.

GERONTE: I am touched by your sentiments.

SGANARELLE: What is your daughter's name?

GERONTE: Lucinde.

SGANARELLE: Lucinde! What a beautiful name for a sick patient.

GERONTE: I will bring my daughter to you. (*Starts R.*)

SGANARELLE: (*Sees Jacqueline, standing by Lucas at R.*) And who — is this fine lady here?

GERONTE: She is my daughter's maid.

SGANARELLE: And properly made in heaven!

GERONTE: I will prepare my daughter to receive you. (*Exits R.*)

SGANARELLE: (*Flirting ourtageously.*) Mademoiselle, I place all my medicine at your service. All my skill, all my knowledge, all my Latin is at your command. (*Starts toward her.*)

LUCAS: (*Steps between them.*) She is my wife.

SGANARELLE: Your wife! (*Aside.*) Your wife?

LUCAS: My wedded wife.

SGANARELLE: Ah, how happy I am to hear that, because the affection I feel for you — (*Embraces Lucas.*) — I can also feel for her.

(*Starts to embrace Jacqueline.*)

LUCAS: (*Pulls him back.*) Save your doctoring for the patient who is sick!

SGANARELLE: You cannot know how delighted I am that you are man and wife. I have the happiness of both of you at heart, and if I embrace you to show my affection — (*Embraces Lucas, then starts for her.*) I embrace her for the same reason.

LUCAS: (*Grabs and sends him across the stage.*) You've said enough.

SGANARELLE: (*Advances again.*) But I must congratulate you both! (*Embraces Lucas, starts for her.*) Her for having such a husband as you — (*JACQUELINE evades him and runs to L. He turns and starts after her, first embracing Lucas again.*) And I congratulate you — (*Crosses to Jacqueline.*) for having so beautiful, so sweet, so shapely a wife. (*Is ready to embrace her.*)

GERONTE: (*Enters R.*) What are you doing, doctor? It is not the maid who needs an examination. It is my daughter.

SGANARELLE: Ah, and I await her with all the remedies of medical science.

GERONTE: Where are they?

SGANARELLE: In here. (*Touches his head. They bow to each other.*) And it is necessary in this case to examine all who are near your daughter. (*Turns and starts to embrace Jacqueline.*)

LUCAS: (*Pulls him away.*) Enough is enough!

SGANARELLE: Beware! I shall give you a fever.

(*LUCINDE, beautiful and beautifully dressed, enters R.*)

SGANARELLE: Is this the patient?

GERONTE: (*Takes Lucinde by the hand, introduces her to the doctor. She makes a graceful curtsey.*) Monsieur, my only daughter. You must act quickly. It would break my heart if she were to die.

SGANARELLE: I forbid it! She must not die without a doctor's prescription.

GERONTE: Come . . . come, a chair for my daughter. (*Lucas places chair D. R. LUCINDE sits gracefully.*)

SGANARELLE: Truly a most beautiful patient. (*Eagerly goes to his patient and puts his hand on her forehead.*)

GERONTE: What is her temperature? Is it hot? Is it cold?

SGANARELLE: It is. (*They bow to each other.*) Now what is the trouble? What is wrong, my dear? Where do you hurt? (*She pantomimes she cannot speak. He comically imitates her. She repeats her pantomime. He repeats his.*) I don't understand. What language is this?

GERONTE: That is the trouble. She cannot speak the language. It has caused her marriage to be postponed.

SGANARELLE: But why?

GERONTE: Monsieur Horace decided to wait until she could speak.

SGANARELLE: Is there such an idiot who would not welcome a wife who is dumb? Oh, would that mine could not say a word.

GERONTE: Monsieur, I beseech you, do everything you can to cure my daughter.

SGANARELLE: Monsieur, I shall. (*They bow to each other.*) Tell me, does she suffer much pain?

GERONTE: (*Looks at Lucinde. She nods.*) Yes, monsieur.

SGANARELLE: All the better! Is the suffering very severe?

GERONTE: (*Looks at Lucinde. She nods.*) Very severe.

SGANARELLE: Splendid! Your hand, mademoiselle. (*Gracefully LUCINDE extends her hand. He holds her wrist romantically.*) the beating — of the pulse — indicates — that your daughter — is — dumb.

GERONTE: Ah, you have discovered it at once!

SGANARELLE: We great physicians know these things immediately. A stupid doctor would puzzle his brains and say, "It is this or that." But I knew immediately — and informed you that — your daughter is dumb.

GERONTE: Yes. Now tell us the cause of it.

SGANARELLE: It is very simple. She is dumb because—she has lost her power of speech.

GERONTE: Exactly, monsieur. But why has she lost the power of speech?

SGANARELLE: All the best authorities would tell you that it is due to an impediment in the use of her tongue.

GERONTE: Of course. But what is the cause of the impediment in the use of her tongue?

SGANARELLE: (*All wait for the answer to this.*) What Aristotle said about this was—very interesting. Ah, Aristotle was a great man! A very great man indeed. A greater man that I am—by that much. (*Raises his arm from his elbow.*) Now I consider that the impediment in the use of her tongue is caused by certain humours—so that the vapours created from the diseased region—coming—so to speak—do you understand Latin?

GERONTE: Not a word.

SGANARELLE: You don't understand Latin?

GERONTE: No.

SGANARELLE: (*Smiles, clears his throat, and begins.*) Cabricius arci thuram, catalamus, singulariter, nominativo baec Musa—the Muse. Bonus, bone, bonum. Deus Sanctus, est ne oratio Latinas? Etiam. Yes. Quare—why? quis substantivo et adjectivum concordat in generi, numerum et casus.

GERONTE: Ah, if only I had been a scholar!

JACQUELINE: What a great man he is.

LUCAS: He must be. I don't understand a word he says.

SGANARELLE: But these vapours which I explained to you, passing the left side where the liver is to the right side where the heart is—

GERONTE: Monsieur . . .? (*Puts hand on left side, then on right side of chest, perplexed.*)

SGANARELLE: It happens that the lungs which we call in Latin *Armyan*, connecting with the brain which in Greek we call *Nasmus*, by means of a vein which we call in Hebrew *Cubile*, encounter — notice this please — encounter the aforesaid vapours — are you listening carefully?

GERONTE: Yes.

SGANARELLE: Having a certain malignant quality — can you hear?

JACQUELINE: Yes.

SGANARELLE: Ossabandus, nequeys, nequer, potarinum, quipsa milus — and that is precisely what makes your daughter dumb.

JACQUELINE: He has explained it all.

GERONTE: One thing, doctor. The position of the liver and the heart. You have them the wrong way about. The heart is on the left side and the liver on the right.

SGANARELLE: True, it used to be; but we have changed all that. Everything is quite different in medicine nowadays.

GERONTE: Forgive my ignorance. (*They bow to each other.*) Now about my daughter. What can be done to regain her power of speech?

SGANARELLE: What can be done?

GERONTE: Yes.

SGANARELLE: My advice is — put her to bed and give her bread dipped in wine.

GERONTE: Why that?

SGANARELLE: Because bread and wine mixed together have a wonderfully pleasant effect that promotes talking. They give parrots nothing else. That is how they learn to talk.

GERONTE: What a great man! Quick, Lucas, fetch a keg of the best wine.

LUCAS: Yes, monsieur. (*Exits L, smiling happily.*)

GERONTE: Come. Help your mistress to her bed and feed her bread and wine every hour on the hour! (*Jacqueline curtsies, and follows Lucinde off at R.*)

SGANARELLE: I will return this evening and see how she is improving. In the meantime, as Aristotle said: Make haste slowly.

GERONTE: Oh, monsieur. I have forgotten an important matter.

SGANARELLE: What is that?

GERONTE: To give you some money.

SGANARELLE: (*Holds out his hand.*) Money? (*Withdraws his hand and turns his back.*) I couldn't take it.

GERONTE: What?

SGANARELLE: No.

GERONTE: You must.

SGANARELLE: No, no, no.

GERONTE: Please.

SGANARELLE: You are joking.

GERONTE: Come, take it.

SGANARELLE: No, I couldn't.

GERONTE: I insist.

SGANARELLE: I do not work for money. (*Puts his hand out behind him.*)

GERONTE: (*Puts small money bag into the hand.*) Of course not, monsieur.

SGANARELLE: (*Holds up money bag.*) Is it full weight?

GERONTE: Yes.

SGANARELLE: I only take it as a favor to you.

GERONTE: (*Aside.*) Such consideration. Good day, monsieur.

SGANARELLE: Good day, monsieur. (*They bow to each other. GERONTE exits R. SGANARELLE looks happily at the money bag.*) As Aristotle said: To sneeze and to swallow at the same time is not easy. But I have done them both!

LEANDRE: (*Enters cautiously from L, a very romantic young lover. He carries a bag.*) Monsieur . . . monsieur . . . I have been waiting . . . (*Looks around, comes to Sganarelle.*) I must see you alone. I implore you. I beg you — help me. (*Holds out his hand.*)

SGANARELLE: (*Takes his wrists. Aside.*) A very fast pulse!

LEANDRE: No, no. I am not ill.

SGANARELLE: Not ill? Then why do you come to a doctor for help?

LEANDRE: I will be brief. My name is Leandre and I am in love with Lucinde, whom you have come to cure. Her father has forbidden me to see her — but I must! The days are sad when I do not see her smile. The weeks are long when I do not hear her laugh. The months are —

SGANARELLE: Let us not have the whole year.

LEANDRE: I have come, monsieur, to ask you to help me. My life, my happiness — her life, her happiness depend on you. I have a plan and with your help I will outwit her father.

SGANARELLE: Outwit her father! Monsieur! I am a doctor! Do you presume that I will serve your amours with plotting a plan against her father!

LEANDRE: Monsieur, sh! Please make no such noise.

SGANARELLE: I will do as I please. I will shout if I please!

LEANDRE: Sh! You will alarm the household.

SGANARELLE: Do not Sh me! I am not a man of two faces. One who gives with his left hand — (*Holds out on opposite side from Leandre.*) and takes with his right. (*Holds out other hand to Leandre.*) No. As a doctor I could never — never — never —

LEANDRE: (*Understands and quickly puts small money bag into Sganarelle's hand.*) Monsieur.

SGANARELLE: Never—never do anything but help you with your plans. (*Puts money bag into his pocket.*) What can I do to serve you?

LEANDRE: First you must know that this illness which you are here to cure is all put on. She is pretending. The truth is that the real cause is love. Mademoiselle Lucinde only assumed the symptoms in order to avoid being forced to marry a man whom she does not love. It is I, monsieur, I with whom she will speak—to whom she will say—"I will." In the meantime, because I cannot see her, the days are sad . . . the weeks are long . . . the months are . . .

SGANARELLE: Yes . . . yes . . . yes. Your plan? What is your plan to see her—and to make her speak?

LEANDRE: First I will—but we must not be overheard. (*Each looks around, then shake their heads at each other.*) No one must know. (*Again they peek around, then shake their heads.*) I will disguise myself. (*They nod. As they speak, LEANDRE takes from his bag an apothecary robe, funny hat, and false nose. With SGANARELLE's help, he quickly puts them on—nose last.*)

SGANARELLE: How?

LEANDRE: As an apothecary. I have borrowed a robe to wear.

SGANARELLE: Ah!

LEANDRE: A hat to cover my head.

SGANARELLE: Ah-ah!

LEANDRE: And a false nose to hide my face.

SGANARELLE: (*Laughs.*) Ha-ha! You have changed completely. Your disguise is perfect.

LEANDRE: Dressed like an apothecary, I can easily accompany you. At last I will see her. At last I will talk with her. Monsieur! I know the right words to say to her, but I know no Latin words to say to her father.

SGANARELLE: Latin words?

LEANDRE: Give me five or six words that I can sprinkle in my conversation.

SGANARELLE: No. I cannot tell you any Latin words.

LEANDRE: Monsieur, if I speak no Latin, her father will suspect me a fraud. Four words? Three?

SGANARELLE: No. I cannot.

LEANDRE: The happiness of two people is in your hands.

SGANARELLE: I cannot.

LEANDRE: One? A single word.

SGANARELLE: I cannot give what I do not have.

LEANDRE: Monsieur, you joke.

SGANARELLE: You are right. It is a joke! (*Laughs.*) I do not know a word of Latin.

LEANDRE: You are a doctor.

SGANARELLE: That is a joke, too. (*Laughs.*) I am not a doctor.

LEANDRE: I don't understand.

SGANARELLE: I will tell you the truth. But swear that you will not reveal my disguise, and I will swear not to tell of yours. (*They raise a hand and nod.*) I am a woodcutter—a poor, simple woodcutter with no schooling at all. It is true I can talk as well as the next—and I once did serve a doctor, but—suddenly they came upon me—whack! And made me into a doctor.

LEANDRE: How?

SGANARELLE: (*Acts out the following speech, changing voices, jumping from side to side, whacking comically.*) They beat me! I said, "I am not a doctor." Whack! "I don't want to be a doctor." Whack. "Why do you pick on me?" Whack. Whack. Whack. "No." Whack. Whack. Whack. Whack. "Yes . . . Yes, I am a doctor." Now dressed in a doctor's hat and robe, I am the wisest man in France. It is the best trade I've found. Whether I help the sick or not I still get my money. And I am never blamed for faulty work. A doctor can make a mess of any man and is never accused. Instead he is paid for it! If I make a mistake, who can blame me? The fault is always the man who died. And the best part of that is that the dead are most silent.

LEANDRE: I never thought of that, but you are right.

SGANARELLE: A doctor is always right!

(*GERONTE enters R.*)

GERONTE: Ah, monsieur, I have been searching — asking for you.

SGANARELLE: How is the patient?

GERONTE: Alas, since taking your medicine she is worse.

SGANARELLE: So much the better! The cure is working.

GERONTE: But my dear doctor, I am worried.

SGANARELLE: Have no fear. My best remedies I save to the last. I am waiting until she reaches death's door.

LEANDRE: (*Clears his throat and speaks in a disguised voice.*) Truly spoken by a great doctor.

GERONTE: Who is this you have brought with you?

SGANARELLE: A most learned — (*LEANDRE bows.*) most clever apothecary. (*LEANDRE bows again.*) He is skilled in the art of making love — Letting blood, and giving sweet potions. Your daughter has a great need for him.

GERONTE: Monsieur, I beg you do all — all in your power to make her happy.

LEANDRE: (*Clears his throat.*) You may be sure I will do all I can!

JACQUELINE: (*Enters R.*) Pardon, monsieur.

GERONTE: What is it?

JACQUELINE: My mistress feels the need of a breath of air and a brief walk.

SGANARELLE: Excellent! It is exactly what I prescribe. Bring Mademoiselle to us at once. (*JACQUELINE curtsies and exits R.*) You, monsieur Apothecary, will walk about, take her pulse — often! — while I explain further her symptoms to her father.

JACQUELINE: (*Enters R.*) Mademoiselle is here. (*LUCINDE enters R. JACQUELINE exits.*)

SGANARELLE: My dear young lady, I have an immediate cure for all your trouble. (*Takes her to Leandre.*) I will put you in the waiting hands of this gentleman — (*LEANDRE removes his nose. She gasps. He puts nose back on.*) — who has a heart-felt interest in your health — and your future happiness.

LEANDRE: Your pulse, mademoiselle. (*Holds her wrist, romantically. She smiles happily.*)

GERONTE: Look — already she appears better.

SGANARELLE. (*Leads Geronte to other side.*) Now let us discuss a most important matter.

GERONTE: (*Turns back to look at Lucinde.*) She is smiling.

SGANARELLE: (*Turns Geronte around so he cannot see the lovers.*) It is a very debatable point among learned doctors. (*GERONTE peeks around, SGANARELLE turns him back around. This business is repeated during the speech, all the while the two lovers sigh and their lips get closer together.*) whether women are easier to cure than men. I would like your opinion. Some say, yes, others say no. I myself say both yes and no. Inasmuch as most of the humours which arise from the nature and temperament of women are the causes for the usual predominance of the body over the mind — (*GERONTE, too curious, turns around and looks at lovers. SGANARELLE circles around him and stands between Geronte and them, still talking. GERONTE bends and tries to see, SGANARELLE bends also to mask them. GERONTE bends to the other side to see around SGANARELLE, who bends that way to mask the view, all the while the lovers are ready to kiss, but the false nose is too large. LEANDRE takes it off.*) are, we observe, the move-ment of the lunary circle: and as the sun shines its rays on the concavity of the earth, it finds —

LUCINDE: (*As they are ready to kiss.*) It is only you that I love.

SGANARELLE: (*He and GERONTE look front, surprised. SGANARELLE quickly starts talking.*) — that the sun and the moon and the tides —

LUCINDE: No, there has never been anyone else. I have not changed my affections.

GERONTE: My daughter's voice! She speaks! She can talk! (*Goes to her, as she breaks away from Leandre.*) Oh wonderful remedy! Oh, greatest of doctors! How grateful I am to you, monsieur. How can I repay you?

SGANARELLE: (*Collapsing.*) It has been a most exhausting case.

LUCINDE: Yes, Papa, I have recovered my speech, but I have recov-ered it only to tell you that I will have no husband but Leandre. (*Looks in his direction. He sighs.*) He is my only choice and there is no use your wanting to give me Horace.

GERONTE: But —

LUCINDE: Nothing will ever change my mind.

GERONTE: What!

LUCINDE: I won't argue.

GERONTE: If —

LUCINDE: Nothing you say will do any good.

GERONTE: But —

LUCINDE: You cannot force me to marry against my will.

GERONTE: I have —

LUCINDE: Never, never, never.

GERONTE: There—

LUCINDE: I'll run away—shut myself in a convent rather than marry a man I don't love.

GERONTE: But—

LUCINDE: No. No. No! I will not do it. That is final, final. Final!

GERONTE: What a torrent of words. What am I to do? I implore you, monsieur, make her dumb again.

SGANARELLE: That is one thing I cannot do. The only thing I can do to help you is—to make you deaf.

GERONTE: Thank you—no. (*To her.*) Young lady—

LUCINDE: I will not listen.

GERONTE: You will listen to what I say and I say—you will marry Horace this very evening. (*LUCINDA gasps and goes to Leandre. GERONTE slaps his hands.*) Attend! Attend! (*JACQUELINE enters R.*) Prepare the church for the wedding tonight. (*JACQUELINE curtsies and exits R.*)

LUCINDE: Never, never, never! I will die first!

SGANARELLE: Peace, I pray. Monsieur, let me prescribe a remedy. It is her illness that is still affecting her, but there is one—only one cure that will make her well.

GERONTE: Then attend her—quickly.

SGARANELLE: In her case, our apothecary is the very man to administer the cure.
  (*To Leandre.*)
A word, monsieur. You see that her ardent affection for Leandre is entirely contrary to her father's wishes. There is no time to lose; the humours are fermenting, and an immediate remedy must be found. Do not delay. I see only one thing for it—a dose of run-away purgative mixed with two drachms of matrimony. If she makes any difficulties,

do your job. Make her follow through. Go. (*He pushes them together. LUCINDE takes his arm.*) Walk her around the garden while I talk to her father here. Above all, lose no time. To the remedy, quick, the one and only remedy to save her!

(*LEANDRE and LUCINDE exit quickly off L.*)

GERONTE: Monsieur, what were the drugs you mentioned?

SGANARELLE: Two special drugs always used in such emergencies. Your daughter — even now — is on her way to a new and happy life.

(*Looks off L, after them.*)

GERONTE: The way she talked to me! It is because of this fellow Leandre. When I discovered how madly she was in love with him, I locked her in — kept her out of his sight.

SGANARELLE: Exactly.

GERONTE: I stopped all communication between the two.

SGANARELLE: Excellent.

GERONTE: And you may be sure I will never let them be together, because I know what would happen —

SGANARELLE: (*Nods toward L.*) I am thinking the same thing —

GERONTE: She would run off with him.

SGANARELLE: My thoughts exactly.

GERONTE: But I have won! The joke is on them.

SGANARELLE: Yes, the joke is on — (*Laughs. They both laugh and start to "elbow" each other.*) They would have to be smart indeed to outwit you. (*They laugh louder, hitting each other.*)

LUCAS: (*Rushes in L, excited.*) Master! Oh, master! It's happened! She is gone. Escaped. Flew the coop!

GERONTE: What is it? What is it?

LUCAS: Your daughter is gone — run away — with young Leandre!

GERONTE: What!

LUCAS: 'Twas Leandre dressed up like an apothecary!

(*SGANARELLE takes one step R.*)

GERONTE: What!!

LUCAS: 'Twas a trick. (*SGANARELLE takes another step.*) And it was him — (*Points at SGANARELLE who stops, frightened.*) the doctor who did this fine operation.

GERONTE: What!! Give me breath . . . you betrayed me! . . . give me air . . . stabbed me in the back! (*Clasps his hands and calls.*) Valere! Valere! Attend! (*VALERE rushes in at L.*) Call the magistrate. Bring the magistrate at once! (*VALERE bows and runs off L. SGANARELLE starts to exit R.*) Stop him! You traitor! You will hang for this!

LUCAS: (*Crosses and grabs him by shoulder.*) 'Twill be a pleasure to hang him myself!

SGANARELLE: (*Knees shaking.*) H—e—l—p.

MARTINE: (*Enters L.*) What are you doing with my husband?

LUCAS: I am going to hang him!

MARTINE: What has he done?

GERONTE: Traitor! Thief! He let my daughter run away, but *he* will not get away. The law will settle this.

SGANARELLE: Couldn't you settle it with a few whacks?

GERONTE: Silence! Justice will be done!

LEANDRE: (*He and LUCINDE enter L.*) Monsieur . . . monsieur.

GERONTE: What do I see? My daughter returns.

LEANDRE: Monsieur, I am Leandre — (*Takes off nose and hat, gives them to Lucinde.*) and I have returned Lucinde to your house. We did intend to run away and to be married, but that intention has given way to a more honourable procedure. I do not wish to rob you of your daughter. Instead I prefer to receive her from you with your blessing.

GERONTE: Give you my daughter? Never, never, never!

LEANDRE: Monsieur, I am to inform you that I have just received letters stating that my *rich* uncle is dead, and I have inherited all his possessions.

GERONTE: Oh, monsieur, what glad — sad news. I extend my sympathy. And now I do see your many shining virtues. I give you my daughter with all the pleasure in the world.

JACQUELINE: (*Enters from R.*) Monsieur, the church is ready for the wedding.

VALERE: (*Enters from L.*) Monsieur, the Magistrate is here to hang the doctor. (*All look at Sganarelle.*)

LEANDRE: My dear — father. You must forgive the doctor, for without his — cure — there would be no happy ending.

GERONTE: That is true. So — the Magistrate, instead of pronouncing death, will pronounce the wedding vows.

SGANARELLE: Ah, a close call for the medical profession.

MARTINE: (*Goes to him.*) My husband, you can thank *me* for making you a doctor.

SGANARELLE: And I can also thank you for the whacking.

MARTINE: But see to what high degree it has raised you.

SGANARELLE: So it has! And so, henceforth, wife, you shall show proper respect to — a doctor — in spite of himself! (*Music. Tableau.*)

The Tricks of Scapin

by Molière
Adapted by Aurand Harris

ROYALTY NOTE

CAST

ARGANTE, *father of Octavio and Zerbinetta*
GERONTE, *father of Leander and Hyacintha*
OCTAVIO, *son of Argante and lover of Hyacintha*
LEANDER, *son of Geronte and lover of Zerbinetta*
ZERBINETTA, *a gypsy girl, later recognized as the daughter of Argante*
HYACINTHA, *daughter of Geronte and lover of Octavio*
SCAPIN, *servant of Leander*
SILVESTER, *servant to Octavio*
NURSE, *companion to Hyacintha*
CARLE, *a rogue*

SCENE: *A street in Naples, Italy*

The Tricks of Scapin

(A *street in Naples, Italy. SILVESTER, servant of Octavio, enters.*
OCTAVIO, a rich, handsome young gentleman, enters.)

OCTAVIO: Silvester! Silvester!

SILVESTER: Yes, my master.

OCTAVIO: Is it true the news I hear from the harbor? Is it true that my
father is coming back today?

SILVESTER: It is true.

OCTAVIO: And he is arriving this very morning?

SILVESTER: This very morning.

OCTAVIO: And he is bringing with him a young lady?

SILVESTER: A very PRETTY young lady!

OCTAVIO: The daughter of Signor Geronte?

SILVESTER: The daughter of Signor Geronte.

OCTAVIO: And—my father intends that I shall marry her?

SILVESTER: You shall marry her.

OCTAVIO: Oh, what a desperate, desperate situation I am in.

SILVESTER: You should have thought of that before WE got into it.

(*SCAPIN, servant to Leander, enters. He is a clever, likeable rascal.*)

OCTAVIO: (*Sees and points at Scapin.*) Scapin.

SILVESTER: Scapin?

OCTAVIO: He is the cleverest scamp in Italy. He can get us out of this trouble.

SILVESTER: Or — get us into more trouble!

OCTAVIO: My dear Scapin. I am in despair.

SCAPIN: Despair?

SILVESTER: We are done for.

SCAPIN: Done for what?

OCTAVIO: My father is bringing the daughter of Signor Geronte back to Naples. He intends for me to marry her.

SCAPIN: And what is there so terrible in that?

OCTAVIO: Oh, you little know my big trouble.

SCAPIN: (*Eager for gossip.*) You have only to tell me.

OCTAVIO: Two months ago Signor Geronte —

SCAPIN: My master.

OCTAVIO: Your master and my father set out on a voyage together. Silvester was to look after me —

SCAPIN: And I was to look after young Leander.

OCTAVIO: Soon afterwards Leander met a young gypsy girl —

SCAPIN: (*Romantically.*) And fell in love with her.

OCTAVIO: And I met a young girl — a stranger in Naples — alone with only her old nurse with her. A sweet, beautiful girl.

SCAPIN: Ah, now we are coming to the point.

SILVESTER: He married her three days ago.

SCAPIN: Married her!

OCTAVIO: So you see, I cannot marry Signor Geronte's daughter.

SILVESTER: Pst. Pst. Oh, master, look. She comes.

OCTAVIO: My dear.

SCAPIN: His dear?

SILVESTER: His wife.

HYACINTHA: (*She enters. She is beautiful, feminine, and proper. She is followed by NURSE, who stands aside.*) Octavio!

OCTAVIO: Hyacintha! (*They rush to each other.*)

HYACINTHA: Oh, is it true, as my Nurse tells me, that your father is back and that he intends you to marry someone else?

OCTAVIO: It is true, dear Hyacintha.

HYACINTHA: Oh, what a dreadful shock for me!

OCTAVIO: Surely you do not doubt my love?

HYACINTHA: Not you. It is your father I fear.

OCTAVIO: He cannot make me give you up. I have never seen the girl he brings for me to marry, but I hate her already. Do not cry, Hyacintha.

HYACINTHA: What are we to do?

OCTAVIO: Help is at hand.

HYACINTHA: So soon?

OCTAVIO: Scapin!

SCAPIN: No, no, no, no. I have sworn that I will never meddle again in other people's business. But — if you both ask very nicely — perhaps —

OCTAVIO: I IMPLORE you. Help us!

SCAPIN: And you?

HYACINTHA: I beseech you. Help us.

SCAPIN: Well—I am persuaded. Go—I will do what I can.

HYACINTHA: Oh, thank you. (*To Octavio.*) Good bye. (*Turns.*) Oh dear. (*Exits, followed by NURSE.*)

OCTAVIO: (*Looking after her.*) My dear.

SCAPIN: Now! First you must prepare yourself to meet your father.

OCTAVIO: I tremble at the thought.

SCAPIN: You must stand firm. Come, pull yourself together. Hold your head up . . . stand tall . . . look fierce.

OCTAVIO: (*Trying.*) Like this?

SCAPIN: We will rehearse. I will be your father and I am coming home. (*Walks and talks like Father.*) "Ah, there you are, you scoundrel, you good for nothing. You have disgraced your father. Stop! How dare you come near me after what you have done. Is this the way you obey me." (*OCTAVIO opens his mouth but no words come out.*) "Is this the way you show your respect for me?" (*OCTAVIO works his jaw but no sound comes. SCAPIN whispers.*) Speak—speak up. (*OCTAVIO nods and takes a deep breath. SCAPIN imitates Father again.*) "Have you married without your father's consent?"

OCTAVIO: I—I—I—

SCAPIN: "Answer me, you rogue!"

OCTAVIO: I—I—I—I—I—

SCAPIN: What is wrong?

OCTAVIO: You sound so much like my father I cannot speak.

SCAPIN: Try again. Be brave. Be commanding!

OCTAVIO: Yes, I will put on a bold front. (*Strikes a pose.*)

SCAPIN: Are you sure?

OCTAVIO: Very sure.

SCAPIN: Good. Because here comes your father!

OCTAVIO: Heaven help me. I am done for! (*Exits.*)

SCAPIN: Stop, Octavio. Be firm. Be—He is gone. Well, WE will meet the old man. Come, Silvester.

SILVESTER: (*Shaking.*) What shall I tell my master?

SCAPIN: Leave the talking to me. Just back me up.

SILVESTER: I will be right behind you. (*SCAPIN stands bravely. SILVESTER hides behind him. ARGANTE enters. He is old and rich and a miser.*)

ARGANTE: Disaster! Ruin! Oh, such a calamity should happen to me!

SCAPIN: He has already heard.

ARGANTE: Such a fool thing to do!

SCAPIN: Let us listen to what he says.

ARGANTE: I'd like to know excuses he will make about this marriage.

SCAPIN: (*Aside.*) We are trying to think of something.

ARGANTE: Will he try to deny it?

SCAPIN: (*Aside.*) No, we never thought of that.

ARGANTE: Or will he try to justify it?

SCAPIN: (*Aside.*) We might do that.

ARGANTE: Or fool me with some made-up story?

SCAPIN: (*Aside.*) That is what we will do!

ARGANTE: He can tell what tale he likes. I will not believe him.

SCAPIN: (*Aside.*) We shall see about that!

ARGANTE: As for that scoundrel Silvester, I will have the hide off him.

SILVESTER: (*Aside.*) I knew I would not come out alive!
(*SILVESTER with high steps starts off. ARGANTE turns and sees him.*)

ARGANTE: Ha, there you are! You are a fine fellow to leave in charge of a family. (*SILVESTER freezes.*)

SCAPIN: Signor Argante! I am happy to see you have returned.

ARGANTE: Good day, Scapin. (*In front of Scapin, speaks sarcastically to Silvester.*) You have carried out my orders nicely, haven't you! My son has behaved well in my absence, hasn't he!

SCAPIN: (*Taps Argante on shoulder.*) You seem in good health, Signor.

ARGANTE: Fairly well, thank you. (*To Silvester.*) You don't say a word. You don't open your mouth.

SCAPIN: (*Taps Argante on shoulder.*) Did you have a pleasant journey?

ARGANTE: Yes, a very pleasant journey! Do let me work off my temper!

SCAPIN: Work off your temper?

ARGANTE: Yes, work off my temper!

SCAPIN: On whom, sir?

ARGANTE: On that scoundrel there! (*Turns to Silvester.*)

SCAPIN: (*Taps Argante on shoulder.*) But why?

ARGANTE: Haven't you heard what has happened while I was away? My son married without my consent!

SCAPIN: But have you heard the whole story?

ARGANTE: The whole story?

SCAPIN: He could not escape from marrying her?

ARGANTE: Escape? Why was he involved?

SCAPIN: Remember he is not as wise as you. Remember he is young, and the young do foolish things. For example, my master, young Leander, he has — in spite of all my teaching — he has done something much worse than your son.

ARGANTE: (*Gloating.*) Young Leander is in trouble?

SCAPIN: Oh, far worse than Octavio. But let me tell you what happened to your son, Octavio. He sees this young lady who takes a liking to him — for he takes after you, who are a favorite with the ladies — he finds her charming, goes to see her, sighs sweet words — and then suddenly he is taken by surprise by her kinsmen and made — by brute force — to promise to marry her.

ARGANTE: Made to by force?

SCAPIN: Would you want him to let them kill him? It is better to be married than to be dead.

ARGANTE: A threat on his life! The law will dissolve this marriage.

SCAPIN: Oh, no!

ARGANTE: They used violence against my son.

SCAPIN: He will never admit it.

ARGANTE: Never admit it?

SCAPIN: Never. He would never admit he was a coward, unworthy of his brave father.

ARGANTE: I will disinherit him!

SCAPIN: Oh, no!

ARGANTE: Who is going to stop me?

SCAPIN: You will.

ARGANTE: I?

SCAPIN: You are too fond of him.

ARGANTE: No, I'm not.

SCAPIN: Oh, yes, you are.

ARGANTE: I tell you, I am not.

SCAPIN: Everyone knows you are a sweet tempered, forgiving, good-natured gentleman.

ARGANTE: I am not a bit good-natured. I can be as ill-natured as anyone. (*Points at Silvester.*) You! Go! Go and find my son, while I go and see Signor Geronte and tell him that his daughter can never marry my son.

SCAPIN: Signor, if I can be of help to you, I am at your service.

ARGANTE: Thank you. Ah, why is he my only child? Why could Heaven not have spared me my little daughter — that I could leave my money to her! (*Exits.*)

SCAPIN: (*Happily.*) Ah, we have started to help.

SILVESTER: Help? You have helped to make him angry.

SCAPIN: Don't you see — the plot is laid. Signor Argante will now meet one of the bride's kinsmen, a fierce, fighting, frightening —

SILVESTER: But she has no kinsmen. She arrived in Naples with only an old nurse.

SCAPIN: We will invent a kinsman. Someone about your height . . . your size . . . your strength . . . you!

SILVESTER: Me!

SCAPIN: You — disguised with a big hat, a big cape, a deep voice —

SILVESTER: No. Leave me out of this.

SCAPIN: You are already in it.

SILVESTER: It will mean three years in the galleys!

SCAPIN: Now, stand straight . . . hand on your sword . . . frown . . .
scowl . . . sneer . . . strut like a scoundrel. (*SILVESTER tries.*) Perfect.
We will disguise your face and voice, and no one will recognize you.
Come. (*SCAPIN marches off, followed by SILVESTER, who imitates
him. ARGANTE enters, followed by GERONTE.*)

ARGANTE: Ah, Signor Geronte, my son has made an old man of me.
He is already married — behind my back — when my one wish was for
him to marry your daughter.

GERONTE: (*He is rich, old, and a miser.*) It is said, bad behavior in a
young man can be the result of bad upbringing.

ARGANTE: What are you getting at?

GERONTE: What am I getting at?

ARGANTE: Yes.

GERONTE: Perhaps if you had brought your son, Octavio, up properly, he would never have played you such a trick.

ARGANTE: Oh, and I suppose you have brought Leander, your son, up
better?

GERONTE: I have. Leander would never treat me the way your son
has disgraced you.

ARGANTE: Oh, he wouldn't? Well, I hear that your precious son
whom you have brought up so well, has done something far worse than
mine.

GERONTE: What are you saying. Have you heard something about
MY son? What? Speak out.

ARGANTE: Ask your servant Scapin.

GERONTE: Scapin?

ARGANTE: He can give you the full details. Good bye. I am off to see
my lawyer and find out what I can do with my son! (*Exits.*)

GERONTE: What can he mean? My son has done something worse
than his son? What can be worse than to marry without your father's
consent! Ah, here comes my son now. I shall find out. Leander!

LEANDER: (*Enters. He is a rich young man, handsome, virile, and impulsive.*) Why, father! Welcome home.

GERONTE: Not so fast. We have something to settle first.

LEANDER: What is it?

GERONTE: That is what I want to know. What has been going on here? What have you been doing while I have been away?

LEANDER: Nothing.

GERONTE: Nothing? That is not what Scapin says.

LEANDER: Scapin?

GERONTE: Ah, ha! That gives you a fright.

LEANDER: He has told you something about me?

GERONTE: We will settle this at home. Be off. And if you have disgraced me, I'll disown you, disinherit you! (*Exits.*)

LEANDER: So Scapin has told my father my secrets. What a rascal he is! But I swear he shall pay for this!

(*OCTAVIO enters, followed by SCAPIN.*)

OCTAVIO: My dear Scapin, I am most grateful. Your plan is excellent. My father will give his consent to the marriage — and he will also give me the money I need.

LEANDER: Ah, Scapin. I am delighted to see you — Signor Troublemaker!

SCAPIN: At your service, master.

LEANDER: Oh, you will make a joke of it, will you? I will teach you to joke with me! (*Hand on dagger.*)

SCAPIN: (*On knees.*) Oh, master —

OCTAVIO: Leander!

LEANDER: No, Octavio, don't interfere.

SCAPIN: But, master —

LEANDER: Just let me get my hands on him!

SCAPIN: But, master, what have I done to you?

LEANDER: What have you done? Traitor! (*Tries to strike.*)

OCTAVIO: Stop—stop!

LEANDER: No, Octavio, I will make him confess. I know what tricks you have been up to. You thought I wouldn't find out, but I have. Now, confess, or I will run you through with my blade!

SCAPIN: Something I have done, master?

LEANDER: Yes.

SCAPIN: I confess I can't think of anything.

LEANDER: (*Threatens.*) You can't think of anything?

SCAPIN: Oh, yes, master. I remember. I confess that one evening you sent me with a watch to the young gypsy girl you are in love with, and I came with my clothes torn and bloody, and I told you that I had been robbed of the watch. It was me, master—I kept the watch for myself.

LEANDER: I am glad to know the truth about that. But—that is not what I mean.

SCAPIN: It isn't?

LEANDER: It is something more serious—and I am going to have it out of you!

SCAPIN: I can't think of anything else, master.

LEANDER: You can't think of anything else? (*Twists his ear.*)

SCAPIN: Ouch!

LEANDER: There is something else. Confess—confess what you just told my father about me.

SCAPIN: Your father?

LEANDER: Yes, my father!

SCAPIN: I have not even seen him since he returned.

LEANDER: But he told me so himself.

SCAPIN: Then, sir, you'll pardon my saying so, but he has not spoken the truth.

CARLE: (*Enters. Carle is a rogue.*) Signor. Signor. I have run . . . run to tell you the news — and bad news it is.

LEANDER: What is it?

CARLE: I come from Zerbinetta. She has sent me to you.

LEANDER: Zerbinetta!

SCAPIN: The gypsy girl.

CARLE: She begged me to come at once and tell you —

LEANDER: Tell me what? Is she in danger?

CARLE: The gypsies are leaving, traveling on. They are going to take her away.

LEANDER: Never!

CARLE: You have not brought the money which you promised them.

LEANDER: I do not have it yet.

CARLE: They say unless you bring the money within two hours she will be gone forever.

LEANDER: Two hours!

CARLE: I must go. Oh, signor, Zerbinetta implores you. Save her.

(*Exits.*)

LEANDER: Of course I will. But how? (*Looks at Scapin.*) Ah, my dear Scapin, help me. I beg you.

SCAPIN: Oh, so now I am your dear Scapin, now that you need me.

LEANDER: I forgive you all that you have done.

SCAPIN: No. No! Do not forgive me anything. Here—run your blade through me.

LEANDER: It was my hasty temper.

SCAPIN: I still remember the insults.

LEANDER: I was wrong.

SCAPIN: You called me a rogue, a villain, a scoundrel.

LEANDER: I am sorry.

SCAPIN: You talked of running a dagger through me.

LEANDER: I will go down on my bended knees. (*Kneels.*) Scapin, I implore you—I need your help.

OCTAVIO: Come, Scapin, say you will help.

SCAPIN: Well—I forgive you. But another time, watch your temper.

LEANDER: Now promise you will help me and Zerbinetta.

SCAPIN: I promise—to think about it.

LEANDER: But there is no time to waste.

SCAPIN: Two hours. How much money do you need?

LEANDER: I promised the gypsies five hundred guineas.

SCAPIN: (*To Octavio.*) And how much do YOU need?

OCTAVIO: Two hundred pounds.

SCAPIN: I will get the money out of each of your fathers. But go. Here comes your father now.

OCTAVIO: My father!

SCAPIN: Be off, both of you! I will start my tricks with Signor Argante. Tell Silvester to come quickly — in his disguise.

OCTAVIO: Disguise?

SCAPIN: (*Puts finger to mouth*). Sh! (*Motions for them to go. They exit. ARGANTE enters.*) Your servant, Signor.

ARGANTE: Good day, Scapin. I have just taken legal steps to get my son's marriage dissolved.

SCAPIN: Take my advice, Signor. Settle it another way — a cheaper way.

ARGANTE: If I only could.

SCAPIN: I can help you. I have just seen the brother of the girl your son has married. He is a professional fighter, free with his sword. He talks of nothing but cutting people to pieces, and thinks nothing of killing a man. Well, I suggested a way to dissolve the marriage, and he said, "Yes — if — "

ARGANTE: If?

SCAPIN: If you will make it worth his while.

ARGANTE: Money?

SCAPIN: Money.

ARGANTE: Never. How much?

SCAPIN: Oh, a huge sum.

ARGANTE: Such as?

SCAPIN: Out of all reason.

ARGANTE: Go on.

SCAPIN: More than five or six hundred pounds.

ARGANTE: Five or six hundred devils!

SCAPIN: That's what I said, and we argued. Then he said, (*Imitates a cut-throat.*) "I am rejoining the army, so I will agree to your proposal." (*Whispers.*) Less money. (*Imitates.*) "First I need a horse. That will be sixty pounds."

ARGANTE: Well, if it is only sixty pounds, I will agree.

SCAPIN: Then he says, "I will need harness and a set of pistols. That will be another twenty pounds."

ARGANTE: That makes eighty.

SCAPIN: Then he says, "I will need a horse for my man. That will cost another thirty pounds."

ARGANTE: What the devil! He will get no horse out of me.

SCAPIN: Oh, sir!

ARGANTE: No, he is a rogue! A cheat!

SCAPIN: But think how much it will cost if you go to law!

ARGANTE: Yes . . . yes. Well, go on.

SCAPIN: Then he says, "I shall need a mule to carry—"

ARGANTE: The devil take his mule! Enough is enough!

SCAPIN: But Signor—

ARGANTE: No, I will have no more to do with him!

SCAPIN: Just a little mule?

ARGANTE: No! Not even a donkey.

SCAPIN: But consider how much—how much more the lawyers will cost in court.

ARGANTE: Well . . . a little mule.

SCAPIN: All in all, he asks for two hundred pounds.

ARGANTE: Two hundred pounds! I'll go to court.

SCAPIN: But going to court will mean money for the summons, money for the writs, money for the warrants.

ARGANTE: Money!

SCAPIN: Give the money to this fellow and you're finished with the whole business. (*He motions for Silvester to enter. SILVESTER struts in, disguised in hat and cape, and stands in a threatening pose.*) Pst! There is the bride's kinsmen, the very cut-throat we have been talking about.

SILVESTER: Scapin! Show me this fellow, Argante, the old miser who is Octavio's father.

SCAPIN: Why Signor?

SILVESTER: Why! Because I have heard he is going to bring the law against me and get my sister's marriage dissolved! I say death and cremation! If I catch him I will cut him to pieces! (*Slices air with sword. ARGANTE hides behind Scapin.*)

SCAPIN: But, Signor, Octavio's father is a man of courage. He will not be frightened of you.

SILVESTER: Won't he? If he were here I would run my sword through him like this! (*Thrusts toward Argante.*) Who is this? Is this the old man? (*ARGANTE shakes his head.*)

SCAPIN: Oh, no, sir.

SILVESTER: One of his friends? (*ARGANTE shakes his head.*)

SCAPIN: No, sir. In fact — one of his deadly enemies!

(*ARGANTE nods his head.*)

SILVESTER: His deadly enemy? Ah, I am glad to meet you! Give me your hand. Give me your hand! (*Shakes hands roughly.*) I swear by the sword if I had old Argante here I would say: you villain, you miserable miser, you bag of hot air! I'll give you a bellyful! (*Recklessly duels with his sword.*) On guard! Stand to! Take that you scoundrel! And that!

SCAPIN: Careful! Easy! We are on your side.

SILVESTER: Ah! Dead! That will teach Argante to play tricks with me! (*Exits.*)

ARGANTE: (*Weakly.*) Scapin—

SCAPIN: Yes?

ARGANTE: I am ready to give him the money.

SCAPIN: Good. I will take it to him.

ARGANTE: But I like to know where my money goes.

SCAPIN: Don't you trust me?

ARGANTE: Well—

SCAPIN: What? Do you think I am a cheat? Ha, then I'll have no more to do with it. Go find someone else to save you from being killed.

ARGANTE: No, no. Take the money.

SCAPIN: Never. You don't trust me.

ARGANTE: I insist. Take it. And let me be off. (*Forces money bag onto Scapin.*) But make sure—to get a receipt from him. (*Exits.*)

SCAPIN: Two hundred for Octavio. And now a trick to help Leander. And here comes his father. (*GERONTE enters. SCAPIN starts wailing.*) Oh, what an unexpected misfortune. Oh, unhappy father. Poor Geronte! Sad, sad news.

GERONTE: (*Aside.*) He speaks my name.

SCAPIN: Can no one tell me where Signor Geronte is?

GERONTE: What is the matter, Scapin?

SCAPIN: I must find him. I must tell him of this disaster.

GERONTE: Disaster?

SCAPIN: I am looking for him, but I cannot find him.

GERONTE: Here I am!

SCAPIN: He has hidden himself well.

GERONTE: I am standing beside you. What is the matter?

SCAPIN: Master!

GERONTE: What is it?

SCAPIN: Your son, Leander.

GERONTE: What about my son?

SCAPIN: Misfortune. Misfortune!

GERONTE: Misfortune?

SCAPIN: I found him a short while ago, terribly upset because of something you said to him — and let me point out, you said I said something I never said! Well, I tried to cheer him up by walking down to the harbour, and there we saw a Turkish galley. Up comes a pleasant-looking young Turk and invites us aboard.

GERONTE: There is no misfortune in that.

SCAPIN: But listen! We are on the boat, eating a delicious meal — and the galley puts out to sea! I am put into a little boat, row to shore, and must find you to tell you that your son will be shipped off to Algiers! Unless you pay immediately five hundred guineas in ransom.

GERONTE: Five hundred guineas!

SCAPIN: Yes, master. And you only have two hours to save him.

GERONTE: Kidnapped my son!

SCAPIN: Think of some way to save him.

GERONTE: I will have the police after him.

SCAPIN: The police on the open sea? Not a chance.

GERONTE: Why the deuce did he go on the galley? I have it. You, Scapin, as a faithful servant will go and take my son's place until I can get the money.

SCAPIN: Oh, master, do you think this Turk will accept a miserable servant like me in place of your noble son?

GERONTE: But what the deuce did he go on the galley for?

SCAPIN: Only two hours.

GERONTE: How much money?

SCAPIN: Five hundred guineas.

GERONTE: Five hundred guineas! Here—here take the key to my cupboard. Open it. There you will find a big key which unlocks my attic. Go take all the old clothes you can find and sell them to redeem my son.

SCAPIN: You won't get five pounds for your old clothes.

GERONTE: Oh, what the deuce did he go in the galley for?

SCAPIN: Forget the galley! Time is passing. Ah, my poor young master. I may never see you again. If you are not ransomed in time, it will be because your father—didn't care.

GERONTE: (*Touched.*) True. True, Scapin. I will give you the money.

SCAPIN: Then be quick.

GERONTE: Four hundred guineas?

SCAPIN: Five hundred.

GERONTE: Here. I have the amount with me. Never did I think I would part with all of it so soon. (*Takes money bag from belt; holds it out to Scapin.*) Take it. Go—go and ransom my son.

SCAPIN: (*Holds out hand.*) Yes, Master.

GERONTE: (*Shaking his fist with the bag.*) And tell that Turk he is a scoundrel!

SCAPIN: (*Reaching for the bag.*) Yes.

GERONTE: (*Shaking bag.*) A villain!

SCAPIN: (*Reaching higher.*) Yes.

GERONTE: A robber!

SCAPIN: I will!

GERONTE: And that if I ever catch him, I will take revenge on him!

SCAPIN: Revenge!

GERONTE: (*Turns away, still with money bag.*) Now go get my son.

SCAPIN: (*Looks at empty hand.*) Master . . .

GERONTE: Well?

SCAPIN: Where is the money?

GERONTE: Didn't I give it to you?

SCAPIN: No, master, You took it back.

GERONTE: Ah, it is grief that blinds me.

SCAPIN: So I see. (*Holds out hand.*)

GERONTE: (*Gives Scapin money bag.*) What the deuce did he go in the galley for! Confound the galley! (*Exits.*)

SCAPIN: Two hundred for Octavio. Five hundred for Leander. And you, Signor Geronte, I will soon settle a score with you. You will pay for my pinched ear! Beware. Scapin will play his best trick on you! (*SCAPIN exits. HYACINTHA and ZERBINETTA enter. Zerbinetta is a beautiful gypsy girl, bubbling with life.*)

HYACINTHA: Oh Zerbinetta, how happy I am that Leander brought us together. We can keep each other company.

ZERBINETTA: Oh, I agree. I — an orphan gypsy girl — am not one to refuse an offer of friendship. We must wait until we hear from our lovers.

HYACINTHA: What is keeping Octavio so long?

ZERBINETTA: What has happened to Leander?

HYACINTHA: It is amazing how alike are our strange adventures. You and I have the same fears and are exposed to the same misfortune.

ZERBINETTA: But you at least know who your parents are. I was taken by the gypsies when I was but a child. You can hope to find your family, while I can hope for nothing.

HYACINTHA: But you have this in your favor. There is no one else but you and Leander. While in my case Octavio's father is bringing another girl for him to marry.

NURSE: (*Enters.*) Oh, my lady, come within. I have just heard of how Scapin tricked Signor Geronte into giving up the five hundred pounds.

ZERBINETTA: The ransom that Leander paid the gypsies for me?

NURSE: The same.

HYACINTHA: Do tell us, Nurse, tell us of Scapin's latest trick.

NURSE: Come inside. It will lift your spirits. (*Laughs.*) "Why the deuce did he go in the galley!" (*NURSE exits, laughing. HYACINTHA and ZERBINETTA follow. SCAPIN enters, followed by GERONTE.*)

GERONTE: Well, Scapin, have you news about my son?

SCAPIN: Good news. Your son is safe. Bad news. You are in danger.

GERONTE: I — in danger?

SCAPIN: At this very minute there are desperados seeking you.

GERONTE: Seeking me?

SCAPIN: To kill you.

GERONTE: But who? Why?

SCAPIN: The brother of the girl Octavio has married, knows that you want to get the marriage dissolved in order to have your daughter take his sister's place. He has sworn to have your blood! He and his cut-throat friends are searching for you.

GERONTE: What am I to do?

SCAPIN: I wish I knew. Oh, I am worried to DEATH about you! Oh, what was that?

GERONTE: (*Shaking.*) Where?

SCAPIN: It is nothing.

GERONTE: Oh, Scapin, you must think of some way to save me.

SCAPIN: There is one way — but no, I would be beaten myself.

GERONTE: Tell me. I will do anything.

SCAPIN: Very well. It is — this. (*Holds up a large burlap sack which he carries.*)

GERONTE: What is your plan?

SCAPIN: A sack!

GERONTE: A sack?

SCAPIN: You will hide inside of it.

GERONTE: I . . .?

SCAPIN: You will get into the sack and I will carry you past your enemies, safely to your home.

GERONTE: No, I don't think —

SCAPIN: Oh! What was that? Footsteps!

GERONTE: Quick! Put the sack over me. (*SCAPIN does. The sack covers Geronte completely.*) Oh, Scapin, I will repay you later — with a suit of my clothes, when I have worn it a bit longer.

SCAPIN: (*Aside.*) And I shall repay you now for the beating Leander gave me because of you.

GERONTE: (*Inside the sack.*) Scapin, I can't see. I can't —

SCAPIN: Ah! Here comes one of the assassins. Don't show yourself — no matter what happens.

GERONTE: I will keep still.

SCAPIN: Don't talk. (*SACK shakes its head.*) Don't move. (*SACK shakes it head bigger.*) Don't breathe. (*SACK is suddenly still.*) He is here.
      (*SCAPIN tip-toes to side, then stomps forward heavily, and comically disguises his voice.*)

"I am looking for the old miser, Geronte. Geronte! Geronte!
(SACK shakes. SCAPIN whispers.)
Do not stir.
(SACK suddenly stops.)
"I will find him. I will find him even if he is hidden in the belly of the earth!"
(Steps heavily. The two top corner points of the sack suddenly fold over each other as GERONTE, holding the corners up, puts his hands over his head.)
"Ah, ha! You there, man with the sack." Yes, Signor.
"Tell me where I can find the old miser, Geronte."
You are looking for Signor Geronte? "I am looking for Geronte — yes!"
(SACK shrinks lower.)
"I will find Geronte — yes!!"
(SACK shrinks lower.)
"And when I find Geronte — Yes? "
(SACK leans to listen.)
"I will beat him blue and black!"
(SACK collapses.)
No, never. I will protect him.
(SACK walks on knees to Scapin.)
"Ah, ha! You are a friend of his?" Yes, a true and faithful friend. "Ah, ha! Then I shall start with my stick on you! Take that. And that!"
(SCAPIN hits the sack repeatedly with slap-stick. At the same time, he cries, "Help! Stop! Ouch!" while GERONTE hops about in the sack.)
"And now take this for — Geronte!"

(He gives the sack a last big whack where Geronte's hips push the sack out.)

GERONTE: *(Covered with sack.)* Oh, help! Help, Scapin. Help!

SCAPIN: Oh, master, I am beaten all over.

GERONTE: You? I got the beating.

SCAPIN: Quiet. Here is another villain. *(SCAPIN pretends again, walking and talking roughly. He may use a comic dialect.)* "Around and around I am running . . . like a dog . . . sniff . . . sniff . . . until I find his trail . . . until I find Geronte!"
(Laughs a frightening villain's laugh.)
Hide yourself well. He is a wild man. "You! You tell me where is this Geronte." Why, Signor? "Why?"

(*Laughs a blood-curdling laugh.*)

"Why to use my club on him! On his back!"

(*SACK starts to inch itself away, feet together, first toe, then heel, then toe, heel, etc.*)

"And to run my sword through his front!"

(*Laughs again. SACK doubles its speed in edging away.*)

"Ha! What is moving in that sack?"

(*SACK stops.*)

Nothing, Signor. Nothing. (*To sack.*) Keep still!

"I will see. I will run my sword through — nothing!"

Stop! Stop! "Ah, then you will show me what is in the sack."

No. It is some — some old clothes. See.

(*Kicks sack. SACK hops on one foot.*)

"Then you will show me the old — clothes."

(*Kicks other side of sack. SACK hops on other foot.*)

No. "You will not show me?" Never. "You will never show me?"

No. "Then I will lay my club on you! Ha ha ha!"

(*Laughs wickedly as he beats the sack with the slap-stick, and at the same time crying for help, "Oh, help. Ouch! Save me.")*

He is gone. Oh, help!

GERONTE: Oh, Scapin! I am beaten to death.

SCAPIN: I am dead already.

GERONTE: But why the devil should he beat me?

SCAPIN: Quiet! Here come more — half a dozen cut-throats with swords and clubs!

(*SCAPIN impersonates many people, with different voices, as he hops about enjoying being each villain.*)

"Geronte! We must find him." "Geronte! We WILL find him!" "Search everywhere. Every house. Every corner." "Every barrel. Every sack!"

(*SACK suddenly kneels on both knees, hands holding the burlap in front in prayer.*)

"There stands his servant." "His obedient servant!" "Tell us where is your master?" Oh, Signors, don't hurt me, please. "Speak then. Speak up! Before I run my sword through you."

(*As SCAPIN waves the slap-stick and continues to impersonate all the enemy, GERONTE slowly lifts the sack up — the difficulty adds to the comedy. When he stands clear of the sack, GERONTE looks around — and sees no enemy.*)

No, never will I give my master away. Run your sword through me. Pull out my tongue. But I will never tell you where he is.

"So you won't talk, eh? Well, get ready. Get ready for what is coming to you."

(*He starts to hit Geronte who now stands exposed.*)

GERONTE: Scapin!

SCAPIN: Help! (*Exits.*)

GERONTE: Traitor! Villain! Scoundrel! For this trick I will hang you!

(*Throws sack off after Scapin.*)

ZERBINETTA: (*Enters, laughing.*) I must have a breath of air. What a funny story the Nurse has told, and what a fool the old miser was!

GERONTE: (*Rubbing his head.*) It is nothing to laugh at.

ZERBINETTA: I am not laughing at you. I am laughing (*Laughs.*) over what has just happened. It is a trick a young man played on his father to get some money out of him. I will tell you. You will laugh, too. First you should know that I was with a band of gypsies and when we arrived here in Naples, a young man saw me and fell in love with me—and I with him. He found that the gypsies were willing to give me up if he would pay them a large sum of money. His father is very rich, but very stingy.

GERONTE: What is his name?

ZERBINETTA: Ronte—no, Monte—no, ah! Geronte, the stingiest man in town. Do you know him?

GERONTE: I know him well.

ZERBINETTA: I do know the servant's name who played the trick.

GERONTE: And so do I! Scapin! Tricked! Tricked by Scapin and my son.

ZERBINETTA: Your son?

GERONTE: You have told me my own story!

ARGANTE: (*Enters.*) Ah, Geronte, I have trouble, trouble, trouble.

GERONTE: You? *I* am the one who has trouble. That scoundrel Scapin has got five hundred guineas out of me.

ARGANTE: Five hundred out of you? The scamp has got two hundred pounds out of me!

GERONTE: And there is more. I have news that my daughter left Taranto some days ago. I fear she has perished at sea.

NURSE: (*Enters, comes to Geronte.*) Ah, Signor Pandolphe!

ARGANTE: Pandolphe? His name is Geronte.

GERONTE: I have two names. Pandolphe is the name I used in Taranto in my second marriage.

NURSE: And what troubles those two names have given me! I have been trying to find you here, but no one knows Signor Pandolphe.

ARGANTE: Who is she?

GERONTE: She is my daughter's nurse. Is my daughter safe?

NURSE: Your daughter is safe — and close at hand.

GERONTE: Lead me to her.

NURSE: But first I have news for you. Hyacintha is married.

GERONTE: Married!

NURSE: I must ask your pardon. We were alone, friendless, and thought we would never see you again.

GERONTE: My daughter is married? To whom?

NURSE: She can best tell you herself.

HYACINTHA: (*Enters.*) Father.

GERONTE: Hyacintha. I feared you were lost at sea.

HYACINTHA: And I feared I would never find you.

GERONTE: (*Sternly.*) I am told you have married without my consent.

HYACINTHA: Yes, to a most noble young man. His name is Octavio.

ARGANTE: My son!

GERONTE: What a coincidence!

ARGANTE: And here he comes now. (*OCTAVIO enters.*) Come my son. We are ready to celebrate your marriage to Geronte's daughter.

OCTAVIO: No, father, I am already married. I will not consider Signor Geronte's daughter.

ARGANTE: But she is —

OCTAVIO: No, father! I will die rather than give up my dear Hyacintha.

ARGANTE: Good. She is the wife I want you to have.

HYACINTHA: Octavio. I am Signor Geronte's daughter by a second marriage.

LEANDER: (*Enters.*) Father, I have just made a most happy discovery.

GERONTE: And so have I.

LEANDER: You need fear no more that I love an unknown gypsy girl. The gypsies say they stole the girl from this city when she was four years old. Here is a bracelet they have given me, which may help to trace her parents.

ARGANTE: It looks familiar. Let me see it. Great heavens! It is the bracelet worn by my little daughter when she was stolen from me.

GERONTE: Your daughter?

ARGANTE: Yes. (*Looks at Zerbinetta.*) My — daughter!

ZERBINETTA: Father!

HYACINTHA: How wonderful!

SILVESTER: (*Enters.*) Gentlemen . . . Gentlemen! A dreadful thing has happened. A dreadful thing! Poor Scapin —

GERONTE: Scapin! I will see that he swings from the tallest tree.

SILVESTER: Oh, sir, you won't need to trouble. He was passing a building when a bricklayer's hammer fell on his head. Injured though he is, he begs to be brought here so that he can speak to you before — he passes on. Here he comes.

SCAPIN: (*Enters. He limps. His head is bandaged.*)
Oh . . . oh. You see what a sad state I have come to. Oh . . . oh! But before I breathe my last — I implore you to forgive me all I have done to you. Signor Argante . . . oh . . . and to you Signor Geronte . . . oh . . . oh!

ARGANTE: Well — (*SCAPIN moans and collapses. SILVESTER supports him.*) I forgive you. Die in peace.

SCAPIN: It is you, master, whom I have offended most. Say . . . say you forgive me.

GERONTE: (*Starts to raise his fist. SCAPIN collapses again.*) I — I also — forgive you.

OCTAVIO: Signor Geronte, you have found one daughter and gained another. Let us celebrate this joyful occasion by pardoning Scapin unconditionally.

ZERBINETTA: He did it only for us.

GERONTE: All right then! He is pardoned for everything!

LEANDER: Prepare a festive supper. Let all dine with us — in honor of this most amazing — most happy — wedding day.

SCAPIN: Carry me to the foot of the table where I will wait until death comes to claim me — where there will be — no more tricks — of Scapin.

(*He winks at the audience.*)

CURTAIN

She Stoops To Conquer
by Oliver Goldsmith
Adapted by Aurand Harris

Introduction

In *She Stoops to Conquer*, Goldsmith attacked the eighteenth century genteel sentimental comedy then in vogue. He hoped to restore "laughing comedy" and banish sentimentality from the theatre. *She Stoops to Conquer* is effective because of the broad characterizations and the farcical humor. The fun is in the situations, characters and dialogue. Various titles were suggested: *The Belle's Stratagem*, *The Old House a New Inn*, *The Mistakes of a Night*. He chose *She Stoops to Conquer* with *The Mistakes of a Night* as a sub-title.

Oliver Goldsmith, a second son of a poor Protestant clergyman, was born November 10, 1728, at Palles, in Langford, Ireland. As a boy he was a poor student and often humiliated because of his small stature, ill-matched features, and pock-marked skin. In 1749 he graduated from Trinity College in Dublin. After briefly studying medicine in Edinburgh and a walking tour through Europe, he arrived in London in 1756, "without friends or money" and only "his brogue and blunders" to recommend him. He earned a meager living by writing articles and poetry for several periodicals. He met and was helped by Dr. Samuel Johnson, who at this time was foremost among men of letters.

In December, 1764, publishing *The Traveler* made Goldsmith famous as a poet. In 1766, *The Vicar of Wakefield* established him as a novelist. These were followed by his first play, *The Good Natured Man;* *The Deserted Village*, his second poem; and *She Stoops to Conquer*, his second play. A year later, April 4, 1774, Goldsmith died. In seven years, he was acclaimed in four — possibly five — different fields — as an English essayist, poet, novelist, playwright — an eccentric.

With his country manners and his Irish brogue, he amazed, amused, horrified and charmed London's elegant society. Physically unattractive, he was vain, a compulsive gambler, extravagant, envious, and often acted the comic buffoon. To some he was "an idiot." Horace Walpole added, "An inspired idiot." David Garrick wondered how anyone could "write like an angel but talk like poor Poll." Even his friend, Dr. Johnson, wrote, "No man was more foolish when he had not a pen in his hand, or more wise when he had." For all his faults, he was for

Joshua Reynolds, "a man of genius," for Thackeray, "the most beloved of English writers," and to Goethe, "To Shakespeare, Sterne, and Goldsmith my debt has been limitless."

After some difficulty, *She Stoops to Conquer* opened on March 15, 1773. Dr. Johnson wrote, "I know of no comedy for many years that has so much exhilarated an audience; that has answered so much the great end of comedy, making an audience merry." However, when one critic, "Tom Tickle," attacked the play in the *London Packet*, Goldsmith attacked the publisher and was fined fifty pounds. The play ran for many months and gave two command performances before the king.

In all Goldsmith's writings he tried to show audiences their errors, to remind them of their blessings, to give them a love of life. And he wrote in terms they could easily understand and heartily enjoy. Because of "his comic vision, his clear insight and sympathetic humor" critics have put Oliver Goldsmith in the great tradition of Chaucer and Shakespeare.

CAST

MR. HARDCASTLE, *an old-fashioned country gentleman*
MRS. HARDCASTLE, *his flighty, fashion-loving wife*
TONY LUMPKIN, *a country bumpkin, son of Mrs. Hardcastle by a previous marriage.*
KATE HARDCASTLE, *the pretty daughter of the Hardcastles*
CONSTANCE NEVILLE, *the pretty niece of Mrs. Hardcastle*
STINGO, *owner of the tavern The Three Pigeons*
YOUNG MARLOW, *a handsome London gentleman*
GEORGE HASTINGS, *best friend of Young Marlow's*
SIR CHARLES MARLOW, *a London aristocrat*
SERVANT, *helper in the Hardcastle household*

SCENES: *The action takes place in the country house of Mr. Hardcastle's and in the nearby tavern The Three Pigeons.*

England, 1770.

She Stoops to Conquer

(The main room of a large country house. MRS. HARDCASTLE enters, followed by MR. HARDCASTLE. She is middle-aged, vain, and foolish. She is comically over-dressed, trying to imitate the fashions of London. Mr. Hardcastle is a hale and hearty country squire.)

MRS. HARDCASTLE: I vow, Mr. Hardcastle, you're very particular. Is there a creature in the whole country, but ourselves, that does not take a trip to London now and then?

MR. HARDCASTLE: Ay, and bring back vanity and affection to last them the whole year.

MRS. HARDCASTLE: Here we live in an old rambling mansion, that looks for all the world like an inn. I hate such old-fashioned trumpery.

MR. HARDCASTLE: And I love it. I love everything that's old; and I believe, Dorothy, you'll own I have been pretty fond of an old wife.

MRS. HARDCASTLE: Mr. Hardcastle, you're forever at your Dorothys and your old wifes. Add twenty to twenty and make money of that.

MR. HARDCASTLE: Let me see; twenty added to twenty — makes just fifty and seven.

MRS. HARDCASTLE: It's false, Mr. Hardcastle! I was by twenty when I wed Mr. Lumpkin, my first husband — Tony's father. And Tony has not come to years of discretion yet.

MR. HARDCASTLE: Nor ever will, I dare answer.

MRS. HARDCASTLE: We must not snub the poor boy, for I believe we shan't have him long among us. I'm actually afraid of his lungs.

MR. HARDCASTLE: And truly so am I! For he sometimes whoops like a speaking trumpet.
   (Off L is heard some loud noises of TONY's calling.)

Listen. Here he comes — truly a very consumptive figure.

(*TONY rushes in from L. He is 21, a loud, crude, country-bumpkin, likeable with his boisterous sense of humor.*)

MRS. HARDCASTLE: Tony! Tony, where are you going, my little charmer?

TONY: I am in haste, mother; I cannot stay. The Three Pigeons expect me down every moment. There's some fun going forward.

MR. HARDCASTLE: Ay, the alehouse.

MRS. HARDCASTLE: Pray, my dear, disappoint them for one night.

TONY: As for disappointing them, I should not so much mind; but I can't abide to disappoint *myself*.

(*Laughs loudly at his own joke.*)

MRS. HARDCASTLE: I say you shan't!

TONY: We'll see which is the strongest, you or I.

(*He suddenly puts her over his shoulder and exits R, laughing loudly. She kicks her feet and calls for help.*)

MR. HARDCASTLE. Ay, there goes a pair that only spoil each other.
(*Looks off L.*)
Ah, but here comes my pretty darling Kate. The fashions of the times have almost infected her, too. By living a year in London, she is as fond of gauze and French frippery, as the best of them.
(*KATE enters. She is young, pretty, and vivacious. She is dressed in a most becoming fashionable gown, which she shows off in entering, then curtsies to her father.*)
Blessings on my pretty innocence! Goodness, what a quantity of superfluous silk hast thou got about thee, girl!

KATE: You know our agreement, sir. You allow me the morning to receive and pay visits and to dress in my own manner.
(*Shows off dress.*)
Then in the evening, I put on my plain housewife's dress to please you.

MR. HARDCASTLE: And remember I insist on our agreement. And, by the bye, I believe I shall have occasion to try your obedience. I expect the young gentleman I have chosen to be your husband from London this very day. I have his father's letter, in which he informs me his son is set out, and that the father intends to follow himself shortly after.

KATE: Indeed! Bless me, how shall I behave? It's a thousand to one I shan't like him.

MR. HARDCASTLE: Depend upon it, child, I will never control your choice. But Mr. Marlow, whom I have pitched upon, is the son of my old friend, Sir Charles Marlow. I am told the young man is of an excellent understanding.

KATE: Is he?

MR. HARDCASTLE: Very generous.

KATE: I believe I shall like him.

MR. HARDCASTLE: Young and brave.

KATE: I am sure I shall like him.

MR. HARDCASTLE: And very handsome.

KATE: My dear papa, say no more! He is mine. I will have him!

MR. HARDCASTLE: And to crown all, Kate, he is one of the most bashful and reserved young fellows in all the world.

KATE: Ah! You have frozen me to death again. A reserved lover, it is said, always makes a suspicious husband.

MR. HARDCASTLE: But before he arrives, I must go prepare the servants for his reception. (*He exits.*)

KATE: Lud, this news of papa's put me all in a flutter. Young — handsome, these he put last, but I put them foremost. Sensible — good-natured, I like all that. But then — reserved and sheepish, that's much against him. Yet . . . can't he be cured of his timidity by being taught to be proud of his wife? Yes! But I vow I'm disposing of the husband, before I have secured the lover.
  (*CONSTANCE NEVILLE enters. She is young, pretty, another romantic young lady.*)
Constance!

CONSTANCE: Kate! (*They rush to each other.*)

KATE: Oh, I'm glad you're come, Constance. Oh, tell me, please, how do I look? Is it one of my well-looking days? Am I in face today?

CONSTANCE: Perfectly, my dear.

KATE: I have been threatened — I can scarce get it out — I have been threatened with a lover!

CONSTANCE: A lover! And his name?

KATE: Is Marlow. The son of Sir Charles Marlow.

CONSTANCE: As I live, the most intimate friend of Mr. Hastings, *my* admirer. They are never asunder.
(*Delicately tries to speak of the unspeakable.*) Your Mr. Marlow . . . he is a very singular character, I assure you. They say . . . among women of reputation and virtue, he is the modestest man alive. But . . . his acquaintance give him a very different character among creatures of — of another stamp. You understand me.

KATE: An odd character, indeed. What shall I do? No . . . we will think no more about him, but trust to occurrences for success. Now tell me, how goes on your own affair, my dear? Has my mother been courting you for my brother Tony as usual?

CONSTANCE: I continue to let her suppose that I am in love with her son, and she never once dreams that my affections are fixed upon another. Ah, my aunt's bell rings for our afternoon's walk. *Allons!* Courage is necessary, as our affairs are critical.

KATE: Would it were bedtime and all were well!

(*They exit. Music. Curtains close. The next scene is played in front of the curtain. A tavern sign, THREE PIGEONS, is placed at the side.*)

STINGO: (*The owner of the tavern, enters.*) Master Tony! Master Tony!

TONY: (*Enters*) Well, Stingo, what's the matter?

STINGO: There be two gentlemen at the gate. They have lost their way, and they are talking something about Mr. Hardcastle.

TONY: As sure as can be, one of them must be the gentleman that's coming down to court my sister.

STINGO: Here they come.

(*YOUNG MARLOW and HASTINGS enter. Marlow is a handsome young man, elegant, and sure of his place in London society. Hastings, his friend, is also a dashing young man. They are both dressed in the height of fashion.*)

MARLOW: What a tedious, uncomfortable day we had of it!

HASTINGS: And all, Marlow, from that unaccountable reserve of yours, that would not let us inquire more frequently on the way.

TONY: Gentlemen, I am told you have been inquiring for one Mr. Hardcastle. Pray, gentlemen, is not this same Hardcastle a cross-grained, old-fashioned fellow, with an ugly face daughter — and a pretty son?

HASTINGS: He has a daughter and a step-son.

TONY: The daughter, a tall, traipsing, trolloping, talkative maypole. The son, a pretty, well-bred, agreeable youth, that everybody is fond of.

MARLOW: The daughter is said to be well-bred and beautiful; the son an awkward booby.

TONY: (*Insulted.*) Then, gentlemen, all I have to tell you is, that you won't reach Mr. Hardcastle's house this night!

HASTINGS: Unfortunate! What's to be done, Marlow?

TONY: I have hit it!
(*Crosses to Stingo, and points out the way.*)
If you go on a mile further to the Buck's Head — the old Buck's Head on the hill, one of the best inns in the whole county!

STINGO: (*Aside to Tony.*) Sure, you be sending them to your father's house as an inn!

TONY: (*Aside to Stingo.*) Mum, you fool. Let them find that out.
(*To Hastings.*)
You have only to keep on straight forward, till you are right by a large old house by the roadside.

HASTINGS: We go to the right, did you say?

TONY: No, no! Straight forward. I'll just step with you myself and show you a piece of the way.
(*He motions, and MARLOW and HASTINGS exit. STINGO bursts out laughing.*)
Mum!
(*Starts off, eager for the fun.*)
So begins — the mistakes of a night.

(*TONY exits. STINGO follows. Music. The sign is pulled back from view. The curtains open. The scene is the main room in the Hardcastle house. SERVANT enters with candles.*)

SERVANT: Welcome, gentlemen, very welcome. This way.

(*SERVANT bows and exits.*)

HASTINGS. (*He and MARLOW enter.*)
After the disappointments of the day, welcome, Charles, to the comforts of a country inn, with a clean room and a good fire.

MARLOW: The usual fate of a large mansion. Having ruined the master, it at last becomes an inn. My life has been chiefly spent in a college or an inn. I don't know that I was ever acquainted with a single modest woman — except my mother.

HASTINGS: And in the company of women of reputation I never saw such an idiot, such a trembler. How do you intend behaving to the lady you are come down to visit?

MARLOW. As I behave to all other ladies. Bow very low, answer yes or no and for the rest, I don't think I shall venture to look in her face.
(*HARDCASTLE enters.*)
Zounds, this fellow here to interrupt us.

MR. HARDCASTLE. Gentlemen, once more you are welcome. Which is Mr. Marlow?
(*MARLOW nods cooly.*)
Sir, you're heartily welcome. I like to give my friends a hearty reception at the gate.

MARLOW: We approve of your hospitality, sir.
(*Talks to Hastings.*)

I have been thinking, George, of changing our traveling dresses in the morning.

MR. HARDCASTLE: I beg, Mr. Marlow, you'll use no ceremony in this house. This is Liberty Hall.

MARLOW: Yet, George, if we open the campaign with too fine a clothes, we may want ammunition later to secure a retreat.

MR. HARDCASTLE: Your talking of a retreat, Mr. Marlow, puts me in mind of the Duke of Marlborough, when we went to besiege Densin. He first summoned the garrison —

MARLOW: Do you think the gold waistcoat will do with the plain brown?

MR. HARDCASTLE: He first summoned the garrison, which might consist of about five thousand men —

MARLOW: The girls like finery.

MR. HARDCASTLE: Which might consist of about five thousand men. "Now," says the Duke of Marlborough —

MARLOW: What, my good friend, if you gave us a glass of punch in the meantime.

MR. HARDCASTLE: Punch, sir!

MARLOW: A glass of warm punch, after our journey, will be comfortable.

MR. HARDCASTLE: Speaking of punch, reminds me of Prince Eugene, when he fought the Turks at the battle of Belgrade.

MARLOW: Instead of the battle of Belgrade, I believe it's almost time to talk about supper.

MR. HARDCASTLE: (*Aside.*) Such a brazen dog sure never my eyes beheld.

MARLOW: And then to see that our beds are aired and properly taken care of.

MR. HARDCASTLE: I entreat you'll leave all that to me.

MARLOW: I always look to these things myself. (*Aside.*) A very troublesome fellow this, as ever I met with. (*Exits.*)

MR. HARDCASTLE: Well, sir, I'm resolved at least to attend you. (*Aside.*) This may be modern modesty, but I never saw anything look so much like old-fashion impudence. (*Exits.*)

HASTINGS: (*Starts to follow, but stops.*)
What do I see? Miss Neville, by all that's happy!

CONSTANCE. (*Enters.*) My dear Hastings! To what unexpected good fortune am I to ascribe this happy meeting?

HASTINGS: Rather let me ask the same question, as I could never have hoped to meet my dearest Constance here — at an inn.

CONSTANCE: An inn? What could induce you to think this house an inn?

HASTINGS: My friend, Marlow, and I have been sent here by a young fellow whom we accidentally met.

CONSTANCE. Ah, certainly it must be one of my cousin Tony's tricks.

HASTINGS: You must know, my dear Constance, I have just seized this happy opportunity of my friend's visit here to get admittance into the family. And when the horses are refreshed, we will soon be landed and wed in France.

CONSTANCE: Though ready to obey you, I should hate to leave my little fortune behind. It chiefly consists in jewels and is in my Aunt's protection.

HASTINGS: Perish the baubles! You are all I desire. In the meantime, my friend Marlow must not be let into his mistake. He would instantly quit the house before our plan was ripe for execution.

CONSTANCE: But how shall we continue to deceive him that this is an inn?

(*CONSTANCE sees MARLOW entering. She motions to HASTINGS, who greets Marlow.*)

HASTINGS: My dear Charles! the most fortunate accident! Who do you think is just alighted? Our mistresses, boy, Miss Hardcastle and Miss Neville.
(*Presents CONSTANCE.*)
Give me leave to introduce Miss Constance Neville to your acquaintance. Happening to dine in the neighborhood, they called on their return to take fresh horses here at the inn. Miss Hardcastle has just stepped into the next room.

MARLOW: (*Acknowledged CONSTANCE'S curtsey without looking at her, is now in a panic.*)
Miss Hardcastle! What if we postpone the happiness of meeting her till tomorrow? Tomorrow at her own hours. Yes, tomorrow it will be.

(*Starts to exit.*)

HASTINGS: (*Stops him.*) By no means, sir. She knows you are in the house.

MARLOW: Oh, the devil! Hastings, you must not go.

HASTINGS: Pshaw, man! It's but the first plunge, and all's over. She's but a woman, you know.

MARLOW: And of all women, she that I dread most.

(*KATE enters R, still in her elegant dress. MARLOW quickly turns away, too nervous to look at her.*)

HASTINGS: Miss Hardcastle, Mr. Marlow. I am proud to bring two persons of such merit together, that only want to know, to esteem each other.

KATE. (*Aside.*) Now, for meeting my modest gentleman with a demure face, and quite in his own manner. I am glad of your safe arrival, sir. I am told you had some accidents by the way.

MARLOW: Yes, madam. No, madam. I mean—yes, madam.

HASTINGS. (*Aside.*) You never spoke better. Well, Miss Hardcastle, I see that you and Mr. Marlow are going to be very good company. I believe our being here will but embarrass the interview.

MARLOW: Not in the least, Mr. Hastings! (*Aside.*) Zounds, George, sure you won't go now!

HASTINGS: You don't consider, man, we want a little *tête-à-tête* of our own.

(*CONSTANCE and HASTINGS exit. KATE, enjoying MARLOW'S discomfort, prolongs the awkward silence. She clears her throat, fans, and finally speaks.*)

KATE: While living in London, I hope the ladies have employed some part of your addresses.

MARLOW: (*Never looking at her.*) I — I — I — have studied, madam — only — to — deserve them, madam.

KATE: And that, some say, is the very best way to obtain them.

MARLOW: I am afraid I — I grow tiresome.

KATE: Not at all, sir. There is nothing I like so much as grave conversation. Do you agree?

MARLOW: In the variety of tastes there must be some — who — wanting a relish — for — a — a —

KATE: I understand you, sir. There must be some who, wanting a relish for refined pleasures, pretend to despise what they are incapable of tasting.

MARLOW: My meaning, madam, but infinitely better expressed.

KATE: (*Aside.*) Who could ever suppose this fellow impudent upon some occasions? You were going to observe, sir . . .?

MARLOW: I was observing, madam — I — I protest, madam, I forgot what I was going to observe.

KATE: (*Aside.*) I vow, and so do I.

MARLOW: But I am sure I tire you, madam.

KATE: Not in the least, sir. Pray go on.

MARLOW: Yes, madam. But I see Miss Neville expecting us in the next room. Madam, shall I do myself the honor to attend you? (*Holds out his arm, still not looking at her, exits.*)

KATE: Was there ever such a sober, sentimental interview? I'm certain he scarce looked in my face the whole time. Yet the fellow, but for his unaccountable bashfulness, is pretty well, too. If I could teach him a little confidence, it would be doing somebody that I know of a piece of service. But who is that somebody? That, faith, is a question I can scarce answer!

(*KATE exits, as TONY enters, followed by CONSTANCE.*)

TONY: What do you follow me for, cousin Con?

CONSTANCE: I hope, cousin, one may speak to one's own relations.

TONY: Ay, but I know what sort of a relation you want to make me. Keep your distance. I want no nearer relationship. (*MRS. HARDCAS-TLE enters, followed by HASTINGS.*)

MRS. HARDCASTLE: Well, I vow, Mr. Hastings, you are very entertaining! There's nothing in the world I love to talk so much as London, though I was never there myself.

HASTINGS: Never there! From your air and manner, I concluded you had been bred all your life at St. James's.

MRS. HARDCASTLE: Pray, Mr. Hastings, what do you take to be the most fashionable age about town?

HASTINGS: Some time ago, forty was all the mode, but I am told the ladies intend to bring up fifty for the ensuing winter.

MRS. HARDCASTLE: Seriously? Then I shall be too young for the fashion.

HASTINGS: Who is the young lady there?

MRS. HARDCASTLE: My niece.

HASTINGS: Your niece is she? And that young gentleman — a brother of yours, I should presume?

MRS. HARDCASTLE: My son, sir. They are contracted to each other. Ah, Tony, child, what soft things are you saying to your cousin Constance?

TONY: I have been saying no soft things. Egad! I've not a place in the house now that's left to myself but the stables.

MRS. HARDCASTLE: (*To HASTINGS.*) Was ever the like for a son!

HASTINGS: Dear madam, permit me to lecture the young gentleman a little.

MRS. HARDCASTLE: Come, Constance, my love. We will leave them. Oh, was ever a poor woman so plagued with a dear, sweet, provoking undutiful boy? Come, Constance.

(*MRS. HARDCASTLE and CONSTANCE exit.*)

HASTINGS: You are no friend to the ladies, I find.

TONY: That's as I find 'em.

HASTINGS: And yet Miss Neville appears to me a pretty, well-tempered girl.

TONY: That's because you don't know as well as I.

HASTINGS: (*Aside.*) Pretty encouragement this for a lover! But you must allow her a little beauty.

TONY: Ah, could you but see Bet Bouncer, you might talk of beauty. Egad, she's make two of she.

HASTINGS. Well, what say you to a friend that would take this bitter bargain off your hand?

TONY: Right away?

HASTINGS: Would you thank him that would take Miss Neville and leave you to happiness and your dear Betsy?

TONY: Ay! But where is there such a friend, for who would take her?

HASTINGS: I am he. If you but assist me, I'll engage to whip her off to France.

TONY: Assist you! Egad, I will. I'll clap a pair of horses to your chaise that shall trundle you off in a twinkling. And — maybe I can get you part of her fortune besides, in jewels.

HASTINGS: My dear Squire, this looks like a lad of spirit.

TONY: Come along then, and you shall see more of my spirit before you have done with me.

(*They exit, TONY singing happily.*)
"We are the boys
That fear no noise
Where the thundering cannons roar."

(*MR. HARDCASTLE enters.*)

MR. HARDCASTLE: What could my old friend Sir Charles mean by recommending his son as the modestest young man in town? To me he appears the most impudent piece of brass that ever spoke with a tongue.

(*KATE enters, wearing a plain, but becoming house dress, with an apron and a cap.*)
Well, my Kate, I see you have changed your dress, as I bid you.

KATE: It is evening and I am keeping my promise.

MR. HARDCASTLE: Kate, I am sorry I recommended my *modest* gentleman to you as a lover today.

KATE: Such a timid look — awkward address — bashful manner —

MR. HARDCASTLE: He is the most brazen first sight that ever astonished my senses.

KATE: Sure, sir, you rally. I never saw anyone so modest.

MR. HARDCASTLE: I never saw anyone so swaggering.

KATE: One of us must certainly be mistaken.

MR. HARDCASTLE: If he be what he has shown himself, I am determined he shall never have my consent.

KATE: And if he be the sullen thing I take him, he shall never have mine!

MR. HARDCASTLE: In one thing then we are agreed — to reject him.

KATE: Yes . . . but upon conditions. For if you should find him less impudent, and I more presuming . . . since one of us must be mistaken, let us make further discoveries!

MR. HARDCASTLE: Agreed. But depend on it, I'm in the right.

KATE: And, depend on it, I'm not much in the wrong!

(*She takes his arm, and they exit. TONY enters, carrying a jewel box.*)

TONY: Egad! I have got them. Here they are. My cousin Con's necklaces, bobs, and all! My mother shan't cheat the poor souls out of their fortune.
(*Frightened at HASTINGS' entrance.*)
Oh, is that you?

HASTINGS: My dear friend, the horses will be refreshed in a short time, and your cousin Constance and I will be ready to set off soon.

TONY: And here's something to bear your charges by the way — your sweetheart's jewels.

HASTINGS: But how did you . . .?

TONY: Ask me no questions, and I'll tell you no fibs. If I had not a key to every drawer in my mother's bureau, how could I go to the alehouse so often as I do?

HASTINGS: Miss Neville is endeavoring to procure them from her aunt this very instant.

TONY: You best keep them. (*Gives box to HASTINGS.*)
When the old lady discovers they are gone — Zounds!
Here they are! Quick! Prance! Depart!

(*TONY pushes HASTINGS off. MRS. HARDCASTLE and CONSTANCE enter.*)

MRS. HARDCASTLE: Indeed, Constance, you amaze me. Such a girl as you wanting jewels! It will be time enough for jewels, my dear, twenty years hence. Besides, I believe I can't readily come at him. They may be missing.

TONY: (*Aside to Mother.*) Say they are lost, and call me to bear witness.

MRS. HARDCASTLE: You know, my dear, I'm only keeping them for you. So, if I say they're gone, you'll bear me witness, will you?

TONY: I'll say I saw them taken out with my own eyes.

CONSTANCE: I desire them but for a day, madam.

MRS. HARDCASTLE: To be plain with you, my dear Constance, they're missing.

CONSTANCE: I'll not believe it.

MRS. HARDCASTLE: Don't be alarmed, Constance. If they be lost, I must restore an equivalent. In the meantime, you shall make use of my garnets till your jewels be found.

CONSTANCE: I detest garnets.

MRS. HARDCASTLE: The most becoming things in the world to set off a clear complexion. You have often seen how well they look upon me. You shall have them. (*Exits.*)

CONSTANCE: I dislike them of all things.

TONY: Don't be a fool. If she gives you the garnets, take what you can get. The jewels are your own already. I have stolen them out of her bureau, and she does not know it. Fly to your spark. He'll tell you more of the matter. Leave me to manage her.

CONSTANCE: My dear cousin!

TONY: Vanish! Here she comes! She has already missed them!
    (*CONSTANCE exits. MRS. HARDCASTLE shouts, off, then enters.*)
Help! Confusion! Thieves! Robbers!
We are cheated, plundered, broken open, undone!

TONY: What is the matter, mamma?

MRS. HARDCASTLE: We are robbed. My bureau has been broken open, the jewels taken out!

TONY: (*Laughs.*) Oh, is that all. By the laws, I never saw it better acted in my life. Egad, I thought you was ruined in earnest. (*Laughs.*)

MRS. HARDCASTLE: Why, boy, I am ruined in earnest. My bureau has been broken open, and all taken away.

TONY: Stick to that. I'll bear witness, you know!

MRS. HARDCASTLE: I tell you, Tony, the jewels are gone.

TONY: By the laws, mamma, you make me laugh — for I know who took them well enough. (*Laughs.*)

MRS. HARDCASTLE: Was there ever such a blockhead, that can't tell the difference between jest and earnest? I tell you I am not in jest, booby.

TONY: That's right. I'll bear witness that they are gone.

MRS. HARDCASTLE: Was ever poor woman so beset with fools on one hand, and thieves on the other?

TONY: I can bear witness to that.

MRS. HARDCASTLE: Do you laugh, you unfeeling brute, as if you enjoyed my distress?

TONY: I can bear witness to that!

MRS. HARDCASTLE: Do you insult me, monster? I'll teach you to vex your mother, I will! Take that!

(*Strikes him with her fan.*)

TONY: I can bear witness to that!

(*He runs off, MRS. HARDCASTLE chasing him and hitting him, both shouting above the other, "Take that." "I can bear witness to that." KATE enters, followed by SERVANT.*)

KATE: What an unaccountable creature is that brother of mine, to send them to this house as an inn.

SERVANT: But what is more, madam, the young gentleman, as you passed by in your present dress, asked me if you were the barmaid.

KATE: Did he? Then as I live, I am resolved to keep up the delusion.

SERVANT: But what do you hope from keeping him in his mistake?

KATE: In the first place, I shall be seen, and that's no small advantage to a girl who brings her face to market. Then — I shall perhaps make an acquaintance, and that's no small victory gained over one who never addresses any but the wildest of her sex. But — my chief aim is to take my gentleman off his guard.

SERVANT: But are you sure you can act and talk like a barmaid?

KATE: It will be like acting in the play last summer.
  (*Speaks with a charmingly funny accent.*)
Did your honor call?

SERVANT: It will do, madam. But he's here.

  (*SERVANT exits. MARLOW enters.*)

MARLOW: What a bawling in every part of the house. If I go to the best room, there I find my host and his stories. If I fly to the gallery there we have my hostess with her talk!

KATE: Did you call, sir? Did your honor call?

MARLOW: As for Miss Hardcastle, she's too grave and sentimental for me.

KATE: Did your honor call?

MARLOW: No, Miss. Besides, from the glimpse I had of her, I think she squints.

KATE: I'm sure, sir, I heard the bell ring.

MARLOW: No, no!

KATE: Perhaps the other gentleman called, sir.

MARLOW: I tell you, no — (*Sees her for the first time.*) Yes, I think I did call. I wanted — I wanted — I vow, you are vastly handsome.

KATE: La, la, sir, you'll make one ashame.

MARLOW: Yes, yes, I did call. Have you got any of your — a — what do you call it in the house?

KATE: No, sir, we have been out of that these ten days.

MARLOW: How old are you?

KATE: O, sir, I must not tell my age. They say women and music should never be dated.

MARLOW: To guess at this distance, you can't be much above forty. Yet nearer, I don't think so much. By coming close to some women, they look younger still: but when we come very close indeed —

(*Tries to put his arm around her, but she gracefully evades him.*)

KATE: Pray, sir, keep your distance. One would think you wanted to know one's age as they do horses, by the number of their teeth.

MARLOW: If you keep me at this distance, how is it possible you and I can ever be acquainted?

KATE: I'm sure you did not treat Miss Hardcastle in this "obstropalous" manner.

MARLOW: Miss Hardcastle is a mere awkward, squinting thing. What work do you do?

KATE: Ay, all work. There's not a screen or a quilt in the whole house but what can bear witness to that.

MARLOW: O? Then you must show me your embroidery.

(*Puts his arm around her.*)

KATE: Ay — but the colors don't look well by candlelight.
(*Pulls away from him.*)
You shall see all in the morning.

(*MARLOW embraces her, as MR. HARDCASTLE enters.*)

MR. HARDCASTLE: Sir!

MARLOW: Zounds! Right when I was making progress!

(*Exits.*)

MR. HARDCASTLE: So, madam! So I find this is your modest lover!

KATE: Trust me, dear papa, but he's still the modest man I first took him for.

MR. HARDCASTLE: I saw him seize your hand. I saw him haul you about like a milkmaid!

KATE: But I will shortly convince you of his modesty.

MR. HARDCASTLE: (*Aside.*) The girl would actually make one run mad! I am convinced. You may like his impudence, and call it modesty; but my son-in-law, madam, must have very different qualifications!

KATE: Sir, I ask but this night to convince you.

MR. HARDCASTLE: You shall not have half the time, for I have thoughts of turning him out this very hour!

KATE: Give me that hour, then, and I hope to satisfy you.

MR. HARDCASTLE: An hour let it be then. But I'll have no trifling with your father. All fair and open in our war! (*Exits.*)

KATE: Agreed! And win I will. Though to win—I stoop to conquer.

(*She exits. CONSTANCE and HASTINGS enter, talking.*)

HASTINGS: You surprise me! Sir Charles Marlow expected here this night. Where have you had your information?

CONSTANCE: I just saw his letter to Mr. Hardcastle, in which he tells him he intends setting out a few hours after his son.

HASTINGS: Then, my Constance, all must be completed before he arrives.

CONSTANCE: The jewels, I hope, are safe.

HASTINGS: Yes, yes, I have sent them to Marlow who keeps the keys of our baggage. I have had the Squire's promise of a fresh pair of horses; and we are off to France.

CONSTANCE: In the meantime, I'll go amuse my aunt with the old pretense of a violent passion for my cousin. Success attend you.

(*Exits.*)

HASTINGS: (*Sees MARLOW entering.*) Marlow here, and in spirits, too.

MARLOW: Give me joy, George! Did you see the tempting, brisk, lovely little thing who runs about the house with a bunch of keys?

HASTINGS: Well?

MARLOW: Tis she! The prettiest girl I've seen!

HASTINGS: You have taken care, I hope, of the box I sent you to lock up? It is in safety?

MARLOW: Yes, yes, it's safe enough. I have taken better precautions for you than you did for yourself. I have—

HASTINGS: What?

MARLOW: I have sent it to the landlady to keep for you.

HASTINGS: To the landlady!

MARLOW: The landlady.

HASTINGS: You did?

MARLOW: I did.

HASTINGS: (*Aside.*) He must not see my uneasiness. Well, Charles, I'll leave you to your meditations on the pretty barmaid. And may you be as successful for yourself as you have been for me. (*Exits.*)

MARLOW: Thank ye, George. I ask no more.
   (*KATE enters.*)
But here she is. A word with you, please.

KATE: Let it be short then. I'm in a hurry.

MARLOW: Pray, I would know you better. What are you, and what may your business be in this inn?

KATE: Inn! O law—what brought that in your head? Old Mr. Hardcastle's house an inn!

MARLOW: Mr. Hardcastle's house! Is this house Mr. Hardcastle's house?

KATE: Ay, sure. Whose else should it be?

MARLOW: To mistake this house, of all others, for an inn, and my father's old friend for an innkeeper! What a swaggering puppy must he take me for! And I mistook you for the barmaid.

KATE: Dear me! I'm sure there's nothing in my behavior to put me upon a level with one of that stamp.

MARLOW: Nothing, my dear, nothing! But it's over — this house I no more show my face in.

KATE: I hope, sir, I have done nothing to disoblige you. I'm sure I should be sorry to affront any gentleman who has been so polite, and said so many civil things to me. (*Crying.*) I'm sure I should be sorry if people said anything amiss, since I have no fortune but my character.

MARLOW: (*Aside.*) By heaven, she weeps. This is the first mark of tenderness I ever had from a modest woman. Excuse me, lovely girl, you are the only part of the family I leave with reluctance.

KATE: (*Aside.*) Generous man. I now begin to admire him.

MARLOW: (*Aside.*) I must make one bold effort and leave her. Farewell. (*Exits.*)

KATE: I never knew half his merit till now. He shall not go, if I have power or art to detain him. And I will undeceive my papa, who perhaps, may laugh him out of his resolution. (*KATE exits. HARDCAS-TLE enters, followed by SIR CHARLES MARLOW, an elderly, rich gentleman.*)

MR. HARDCASTLE: Come, Sir Charles. We will find your son. He who mistook my house for an inn and me for a common innkeeper.

(*Laughs.*)

SIR CHARLES. I can see it was all a mistake. But I believe he took you for an un-common innkeeper. (*Laughs.*)

MR. HARDCASTLE: Well, I'm in too good spirits to think of anything but joy.

SIR CHARLES: And so am I. If, as you say, your daughter and he like each other, then I strongly approve of their marriage.

MR. HARDCASTLE: I saw him grasp her hand in the warmest manner. And here he comes to put you out of your ifs.

MARLOW: (*Enters.*) Sir, once more, I ask pardon for my strange conduct to you.

MR. HARDCASTLE: Tut, boy, a trifle. You take it too gravely. An hour or two with my daughter will set all to rights again.

MARLOW: Miss Hardcastle!

MR. HARDCASTLE: Come, boy, I know what has passed between you.

MARLOW: Sure, sir, nothing has passed between us but the most profound respect on both sides.

MR. HARDCASTLE: I tell you she don't dislike you; and as I am sure you like her—

MARLOW: But hear me, sir—

MR. HARDCASTLE: Your father approves the match, and so do I!

MARLOW: By all that's just and true, I never gave Miss Hardcastle the slightest mark of my attachment.

SIR CHARLES: And you never grasp'd her hand, or made any protestations.

MARLOW: As heaven is my witness, no. And now I wish to leave before I suffer more. (*Bows stiffly and exits.*)

SIR CHARLES: I am astonished at the air of sincerity with which he parted.

MR. HARDCASTLE: And I am astonished at the deliberate intrepidity of his assurance.

SIR CHARLES: I dare pledge my life and honor upon my son's truth.

MR. HARDCASTLE: Here comes my daughter, and I would stake my happiness upon her veracity.

(KATE enters.)
Kate, come hither, child. Answer us sincerely; has Mr. Marlow made you any profession of love and affection?

KATE: The question is very abrupt, sir! But — I think — he has.

MR. HARDCASTLE: You see.

SIR CHARLES: But did he profess any attachment?

KATE: A lasting one.

MR. HARDCASTLE: You see!

SIR CHARLES: Amazing!

KATE: Sir, you may even witness his affection. If you and papa will place yourselves behind that screen, you shall hear him declare his passion to me in person.

SIR CHARLES: Agreed. And if I find him what you describe, all my happiness in him must have an end.

KATE: And if you don't find him what I describe — I fear my happiness must never have a beginning! But here he comes.

(SIR CHARLES and MR. HARDCASTLE hide behind screen. MARLOW enters.)

MARLOW: Madam, though prepared for setting out, I come once more to say goodby.

KATE: Then go, sir. I must remain contented with the memory — of our meeting.

MARLOW: Madam, your beauty at first caught my eye; for who could see that without emotion?

SIR CHARLES: *(Peeks out from one side of the screen.)* Such boldness. He amazes me! *(Hides again.)*

MR. HARDCASTLE: *(Peeks out from other side of screen.)* I told you how it would be. Hush! *(Hides again.)*

MARLOW: I am now determined to stay, madam. I cannot leave you. By all that's good, I can have no happiness but what's in your power to grant me!

KATE: Sir. I must entreat you'll desist. Do you think I could ever catch at the confident addresses of a secure admirer?

MARLOW: (*Kneels.*) Does this look like security? Does this look like confidence?

SIR CHARLES: (*He and HARDCASTLE come out from hiding.*) I can hold it no longer, Charles. Charles, how hast thou deceived me! Is this your inference to the girl?

MR. HARDCASTLE: What have you to say now?

MARLOW: That I'm all amazement! What can it mean?

MR. HARDCASTLE: It means that you have one story for us, and other for my daughter.

MARLOW: Daughter! This lady — your daughter?

MR. HARDCASTLE: Yes, sir, my only daughter — my Kate.

KATE: Yes, sir, that tall, squinting lady you were pleased to take me for.

MARLOW: Zounds, there's no bearing this. I must be gone.

MR. HARDCASTLE. By the hand on my body, you shall not. I see now it was another mistake.

MRS. HARDCASTLE: (*She enters, followed by TONY.*) So, so they're gone off. Let them go. I care not.

MR. HARDCASTLE: Who gone?

MRS. HARDCASTLE: My dutiful niece and Mr. Hastings. Well, if he has taken away the lady, he has not taken her fortune. (*HASTINGS and CONSTANCE enter.*)

MR. HARDCASTLE: What! They return!

HASTINGS: Excuse my attempt to fly off with your niece. We are now come back to appeal from your justice to your humanity.

CONSTANCE: Since my father's death, I have been obliged to stoop to dissimulation to avoid oppression. I now hope to receive from your tenderness what is denied me from a nearer connection.

MR. HARDCASTLE: I'm glad you've come back to reclaim your due. Come hither, Tony, my boy. Do you refuse this lady's hand whom I now offer you?

TONY: You know I can't refuse her till I'm of age, father.

MR. HARDCASTLE: I thought concealing your age was likely to conduce to your improvement, but I must now declare you have been of age this three months.

TONY: Of age! Am I of age, father?

MR. HARDCASTLE: Above three months.

TONY: Then you'll see the first use I'll make of my liberty. Witness all men by these presents, that I, Anthony Lumpkin, Esquire, of BLANK place, refuse you, Constania Neville, spinster, of no place at all, for my true and lawful wife. So Constance Neville may marry whom she pleases and — Tony Lumpkin is his own man again.

MARLOW: Joy, my dear George, I give you joy sincerely. And could I prevail upon my little tyrant here to be less arbitrary, I, too, should be the happiest man alive.

HASTINGS: Come, madam, you are now driven to the very last scene of all your contrivances. I know you like him. I'm sure he loves you, and you must and shall have him. (*KATE smiles and nods her head.*)

MR. HARDCASTLE: And I say so, too. So boy, take her; and as you have been mistaken in the mistress, my wish is, that you may never be mistaken in the wife.

KATE: (*All line up for the epilogue.*) So having stooped to conquer with success,

MARLOW: She gained a husband without aid from dress.

CONSTANCE: And I, my constant love am free to wed,

HASTINGS: Not a country squire, but me instead.

SIR CHARLES: Because the country squire did renounce her.

TONY: Ay! I'm off to court Bet Bouncer!

MR. HARDCASTLE: So, two by two — all comes out right.

ALL: Thus we end — the MISTAKES ALL OF A NIGHT.

CURTAINS CLOSE

Fashion

by Anna Cora Mowatt
Adapted by Aurand Harris

Introduction

Anna Cora Mowatt's social comedy, *Fashion: or Life in New York*, is ranked the best, and perhaps the first, of the early satiric treatments of "fashionable" society in American life. With simple virtue rewarded and with thrusts at snobbishness, the play is a spirited burlesque of the folly of the newly rich Americans who in the 1840's regarded everything French as elegant and everything American as commonplace. Although the play shows the influence of Sheridan's English comedies of manners, Mrs. Mowatt endows her characters with a distinctive American flavor.

Fashion was initially produced in 1845 at the Park Theatre in New York and was an instant success. It ran for twenty-eight nights, a long run at that time, and then was given a second production in Philadelphia.

Mrs. Mowatt was born of a good family in New York City, (1819–1870). Married at fifteen, she wrote her first play at seventeen, *The Gypsy Wonder*. She was an acclaimed public reader, and after the success of *Fashion*, she became a successful actress, first appearing in Bulwer-Lytton's romantic play, *The Lady of Lyones*. Later she formed her own company and performed *Fashion* in London. She wrote several other plays, novels, short stories and magazine articles, but *Fashion* is what she is remembered for.

Edgar Allan Poe reviewed *Fashion* in the *Broadway Journal* of March 24, 1845, complaining about the trite melodramatic staging of the play but added, after seeing the first five performances, "Compared with generality of modern drama, it is a good play; estimated by the natural spirit of dramatic art, it is altogether unworthy of notice." In his second review he was more generous. He applauded her satirizing of fashion and saw in her play a clear indication of a revival of the American drama.

About a December 7, 1926, revival of *Fashion*, a critic for the *Chicago Journal* wrote that it was "one of the earliest manufacturers of hokum."

Quinn's *History of the American Drama* states, "Real as her (Mowatt's) contribution to our drama was, her influence upon our theatre was probably even greater. She proved triumphantly that an American gentlewoman could succeed in it. She took into the profession her high heart, her utter refinement, her keen sense of social values, and her infinite capacity for effort, and her effect was a real and great one."

Mrs. Mowatt said she wrote *Fashion* to be performed, to be seen on the stage. She wanted "a dramatic, not a literary success." She got what she wanted. *Fashion* may not be literature; but as theatre, it succeeded. Even today it can still be performed as a classic theatre period comedy.

CAST

ADAM TRUEMAN, *a Farmer from Catteraugus*
COUNT JOLIMAITRE, *a fashionable European Importation*
COLONEL HOWARD, *an Officer in the U.S. Army*
MR. TIFFANY, *a New York Merchant*
SNOBSON, *a rare species of Confidential Clerk*
MRS. TIFFANY, *a Lady who imagines herself fashionable*
SERAPHINA TIFFANY, *her daughter, a Belle*
GERTRUDE, *a Governess*
MILLINETTE, *a French Lady's Maid*

SCENE: *New York City*

TIME: *1850*

FASHION

(*SETTING: A splendid Drawing Room in the house of Mrs. Tiffany. Down Left is a large doorway leading to the main hall and stairs. Down Right is a door leading to the music room. At the back is a large archway leading to the conservatory, which is bright with flowers and sunlight. There are two small doors, one Up Right and one Up Left. MILLINETTE, a French Maid, is arranging some pillows. She sings a lively French Song.*)

MILLINETTE: *Parfait!* (*Looks about the room*) Ah, de room *resemble* exactly like de great *salons de Paris*. Madame Tiffany vill be *très* proud of Millinette. (*Confidentially to audience*) I tell you in *confidence* Madame Tiffany is a lady of fashion. Monsieur make de money. Madame spend it. Monsieur nobody at all. Madame everybody altogether. Ah! De money is all dat is *nécessaire* in dis country to make one lady of fashion. I teach Madame de latest *les modes de Paris*, and Madame set de fashion for all New York.

MRS. TIFFANY: (*Off*) Millinette!

MILLINETTE: *Oui*, Madame.

MRS. TIFFANY: (*Enters D. L., dressed in the most extravagant height of fashion*) Is everything in order, Millinette? Ah! Very elegant, very elegant indeed! There is a *jenny-says-quoi* look about the room. Is there not, Millinette?

MILLINETTE: Oh, *oui*, Madame!

MRS. TIFFANY: Miss Seraphina is not dressed yet? Oh, but I remember that nothing is more fashionable than to keep people waiting.
(*Aside*) This girl is worth her weight in gold. Millinette, how do you say "arm-chair" in French?

MILLINETTE: *Fauteuil.*

MRS. TIFFANY: Fo — tool! How refined. Fow-tool! Armchair! What a difference. Like hat — so common. *Chapeau* — so elegant. Tell Seraphina to hurry.

MILLINETTE: *Oui*, Madame.

MRS. TIFFANY: (*Talks to herself in the mirror, thinking she is alone*) I remember when I worked as a milliner, sewing and tying ribbons on hats —

MILLINETTE: Madame, sewing?

MRS. TIFFANY: (*Startled*) I mean — when I visited a millinery shop, TRYING on *chapeaux*, I — Oh, do tell Seraphina to come immediately!

MILLINETTE: I sink she *raide. Oui.* She *arrive.* (*She curtsies and exits D.L. after SERAPHINA enters D. L. Seraphina, too, is very extravagantly dressed*)

MRS. TIFFANY: My dear, how bewitchingly you look. Does Millinette say that that head dress is strictly Parisian?

SERAPHINA: Oh, yes, Mama, all the rage!

MRS. TIFFANY: Count Jolimaitre will soon be here. He is the most fashionable foreigner in town. Yes, he would be quite eligible as a husband for a daughter of the Upper Ten Thousand! (*Bell rings*) Oh, he is here! A-dolph will let him in. Good gracious! I am so flurried, and nothing is so ungenteel as agitation. He's coming up! Smooth your dress. Stand by the *faw-tool.*

SERAPHINA: Stand where?

MRS. TIFFANY: By the *faw-tool! Faw-tool!*

COUNT: (*Enters D. L., very dashingly dressed*) Madam.

MRS. TIFFANY: *Entray, sol vous plaît.* Oh, Count, this unexpected honor — (*Curtsies*)

SERAPHINA: Oh Count, this inexpressible pleasure —

COUNT: (*Bows to each*) Beg you won't mention it, Madam. Miss Seraphina, your most devoted. Ah, I find there is one redeeming charm in America — the superlative loveliness of the feminine population. (*Aside*) And the wealth of their obliging papas.

MRS. TIFFANY: My dear Count, I am sure you are at home in all the courts of Europe.

COUNT: Courts? Oh, yes, Madam. I am known in many courts in Europe. (*Aside*) Including a few POLICE COURTS. But I find very little refinement, very little *élégance* outside of Paris.

SERAPHINA: America, then, has no charm for you?

COUNT: I find you particularly *charmante*. Your smile transports me to the summit of Olympus.

SERAPHINA: Then I must frown, for I would not send you so far away.

(*Bell rings*)

MRS. TIFFANY: The bell! Who? *Excusay.* (*Calls D. L.*) A-dolph, announce—I am NOT AT HOME.

COUNT: In a word, Madam, I was tired of civilized life and I had *le désire* to refresh myself in a barbarous country, so I came to New York.

TRUEMAN: (*Off*) Out of my way! Don't tell me I can't come in. Can't you see? I am in!

MRS. TIFFANY: Who can it be? So *vul-gaire!*

TRUEMAN: (*Off*) I've come to see my old friend, Antony Tiffany. (*Enters D. L. dressed as a farmer, a stout cane in hand*) Where is this woman that's not AT HOME in her own house?

MRS. TIFFANY: Sir, how dare you intrude yourself into my parlor?

TRUEMAN: Oh, you're the one.

MRS. TIFFANY: I am Mrs. Tiffany.

TRUEMAN: Antony's wife, eh? Well, I'll shake on that.

MRS. TIFFANY: Sir, it is not the fashion in Paris to shake hands.

TRUEMAN: (*Aside*) Poor woman, she doesn't know what country she's in. Madam, I've known your husband since he was a little lad. His father was my best friend. Now I hear he's grown rich, and of course grown older—like me and you.

MRS. TIFFANY: Sir, a woman of fashion never grows old.

TRUEMAN: Eh?

MRS. TIFFANY: Age is always out of fashion. Now I will say, good day, Sir.

TRUEMAN: I thought city folks had better manners, or I wouldn't have come all the way from Catteraugus for a visit with you and yours.

MRS. TIFFANY: A visit!

TRUEMAN: Yes, I've come to see my old friend, Antony. (*Aside*) And to see what's happened to young Gertrude. I hope she's not that dressed-up critter. I don't believe, Madam, you've introduced me to the young lady?

MRS. TIFFANY: It is not the fashion in Paris, Sir, to introduce.

TRUEMAN: Thunder and lightning, woman! This is America.

MRS. TIFFANY: (*Aside*) How shall I get rid of him? Count Jolimaitre, please *par-doan* the errors of this rustic.

COUNT: (*Inspecting Trueman through his eye-glass*) Pray, Madam. To what tribe of Indians does he belong? Does he carry a tomahawk?

TRUEMAN: Something quite as useful — do you see that? (*Shakes stick*)

MRS. TIFFANY: Oh, dear! I shall faint. Millinette! Millinette!

MILLINETTE: (*Enters D. L.*) *Oui*, Madame.

MRS. TIFFANY: A glass of water. *Toot-de-sweet!* (*Rising to her full dignity*) Sir, the gentleman to whom you speak is *très distinguished*. He is a count. (*MILLINETTE looks at Count, starts and screams. COUNT, after a short surprise, plays with his eye-glass, and looks perfectly unconcerned*) What is the matter? What is the matter?

MILLINETTE: Noting, noting — only — (*Looks at Count and turns away*) only — noting at all.

MRS. TIFFANY: Millinette, send for Mr. Tiffany instantly.

MILLINETTE: He *arrive* now, before, dis *moment*. (*Curtsies and Exits D. L.*)

TRUEMAN: My old friend! Where is he? I long to see his friendly smile.

MRS. TIFFANY: Count, *voo-ley-oo a-com-po-nay* Seraphina and *moi* into the *con-sir-va-twire*. (*COUNT bows and takes Seraphina's arm*) Pray walk this way, *sal vous plaît*. (*They Exit at back*)

TRUEMAN: *Sal vous plaît*. Ha, ha, ha! She's so fashionable she's forgot how to speak her mother's tongue. (*Turns to doorway D. L.*) Where are you Antony? (*Aside*) We'll see what fashion has done for him.

MR. TIFFANY: (*Enters D. L., followed by SNOBSON, his clerk*) My old friend! Adam Trueman! (*Shakes hands formally*) We are happy to welcome you, Sir.

TRUEMAN: Happy? I'm not so sure. Your fine lady of a wife greeted me with the message SHE WAS NOT AT HOME. Refused to shake my hand. It's not the fashion, she says. And now I look at you—and see your face is criss-crossed with worried frowns. I'm afraid it's many a day since you were HAPPY at anything.

MR. TIFFANY: True, my work is heavy.

TRUEMAN: Your business is sound I hope? Nothing rotten at the core? (*SNOBSON coughs*) Who's that puppy barking at his fleas?

MR. TIFFANY: My confidential clerk.

TRUEMAN: Confidential? I wouldn't trust him with my spittoon.

SNOBSON: What I have to say, Sir, is an HONEST matter of importance to the CREDIT of the concern, Mr. Tiffany.

MR. TIFFANY: Oh, yes. (*To Trueman*) Excuse me for a moment. Urgent business.

TRUEMAN: (*Aside*) From the looks of that one—UNDERHANDED business.

MR. TIFFANY: If you will please make yourself comfortable in the library. This way, Sir. (*Goes to door U. L.*)

TRUEMAN: (*Aside*) I'll be more comfortable after I see young Gertrude. I worry. Will she, also be bitten by the FASHION bug? (*Goes U. L.*) Thank you, Antony. I can do with a bit of a rest. (*Exits U. L.*)

MR. TIFFANY: (*Shuts door*) Now, Mr. Snobson, proceed.

SNOBSON: My salary, Mr. Tiffany. It is insufficient for the necessities of an honest man — mark me, an HONEST man, Mr. Tiffany.

MR. TIFFANY: (*Aside*) Will I never be rid of his blackmail? Very well, another hundred shall be added.

SNOBSON: There is one other subject which I have before mentioned, Mr. Tiffany — your daughter.

MR. TIFFANY: (*Aside*) Villain! Only the hand of my daughter will seal his lips. Very well, Sir. It shall be as you desire.

SNOBSON: And Mrs. Tiffany shall be informed that I'm to be THE MAN?

MR. TIFFANY: Yes, I'll to her at once. (*Aside*) How low have I bowed to this insolent rascal! (*Exits at back*)

SNOBSON: And now I'll find Miss Seraphina and state my case. (*Looks at watch*) Bless me! Half past and I haven't had my julep yet! Snobson, I'm ashamed of you! (*He Exits D. L. GERTRUDE enters U. R., humming a popular song. She is a young girl, simply but becomingly dressed. She sees no one is about, goes to conservatory entrance. As she picks a rose, COLONEL HOWARD enters D. L. He is a handsome young army man, dressed in uniform. He sees her and comes to her quickly*)

HOWARD: Miss Gertrude.

GERTRUDE: Colonel Howard!

HOWARD: It is quite fitting that I find you among the roses.

GERTRUDE: I enjoy tending the flowers. They remind me of the country.

HOWARD: You came from a pleasant little town.

GERTRUDE: Geneva. Where I prefer a ramble in the woods to a promenade in Broadway.

HOWARD: I, too, like a simple life. And I admire you — and your truthfulness.

GERTRUDE: I have no reason to conceal the truth. I was brought up, an orphan, by two kind sisters in Geneva. I had abilities and desired to use them. I came here and am employed to teach music to Miss Seraphina. You see, I have my independence.

HOWARD: I—admire your spirit, Gertrude. I admire—

GERTRUDE: Colonel Howard, I must remind you that Mrs. Tiffany only receives visitors on her reception day. (*TRUEMAN enters U. L. stops, listens, and remains unseen*)

HOWARD: Nay, Gertrude, it is not Mrs. Tiffany, nor Miss Tiffany, whom I came to see. It—it is—(*Aside*) If I only dared to give utterance to what is hovering upon my lips.

GERTRUDE: Yes, Colonel Howard?

HOWARD: Gertrude, I must—must—

GERTRUDE: Yes, indeed, you MUST, must leave me!

HOWARD: Your book—(*Starts to give her book*)

GERTRUDE: Mrs. Tiffany would not be pleased to find you here. And we should not be found alone. Pray, pray leave me. (*She hurries him out D. L.*) What a strange being is man! Why should he hesitate to say— nay, why should I prevent his saying, what I would most delight to hear? Truly man IS strange—but woman is quite as incomprehensible!

TRUEMAN: (*Aside*) It is Gertrude. Yes, there is a light in her face—the same light that was in another face, which I remember so well.

GERTRUDE: Sir?

TRUEMAN: You are Gertrude?

GERTRUDE: Yes.

TRUEMAN: I am an old friend of Mr. Tiffany, from Catteraugus.

GERTRUDE: Mr. Trueman! Yes, Mr. Tiffany has spoken of you. I am glad to meet you, Sir. I, too, come from the country. Geneva.

TRUEMAN: Ah, Geneva. The Wilson sisters?

GERTRUDE: You are acquainted with them?

TRUEMAN: I shouldn't wonder if I was.

GERTRUDE: Then we have much to talk about!

TRUEMAN: (*Aside*) Ah, much more than she knows.

GERTRUDE: (*Listens*) They are coming in from the conservatory.

TRUEMAN: Thunder and lightning! Right when we were getting acquainted.

GERTRUDE: I must prepare for Miss Seraphina's lesson. Oh, Mr. Trueman, I feel already we are friends. Thank you for coming!

(*Exits U. R.*)

TRUEMAN: (*Looking after her*) If falsehood harbours there, I'll give up searching after truth! (*He exits*)

SERAPHINA: (*She and the COUNT enter at back*) We must not tarry so long. Mama will be worried. No one here.

COUNT: Then we are alone — again. (*Clock chimes*)

SERAPHINA: Two o'clock. Time for our afternoon drive. It's all the rage! You must ride with us in our carriage.

COUNT: Ah, there's no resisting you, Miss Tiffany.

MILLINETTE: (*Enters with wrap*) Mademoiselle, I bring dis scarf for de ride. Keep you cozy in de breeze.

SERAPHINA: You are certain the scarf is the latest fashion?

MILLINETTE: (*Gives Count a threatening look, arranges scarf over Seraphina's shoulders, turns her around so she is facing the other way*) Mademoiselle, *permettez-moi* (*Aside to Count*) Traitor! If Mademoiselle vill stand *tranquille* one *petit moment*. (*Aside to Count*) I must speak vid you!

COUNT: Sh!

MILLINETTE: I tell all.

COUNT: Sh. We will talk later.

MILLINETTE: (*Nods*) Ve vill return here.

COUNT: No.

MILLINETTE: I tell all!

COUNT: Yes! Return here.

SERAPHINA: What is that you say, Millinette?

MILLINETTE: Dis scarf make you so very beautiful, Mademoiselle. *Très parisienne!* (*Whispers to Count*) Ve meet here. (*He nods. She curtsies to Seraphina and exits D. R.*)

COUNT: (*Aside*) Not a moment to lose! Or — I am exposed! Miss Tiffany, I have an unpleasant piece of intelligence. You see, I have just received a letter from the — aw — Earl of Airshire; the truth is, the Earl's daughter has distinguished me by a tender *penchant*.

SERAPHINA: And they wish you to marry the young lady. But surely you will not leave us, Count?

COUNT: If YOU bid me stay, I couldn't AFFORD to tear myself away. (*Aside*) I'm sure that's honest. Say the right word — say that you will be my Countess —

SERAPHINA: Oh, you must not think of leaving. I — yes — yes, Count, I do consent.

COUNT: (*Aside*) I thought she would. (*Embraces her*) Enchanted, rapture, bliss, ecstasy, and all that sort of thing — words can't express it. But our wedding must be kept a secret. We will elope. Sh! (*Whispers*) Now.

SERAPHINA: (*Whispers*) Elope?

COUNT: It is the latest fashion. (*She nods*) Hurry. Pack some things. We will get the carriage — before your mother does. Ah, we part — but only for a moment — my petite bird of paradise.

SERAPHINA: I fly! (*Exits D. L.*)

COUNT: Ah, if only I were not so irresistible! But I find handling two women at once is TOO much. The only course of valor is — to be off! (*He starts D. L., freezes when he hears Millinette*)

MILLINETTE: (*Enters D. R., whispers*) Gustave . . . We be all of us alone?

COUNT: Ah, Millinette, my *chérie*, you see I am here as you bid.

MILLINETTE: Vat for you leave me in Paris? Vat for you leave me — and I love you so much?

COUNT: I was forced by uncontrollable circumstances.

MILLINETTE: Vat you do vid all de money I give you? The last *sous* I had — did I not give you?

COUNT: I dare say you did, *ma petite*. (*Aside*) And I wish you'd been better supplied. (*GERTRUDE enters U. R., unperceived*) But we must not talk here. I will explain everything later.

MILLINETTE: No! You not deceive me no more.

SERAPHINA: (*Off*) Millinette? Millinette!

COUNT: Go. I will meet you —

MILLINETTE: Ven? Vere?

COUNT: In the music room. (*Points D. R.*) Alone . . . in five minutes. I will explain it all, my sweet, *adorable*, Millinette.

MILLINETTE: I vill be dere. You be, also. And you give me one grand *explanation*!

SERAPHINA: (*Off*) Millinette!

MILLINETTE: *Oui*, I come. Five minutes. Or I vill tell all. (*Exits D. L.*)

COUNT: Haste is the word. Hold the carriage at the side door. Appease Millinette. And marry Seraphina. (*Exits D. L.*)

GERTRUDE: (*Advancing from hiding*) Meet in the music room. Explain — what? This man is an imposter! If I tell Mrs. Tiffany — No, she will disbelieve me. I must devise some plan for opening their eyes. (*Has an idea*) Ah, if I could expose the Count . . . if I could learn the truth from his own words. I will hide myself in the music room, pull the draperies, disguise my voice, use my best French, and unmask this insolent pretender. But this is impudence — if I should fail? Fail! To lack courage when faced with difficulty is not a woman's failing. (*She Exits into music room, D. R. as COLONEL HOWARD enters D. L.*)

HOWARD: Miss Gertrude — Gertrude, I — (*She has gone. He is left holding the book*) In my haste I forgot — your book. (*Aside*) I — I will speak. I will ask her hand in marriage. Gertrude, I have returned to ask you — (*He looks into the room, Aside*) Whatever is she doing? Darkening the room — closing the window curtains. I wonder what . . .? But it is without honor to spy. Yet — (*He looks again. The door swings shut*) And now the door is shut. Footsteps. I must not be caught eavesdropping. (*He hides*)

COUNT: (*Enters, D. L., cautiously*) Caution is the word. Ah, the door is shut. She is there. (*Tiptoes to door. Knocks*) Open, my *petite chérie.* (*Door opens*) Where are you? I cannot see you in the dark.

GERTRUDE: (*Off, imitating Millinette's voice*) Hush. *Parle bas.*

COUNT: (*Enters doorway*) Come and give me a kiss! (*Door shuts behind him*)

HOWARD: (*Steps out from hiding, speaks aside*) A kiss! Oh, Gertrude!

   (*Hides again*)

MILLINETTE: (*Enters D. L.*) Now I vill know de truth. I vill make one grand discovery! (*Opens door D. R.*) *Mon Dieu!* Vat do not I see?

COUNT: (*Off*) Millinette! Out there! Who is this in here?

MILLINETTE: Ma'mselle Gertrude! Vat you do? Together! In de dark! I vill scream! (*She screams, looks at door, screams again, gasps for breath, and again screams and cries*)

MRS. TIFFANY: (*Enters D. L., followed by TRUEMAN*) What is the noise? How dare you create this disturbance in my house?

MILLINETTE: Look! You vill not believe. See! In de dark. Together!

MRS. TIFFANY: Who? (*COUNT enters*) The Count! (*GERTRUDE enters*)

TRUEMAN: Gertrude!

MILLINETTE: Oh, I not feel vell! My poor heart—broken a *million* pieces. You traitor! You villain! You—Oh, I go—I die of de broken heart. (*Exits D. L.*)

MRS. TIFFANY: (*To Gertrude*) What is the meaning of this?

TRUEMAN: (*To Count*) You scoundrel! I'll beat the truth out of you.

(*Raises stick*)

COUNT: (*Rushes to Mrs. Tiffany*) Madam—my dear Madam—keep off that barbarous old man, and I will explain! When I entered that room, Madam, I—I did not know SHE was there. Miss Gertrude, say if that is true or not true.

GERTRUDE: Sir, you know that you planned to meet—

COUNT: Answer a simple yea or nay. Did I know YOU were in that room?

GERTRUDE: I will be truthful. No, he did not know *I* was there, but he—

COUNT: You hear, Madam, I am innocent!

MRS. TIFFANY: Then YOU, you shameless girl, you planned it!

TRUEMAN: I won't believe it.

HOWARD: (*Steps forward from hiding*) It is true.

MRS. TIFFANY: Colonel Howard!

HOWARD: Would that I could tear out my tongue, but honor is at stake. She drew the curtains. She arranged—the rendezvous. Oh, Gertrude, I have striven to find some excuse—but this is beyond all endurance. I take my leave. (*Exits D. L.*)

MRS. TIFFANY: Get out, you *ow*dacious—you ruined woman! Never let me see your face again. Pack!

COUNT: Mrs. Tiffany—Madam—try to keep calm, control yourself. Let me help you, conduct you to the *silence* of your sitting room.

MRS. TIFFANY: (*Count takes her arm. She is dramatically exhausted*) *Merci bow-coop.*

COUNT: (*Helping her to the door*) You must rest. You must relax. (*Aside*) And I must quick, be off with Seraphina. (*They exit D. L.*)

GERTRUDE: Mr. Trueman, I insist upon being heard. I claim it as a right!

TRUEMAN: Right! Ah, my girl you had more rights than you knew of, but you have forfeited them all. I'll start back to Catteraugus tomorrow. (*She starts toward him*) No. I have seen enough of what fashion can do! (*Exits D. L.*)

GERTRUDE: Oh, how heavy a penalty has my impudence cost me! I will go back to Geneva. Yes, but I must hurry and write them that I am coming. (*Sits at desk*) What shall I say? I will write the truth. (*Writes*) I shall tell them how in trying to help, I was caught in my own web of innocence. Ah, what true pleasure there is in daring to be honest.

TRUEMAN: (*Enters D. L.*) There she is. If this girl's soul had only been as fair as her face — yet — she dared to speak the truth. I'll not forget that! A woman who refuses to tell a lie still has in her one spark of heaven. I will say goodby to her. Gertrude. What are you writing there?

GERTRUDE: I am writing the truth of what happened. I have done nothing of which I am ashamed. There, read it if you like. (*Hands him the letter*)

TRUEMAN: So I will. (*Reads*) What's this? "French maid — the Count — an imposter! — disguised myself — to expose him." Thunder and lightning! I see it all. (*Aside*) Ah, she's a rare girl! Gertrude, I have found one true woman at last. Now, my girl, one more truth. It is important that I know if your heart is free or taken? Ah, you blush. There is a man. Who is he? Out with the truth. (*HOWARD enters D. L.*)

GERTRUDE: Colonel Howard here!

HOWARD: I have returned —

GERTRUDE: Yes?

HOWARD: I have returned with your book.

GERTRUDE: Thank you. (*Takes it*)

HOWARD: I have returned to bid you farewell.

GERTRUDE: Colonel Howard, if you will read this letter it will explain everything. (*Hands letter to HOWARD who reads*)

MRS. TIFFANY: (*Enters D. L., followed by MR. TIFFANY*) Mr. Tiffany, not another word. There is nothing more ungenteel than fretting over one's unpaid bills. Oh, what a *fa-tee-ging* day!

TRUEMAN: Ah, Antony, you are here just in time. I now can tell you and tell Gertrude why I came. You remember, Antony, a blue-eyed, smiling girl —

MR. TIFFANY: Your daughter, Sir?

TRUEMAN: (*Remembers with emotion*) Yes, my only daughter. Twenty years ago I found myself the richest farmer in Catteraugus. This cursed money made my girl an object of speculation. Every idle fellow came to court Ruth. There was one — ah, Ruth was taken with him. And one morning — the rascal robbed me of the only treasure I cherished — my daughter.

MR. TIFFANY: But you forgave her.

TRUEMAN: I did. The scoundrel thought he was marrying my gold, but he was mistaken. A year later, he forsook her! She came back to her old father. It couldn't last long — she pined — and pined — and — then — she died, and left a little girl. I swore that my unlucky wealth should never curse her, so I sent the child away, to be brought up by relatives in Geneva.

GERTRUDE: Geneva?

TRUEMAN: There she was taught true independence. For I resolved not to claim her until she'd found the man who was willing to take her for herself alone, not her money. Today I am going to claim her. There stands Ruth's child! Old Adam's heiress! Gertrude, Gertrude! My child! (*Gertrude rushes into his arms*)

MRS. TIFFANY: Gertrude! An heiress!

MILLINETTE: (*Enters D. L. with letter*) Madame! Madame! De letter! Mademoiselle Seraphina left de letter! She going. She *gallop* avay vid de carriage.

MRS. TIFFANY: Letter? Gone away?

MR. TIFFANY: (*Snatches letter, reads*) "My dear Mama—when you receive this I shall be a countess! The Count and I were forced to be married privately . . ."

MILLINETTE: (*Horror-stricken*) Married! Oh, Madame, I vill tell everyting! Oh, dat *animal*! Dat *monstre*! He give de promise to marry me.

MRS. TIFFANY: The Count marry YOU!

MILLINETTE: *Oui.* But, Madame, de truth is dat he is not one Count, not at all! He not one Frenchman at all, but he do live one long time *à Paris.* He do live vid Monsieur Vermicelle—dere he vas de cook.

MRS. TIFFANY: A COOK!

MILLINETTE: *Voilà*, now I tell de truth, Millinette feel one great deal better!

SNOBSON: (*Enters, D. L., evidently a little intoxicated.*) I won't stand for it. I say, Snobson, I won't stand for it. That extra mint julep has put the true puck in me. Mr. Tiffany, Sir, I'd like to know, Sir, why you assisted your daughter, Sir, in running away? I have been swindled, Sir.

MR. TIFFANY: This is not the place—

SNOBSON: Place? Your place, Mr. Tiffany, Sir, is in the STATE'S PRISON! He's a FORGER! (*There is general confusion:* "Oh! What? No!")

TRUEMAN: (*To Snobson*) You! I assume you have been aware of, and a witness to, all his forgeries!

SNOBSON: You've hit the nail, Catteraugus!

TRUEMAN: You saw him forge the name?

SNOBSON: I did.

TRUEMAN: Repeatedly?

SNOBSON: Re-pea-ted-ly.

TRUEMAN: Then if he goes to the State's Prison, YOU'LL go, too. You are an accomplice, and ACCESSORY!

SNOBSON: (*Bewildered*) The deuce, so I am! I must make myself scarce, I'll be off. They want men of genius in the West. Which is the way to California? (*Exits D. L.*)

TRUEMAN: Antony, I'm not given to preaching. Your face speaks for itself — the crime has brought its own punishment. And I will assist you financially, but upon one condition. You must sell your house and bundle your wife and daughter off to the country. There let them learn economy, true independence, instead of dependence upon a dressmaker; learn to live with home virtues, instead of foreign fashion.

MR. TIFFANY: We will go with you to Catteraugus!

TRUEMAN: Thunder and lightning, no! Keep clear of Catteraugus. I want none of your fashion there!

SERAPHINA: (*She and Count enter D. L.*) I returned for my jewels — before we are married.

MILLINETTE: (*Sees Count, rushes to him, holds him*) He is here! Ah, Gustave, *mon cher* Gustave! I have you now and ve never come apart no more.

TRUEMAN: Step forward, Mr. Count. And for the edification of fashionable society confess that you are an impostor.

COUNT: I? An impostor?

MILLINETTE: I lost you. I re-find you. I tell all. I love you so!

COUNT: Well, then I do confess I am no Count, but ladies and gentlemen, may I recommend myself as the best French cook, *à la mode de Paris*.

MRS. TIFFANY: Oh, Seraphina!

SERAPHINA: Oh, Mama!

TRUEMAN: If you promise to dress in your cook's attire and call upon all your fashionable acquaintances, I will set you up in business tomorrow.

COUNT: Madam, Mademoiselle, I hope you will pardon my conduct, but I heard in America where FASHION makes the basest coin current, where you have no kings, no princes, no NOBILITY—

TRUEMAN: Stop! We have NOBILITY. We have people noble with the stamp of NATURE, not of FASHION. Yes, we have honest men, warm-hearted and brave and we have women—gentle, fair and true. I raise my stick and salute them. In America, good people do not need a title, for they ARE the finest of NOBILITY! (*Tableau. Music*)

GERTRUDE: (*Steps forward, addresses audience*). But ere we end our play, a word with you—

HOWARD: (*He and each actor step forward, making a line for the epilogue*) On honor say—Is our picture true?

MR. TIFFANY: Fashion drove me close to a prison wall.

TRUEMAN: Fashion made hypocrites of you all.

MRS. TIFFANY: I've been deceived. Fashion, I thought was vital.

SERAPHINA: Fashion lost me both a husband and a title.

COUNT: A Count no more, I'm no more account.

TRUEMAN: But to a nobler title you may mount,
And be in time—who knows?—an honest man.

MILLINETTE: Oh, *oui*, my *adorable* hero, I know you can.

SNOBSON: (*Enters D. L. and stands in line*)
I aspired to rise, a fashionable gent to be,
But, damn it, fashion didn't take up me.

GERTRUDE: Thus our play has shown in its ruling passion,
And portrayed, we hope, the tinsel value—of Fashion.

CURTAIN

The Romancers

by Edmond Rostand
Adapted by Aurand Harris

NOTICE

Introduction

Edmond Rostand, born 1868, died 1918, was a French playwright and poet. At the height of the naturalistic period, dominated by the plays of Ibsen, Rostand rewakened briefly and popularized again the Romantic spirit of seventy years before with his romantic verse dramas.

Les Romanesques, his first play to be produced, was immediately put in the repertory of the *Théâtre Français*. The play is frankly theatrical—a romantic fanciful variation of the Romeo and Juliet theme, taking place "wherever you please, provided the costumes are pretty." The theme delightfully satirizes the romantic naiveté of adolescent lovers. Unfortunately the lyric beauty of his original poetry loses some of its charm when translated into English prose.

Since its first production the comedy has been popular throughout the world. In 1969, Tom Jones and Harvey Schmit wrote an American musical, *The Fantasticks*, based on Rostand's play. It opened off Broadway in New York City and has been running ever since, with over six thousand performances elsewhere in the United States, and over three hundred productions in fifty-four other countries, in fourteen languages.

Cyrano de Bergerac is Rostand's masterpiece. The play, a neo-romantic "heroic comedy" in verse, is wholly of the theatre. A showcase for Rostand's wit, idealism and technical skills, the script combines gentle satire and lyrical grace, comedy and pathos, all expressed with poetic beauty.

The play was written for Coquelin, the greatest romantic actor of his day; and he may well have helped shape the play with his theatrical knowledge. The story is based on the life of an actual French philosopher-poet-soldier, Cyrano, (1619–1655), who wrote plays and satires. Rostand captures both the swagger and the adventurous feeling of the seventeenth century.

On the opening night, December 28, 1897, Rostand from his place on the stage where he played the part of one of the Cadets, heard the thunderous applause—"the most enthusiastic popular reception in dramatic history." It ran for two hundred performances, followed by many productions in Europe and abroad.

The play has been made into an opera, two musical comedies and several films. After a modern theatre revival by Jose Ferrer in 1946, a critic observed, "When a great play meets a great performer that's good news on Broadway." Louis Kronenberger may have given the play a final evaluation: "Rostand's play offers all the dashing, poetic, impossible romantic things for which the human heart secretly hungers; offers them in abundance, moreover, and offers them with authority."

CAST

SYLVETTE, *a romantic young lady*
PERCINET, *a romantic young man*
BERGAMIN, *father of Percinet*
PASQUINOT, *father of Sylvette*
STRAFOREL, *a bravado*
Swordsmen, musicians, and torchbearers

TIME: *Eighteenth Century*

PLACE: *France*

SETTING: *Two gardens separated by a wall*

The Romancers

(Dividing the stage in the Center is a picturesque wall. On one side is the garden of BERGAMIN and on the other side is the garden of PAS-QUINOT. There is a bench against the wall on each side. PERCINET is discovered sitting on the wall, holding a book of verse. He is young and romantic. He is reading to SYLVETTE who sits gracefully on the bench on her side of the wall. She listens in rapture at PERCINET's reading.)

SYLVETTE: *(Sighs)* Ah, Monsieur Percinet! How beautiful it is!

PERCINET: Is it not? Listen to Romeo's answer: *(Reads with passion)*
"It was the lark, the herald of the morn,
No nightingale: look, love, what envious streaks
Do lace the severing clouds in yonder east:
Night's candles are burnt out, and jocund day
Stands tiptoe on the misty mountain tops:
I must begone—"

SYLVETTE: *(Rises, interrupting)* Sh! Someone is coming! *(Goes to Right, looks nervously)*

PERCINET: *(Looks anxiously to Left)* No one. *(Motions her back to bench. She sits, looking fondly at him)* Now, Mademoiselle, you must not be frightened like a startled bird, who at the slightest noise, flies off the branch. Listen to what the immortal lovers say to each other: *(Reads, dramatically)*
Romeo. "Let me be ta'en, let me be put to death;
I am content, so thou will have it so.
I'll say, yon gray is not the morning's eye,
'Tis but the pale reflex of Cynthia's brow;
Nor that is not the lark, whose notes do beat
The vaulty heaven so high above our heads:
I have more care to stay than will to go:
Come, death and welcome. . . ."

SYLVETTE: Oh, no! I do not wish him to speak of death. No . . . I shall cry.

PERCINET: Then we will close our book until tomorrow. Since you wish it, we will let Romeo live! (*Shuts book, looks at gardens*) What a lovely spot. It seems to me it was made especially to cradle the beautiful verses of the great Shakespeare.

SYLVETTE: Oh, the verses are beautiful . . . and the gardens are beautiful . . . but what makes it more beautiful to me is the music of your voice.

PERCINET: Flatterer.

SYLVETTE: (*Rises and walks to Right*) Poor lovers. How cruel their fate. How sad for them. Ah, I think that Romeo and Juliet —

PERCINET: (*Leaning far over the wall toward her*) Yes?

SYLVETTE: (*Turns away shyly*) Nothing.

PERCINET: Yes. Something which suddenly made you blush.

SYLVETTE: Nothing.

PERCINET: You cannot deceive me. Your eyes are too transparent. Ah, I understand! I see what you meant. You are thinking of us . . . of our families.

SYLVETTE: Perhaps.

PERCINET: Of your father . . . of my father . . . of the hate they have for each other.

SYLVETTE: Oh, yes! That is what grieves me. That is what makes me cry . . . often . . . when I'm alone. I remember last month, when I returned from the convent, my father showed me your father's park and said to me, "*Mon enfant*, you see there the domain of my mortal enemy, Bergamin. Never let your path cross that of his or of his rascal son, Percinet. Promise me that, or else, I shall disavow you as an enemy. Their family has always hated yours!"
(*Weakly*) I promised. (*Runs to wall and to him*)
But you see how I keep my word.

PERCINET: And did not I also promise my father to hate you . . . always, Sylvette? But . . . I love you.

SYLVETTE: (*Nods happily*) Yes . . . (*Then naively fearful*) and it is so sinful.

PERCINET: Yes. But what can we do? (*They sigh and gaze at each other*) The greater the barriers to love, the stronger the desire. Sylvette, kiss me!

SYLVETTE: Never!

PERCINET: But you do love me?

SYLVETTE: (*Aside, and pleased*) What does he say?

PERCINET: I am saying only what you yourself said a short while ago. Yes, you yourself, Sylvette, compared Romeo and Juliet with us . . . here.

SYLVETTE: But I didn't say—

PERCINET: But you did! And it is true! My father and your father are Juliet's father and Romeo's father—and we are Romeo and Juliet! Yes, and that is why we are so recklessly in love, and I dare to face the terrible hatred of Pasquinot-Capulet and Bergamin-Montague!

SYLVETTE: Then, we are in love? But, Monsieur Percinet, how has it happened so quickly?

PERCINET: Love is born, one knows not how, because it must be born. I often saw you pass my window . . .

SYLVETTE: I, too . . .

PERCINET: And our eyes spoke secretly.

SYLVETTE: One day, near the wall, by chance I was gathering flowers.

PERCINET: By chance I was reading Shakespeare. And—see how everything has conspired to unite two hearts.

SYLVETTE: And then the wind whisked my scarf . . . whoosh . . . over to you.

PERCINET: And I climbed the wall to return it . . .

SYLVETTE: And I, too, climbed the wall . . .

PERCINET: And since then, I have waited for you each day, and each day my heart beats faster until finally from behind the wall, I hear your soft gentle laugh and then your head appears and you are here. (*Face to face over the wall they are close enough to kiss*)

SYLVETTE: (*Pulls away*) But our fathers forbid us to see each other. If only their hatred would end.

PERCINET: I doubt that it will.

SYLVETTE: (*Walks to Right*) I have faith in the future. I have already thought of five or six possible things which could happen . . . very possible.

PERCINET: (*As far as he can get over the wall toward her*) Really? What are they?

SYLVETTE: (*Excitedly acts each scene for him*) Now just suppose . . . I've read in more than one novel of a similar occurrence . . . suppose the reigning Prince happened to be passing one day . . . I run . . . I appeal to him . . . I tell him of our love . . . and how our fathers harbor an ancient hatred. The Prince summons my father and your father, and they are reconciled!

PERCINET: And he gives me your hand!

SYLVETTE: (*Runs to him*) Yes! (*Again they are close enough to kiss. She turns away, and dramatizes the next scene*) Or else . . . it can be arranged as it was in another novel. You languish . . . become pale and ill . . . and the doctor says you will surely die . . .

PERCINET: My father asks me, "What is your last desire?"

SYLVETTE: And you answer, "I desire Sylvette." (*She runs to him*)

PERCINET: And his stubborn pride is forced to yield. (*He almost kisses her, but she turns away*)

SYLVETTE: Or else . . . (*Goes to Right, acting the scene*) this adventure could happen: an old duke, having seen my portrait, falls in love with me and offers to make me his duchess.

PERCINET: (*Jealously*) And you answer, "NO!"

SYLVETTE: (*Nods*) He is offended! One night, late on a dark path in the park where I have gone to meditate, I am kidnapped! I cry out!

PERCINET: And I lose not a second in leaping to your side. Dagger in hand, I fight the assassins like a lion!

SYLVETTE: You put to chase three or four men! My father runs out, takes you in his arms. You identify yourself. His hatred melts. He gives me to my rescuer. And your father, proud of our courage, gives his consent. (*Goes to him*)

PERCINET: And we live forever and ever, happily together. (*So close together that their lips meet, but PERCINET suddenly pulls away*) Someone is coming! (*They each look toward their house, then speak quickly to each other*) This evening again? Here? At the hour of eight. You will come? Tell me you will.

SYLVETTE: I can't. No.

PERCINET: You must. Yes.

SYLVETTE: (*Nods. Then points to Left*) Your father!

(*They each ad-lib, "At eight . . . this evening . . . Yes . . . etc.", and quickly sit on a bench, each on his side of the wall. SYLVETTE trying to listen, PERCINET innocently reading his book. BERGAMIN enters from Left. He is an elderly gentleman and a comic. He sees his son and shouts to him*)

BERGAMIN: Aha! Here I find you . . . alone . . . dreaming . . . in this corner of the park.

PERCINET: Father, I adore this corner of the park. I love sitting on this bench which is sheltered by this drooping vine. See how graceful it falls. (*Inhales romantically*) Ah, the air is purer here.

BERGAMIN: (*Inhales vigorously*) By *this* wall?

PERCINET: (*Looks adoringly toward wall*) I have fallen in love— (*SYLVETTE sighs on the other side of the wall*) with it.

BERGAMIN: I see nothing lovable about it!

SYLVETTE: (*Aside*) He can't see why!

PERCINET: But it *is* lovely . . . this ancient wall, topped with greenery and scarlet vines . . . with honeysuckle which peeping through each crack and cranny . . . like eyes . . . is kissed by the warm sun.

BERGAMIN: Eye? Does the wall have eyes?

PERCINET: Ah, what lovely eyes . . . soft azure smiles, gentle blue wonders, you are my delight, and if ever tears bedim them, I shall dispatch them with a single kiss. (*Blows a kiss, toward wall. SYLVETTE shivers with delight*)

SYLVETTE: How clever.

BERGAMIN: How stupid. Ah, but now I see what has made you lose your senses. You come here to read in secret. (*Takes book from PERCINET*) And drama! In verse! That is why you dream and talk of honeysuckle and a wall with bluer eyes! Poetry! (*He throws the book away*) A wall, my son, is meant for protection, not beauty. Protection from our neighbor's spying eyes! (*Studies the wall*) I am going to rebuild this wall, re-lay the bricks. I want a white wall, very tidy, very high. No vines or honeysuckle. Instead we shall decorate the top with pieces of sharp, broken glass.

PERCINET: Oh, pity!

BERGAMIN: No pity. (*Gleefully*) I will sprinkle glass all along the top.

PERCINET AND SYLVETTE: Oh!

BERGAMIN: Now I want to talk with you, my son. I have something important to say to you. (*Starts to speak, stops, looks at wall, and whispers*) If the wall doesn't have eyes, it may have ears. (*SYLVETTE, eavesdropping, reacts*) See if some curious listener is listening.

PERCINET: (*Stands on bench and looks over wall, whispers to SYLVETTE*) Until tonight.

SYLVETTE: I will come as the chimes strike eight.

BERGAMIN: Well?

PERCINET: (*Turns, innocently*) No one.

BERGAMIN: Good. This, my son, is what I have to tell you. I wish you to marry. (*SYLVETTE gives a startled cry*) What was that?

PERCINET: Nothing.

BERGAMIN: Someone cried out.

PERCINET: (*Looking tragically toward wall*) Perhaps . . . a wounded bird.

SYLVETTE: Alas!

PERCINET: . . . In the branches.

BERGAMIN: Now to continue our discussion. After some lengthy reflection, I have chosen you a wife. (*Startled, PERCINET begins to whistle and walks away. BERGAMIN follows him*) I am firmly resolved in this. (*Louder whistling, and following*) I tell you I shall force you. . . . (*Loudest whistling*) Will you stop that idiotic whistling! The lady is still young and very rich . . . a pearl!

PERCINET: And what if I do not want your pearl?

BERGAMIN: You will. Just wait. I'll show you!

PERCINET: (*He walks, romantically reciting. BERGAMIN follows, fuming and threatening*) Spring has filled the trees with sounds of wings, and the brooklets murmur with the birds cooing to each other.

BERGAMIN: You scallywag!

PERCINET: All laugh and sing farewell to April. The butterflies . . .

BERGAMIN: Rascal!

PERCINET: . . . skim across the meadows to make love to the flowers they adore! Love . . .

BERGAMIN: Scamp!

PERCINET: . . . makes all hearts open. (*Turns on BERGAMIN*) And you wish to make a marriage of convenience!

BERGAMIN: Certainly I do.

PERCINET: Then my answer is no, no, no, father. I swear . . . by this wall which hears me I hope . . . that I shall not marry one of your choice.

BERGAMIN: Yes, you will!

PERCINET: I will marry only the one of *my* choice. (*Starts to exit Left*)

BERGAMIN: (*After him with raised fist*) Villain!

PERCINET: My own bright, dazzling, beautiful jewel. (*Exits*)

BERGAMIN: Wait until I catch you! You knave! Scoundrel! Scallywag!

(*Exits after him*)

SYLVETTE: Now I can truly understand my father's hate for that miserable man.

(*PASQUINOT enters from Right. He, too, is an elderly gentleman and a comic. He sees his daughter*)

PASQUINOT: Ah! What are you doing here, mademoiselle?

SYLVETTE: (*Too innocently*) Nothing. Walking in the garden.

PASQUINOT: Here! Alone! But foolish girl, aren't you afraid?

SYLVETTE: I am not easily frightened.

PASQUINOT: But alone near this wall! Remember, I forbid you to come near this wall! My child, take a good look at that park. Over there you see the estate of my ancient mortal enemy.

SYLVETTE: I know, father, you have told me often enough.

PASQUINOT: And still you come to expose yourself to insults. Heaven knows what those two are capable of! If that rascal, or his son, knew that my daughter comes here alone—oh-oh! (*Shivers*) Just thinking about it makes me shudder! (*Looks at wall and has an idea*) Ah, I have an idea! I shall rebuild the wall. Make it higher! And on the top put sharp steel spikes!

SYLVETTE: (*Aside*) He will never do it. It would cost too much.

PASQUINOT: And now, my dear, go into the house. At once! Away from this wall. Quick . . . quick . . . quick. (*He watches her hurry off Right, then looks Left at wall, and with excited anticipation goes to it and calls cheerfully*) Bergamin . . . Bergamin! (*Looks over wall*)

BERGAMIN: (*Enters from Left, also excited and happy*) Pasquinot!

(*Hurries to wall, climbs upon the bench with comic difficulty*)

PASQUINOT: My dear friend (*They embrace, over the wall, kissing each other on one cheek in the French fashion*)

BERGAMIN: My dear friend. (*They embrace again, and kiss each other on the other cheek*)

PASQUINOT: How are you?

BERGAMIN: Not badly.

PASQUINOT: How's your gout?

BERGAMIN: Better. And how is your cold?

PASQUINOT: Still in my head, devil take it.

BERGAMIN: Well, my dear friend, I have news for you, about our children. It is all settled. The wedding will be soon.

PASQUINOT: Wedding?

BERGAMIN: I heard them talking while I was hidden by the foliage. (*He, too, is a romantic*) They adore each other!

PASQUINOT: Bravo! Bravo!

BERGAMIN: The time has come to bring matters to a head. What has always been our one goal?

PASQUINOT: To remove this wall . . .

BERGAMIN: In order that we may live together . . .

PASQUINOT: And merge our two estates!

BERGAMIN: And how is this going to be accomplished?

PASQUINOT: By marrying our two children.

BERGAMIN: But arranged marriages are never tempting to poetic young lovers. So my scheme has worked admirably. Percinet, home from college, and Sylvette home from the convent, when forbidden never to speak to each other, have, of course, sought each other out and fallen in love. Now we have only to say, "Yes" to them.

PASQUINOT: Agreed! But how can we give our consent without telling them of the trick? I have called you "scoundrel" . . . and "idiot" . . .

BERGAMIN: Idiot? Scoundrel was enough!

PASQUINOT: But what pretext can we give for suddenly becoming friends?

BERGAMIN: Your daughter herself has just given us the perfect strategy. While she was talking to Percinet, she described the very plan I was considering. This evening, they will meet here by the wall at eight. Percinet will come first. Then just as Sylvette appears, some dangerous characters leap from a hiding place and seize her! She cries out! Then my young hero leaps over the wall on to the ravishers. Swords meet swords! The kidnappers flee. You appear. I arrive. Your daughter and her honor are saved. Your joy is unbounding. You give your blessing to them both, dropping a few appropriate tears. I am equally touched by the heroic rescue and give my consent. Embraces. End of scene.

PASQUINOT: Ah, you are a genius!

BERGAMIN: Yes, I think it is rather good. Sh! (*Points off Left*) Look! You see who is coming? It is Straforel, the bravado whom I sent a note to about this plot. Yes, if this is going to be an abduction with style, he is the one to do it.

(*STRAFOREL struts in from Left, an overly dressed, affected, comic swordsman. BERGAMIN goes to him and bows*)

BERGAMIN: Monsieur.

STRAFOREL: (*Bows with a great* flourish)

BERGAMIN: Allow me to introduce you to my friend Pasquinot.

STRAFOREL: (*Bows with a flourish*) Monsieur. (*But sees he has bowed to no one*)

BERGAMIN: No, no. There—on the wall. (*Points to PASQUINOT whose head appears over the wall*)

STRAFOREL: Ah. (*Walks to wall and bows elaborately*) Monsieur.

PASQUINOT: (*Bows, with even a greater flourish*) Monsieur.

BERGAMIN: You have read my note in which I explained my plan? How does it impress you?

STRAFOREL: It is—elementary.

BERGAMIN: You will act quickly . . .

STRAFOREL: And be discreet!

BERGAMIN: A pretended kidnapping . . . a make-believe sword fight . . .

STRAFOREL: I understand exactly.

BERGAMIN: Make sure you have skilled swordsmen, so that they do not harm my boy. He is my only child.

STRAFOREL: I will duel with him myself.

BERGAMIN: Excellent. In that case, I will have no fears.

PASQUINOT: (*Motions for BERGAMIN, who comes to wall*) Psst! Psst! Ask him how much it will cost.

BERGAMIN: What do you charge, Maestro, for an abduction?

STRAFOREL: That depends, Monsieur, on what one is willing to pay. There are abductions at every price. But, in this case, if I understand correctly, money is no object, so if I were you, I would have a first class abduction.

BERGAMIN: You have several classes?

STRAFOREL: Numerous! There is the common abduction by cab with two sinister characters—that is hardly ever used. A midnight abduction, a daylight abduction, the pompous abduction in a court carriage with servants—wigs are extra. The post-chaise abduction with two, three, four, five horses—one plays the number by ear. The discreet abduction in a little carriage—which is a bit dreary. The droll abduction in a sack. The romantic one by boat—but one needs a lake for that. The Venetian abduction by gondola—one, of course, would need a lagoon! The sinister abduction with combat. The brutal abduction; the polite abduction; the abduction by torchlight—very pretty. The classical abduction with masks. The gallant abduction with music. But the gayest, the newest, and the most distinguished of all is the full moon abduction!

BERGAMIN: (*Eagerly to PASQUINOT*) What do you think?

PASQUINOT: (*Eagerly to BERGAMIN*) What do you?

BERGAMIN: (*Excited*) I think we should have the best—spare no expense! Let us give our young fantasists something they will long remember. Let us have masks, music, torches, and a full moon!

STRAFOREL: A first class abduction—with all the trimmings!

BERGAMIN: Bravo! Bravo!

STRAFOREL: I shall return. Remember, monsieur, you must leave the park gate open.

PASQUINOT: It will be open.

STRAFOREL: My compliments. (*Bows profusely*)

PASQUINOT: Monsieur. (*Bows, almost falling off bench*)

STRAFOREL: (*Bows to BERGAMIN*) Au revoir.

BERGAMIN: Monsieur. (*Out bowing STRAFOREL*)

STRAFOREL: (*Crosses to Left*) One first class abduction with all the extras! (*Exits grandly*)

PASQUINOT: The honest man, he went without setting a price.

BERGAMIN: (*Almost dancing with joy*) Ah, it is all settled. Soon we will demolish the wall. Our wishes are about to be fulfilled!

PASQUINOT: We will grow old together.

BERGAMIN: Your daughter is provided for.

PASQUINOT: Your son, too!

BERGAMIN: (*With comic difficulty climbs on bench by the wall*) Ah! My dear old Pasquinot.

PASQUINOT: Ah! My dear old Bergamin.

BERGAMIN: Dear friend. (*They embrace, kissing on one cheek*)

PASQUINOT: Old friend. (*They embrace again, kissing on the other cheek*)

SYLVETTE: (*Enters at Right, sees the men at the wall. She is startled*) Oh!

BERGAMIN: (*In a panic to PASQUINOT*) Your daughter!

PERCINET: (*Enters at Left, sees the men at the wall. He is startled*) Oh!

PASQUINOT: (*In a panic to BERGAMIN*) Your son!

BERGAMIN: Quick! We must pretend we are fighting. (*Starts shouting and hitting*) You — you rogue!

PASQUINOT: (*Takes up the fight*) You scoundrel!

BERGAMIN: Rascal!

PASQUINOT: Fool!

SYLVETTE: (*Runs to father and pulls at his coat*) Papa!

PERCINET: (*Runs to father and pulls at his coat*) Papa!

BERGAMIN: Leave us alone!

PASQUINOT: He insulted me!

BERGAMIN: He struck me!

PASQUINOT: Coward!

SYLVETTE: Papa!

BERGAMIN: Thief!

PERCINET: Papa!

PASQUINOT: Bandit!

SYLVETTE: Papa!

PERCINET: Come home. It is late!

BERGAMIN: Let me go! Let me at him! (*He winds up, swings, and hits PASQUINOT unexpectedly hard*)

PASQUINOT: (*Surprised, then dangerously swings an upper cut*) I'll kill him! (*BERGAMIN is knocked off the bench, falling into PERCINET's arms*)

SYLVETTE: (*Pulls her father off the bench*) Please, Papa. Come! The air is getting cooler. Remember your rheumatism.

BERGAMIN: (*As PERCINET guides him off Left*) Fool!

PASQUINOT: (*As SYLVETTE pushes him off Right*) Scoundrel!

BERGAMIN: (*Shouts Off-stage*) Villain!

PASQUINOT: (*Shouts Off-stage*) Idiot!

SYLVETTE: (*Following him off*) Papa.

PERCINET: (*Following him off*) Papa.

(*Slowly the stage becomes darker, until it is a beautiful romantic evening. STRAFOREL enters Right, creeping comically and mysteriously*)

STRAFOREL: Ah! One star already brightens the evening sky. Day is dying. (*Motions to his men. Swordsmen, torchbearers, musicians enter in the shadows from Right*) You — there. You — there. And you — there. (*Like an artist, he sets the stage. Satisfied, he enjoys the romantic scene*) Ah, the hour is near. When the chimes sound eight, a girl will appear —

there. Then I will whistle— (*Whistles loudly. The large moon in the back suddenly lights up*) The moon . . . ah, perfect! Everything is ready. (*Comically inspects his men's attire*) Spread your capes—excellent. Turn up your collar a bit more. Stand here—in the shadow. Ah, the swordsmen are not bad! Torches! You do not appear until my signal. Musicians—there! Down more in the back. Now—oh some grace, please. (*Shows them a graceful pose, which they all imitate*) No, no! Vary your poses. Stand straight, mandolin! Sit, alto! This is a first class abduction. (*Turns suddenly*) First masked man—what are you doing? No, no! A desperado never waddles! Come—show some character! A dangerous villainous walk! Good. Now instruments, tune up. *Sol . . . mi . . . si . . .* Ah. Listen . . . Quick! Someone comes. (*STRAFOREL waves his arms in a wild dramatic signal. All his helpers, hurry to a hiding place. STRAFOREL tip-toes Down Right and hides his face behind his cape. All is silent. PERCINET enters at Left*)

PERCINET: My father is calmer now. I can slip away. (*Romantically*) It is the end of the day. The scent of the elders intoxicates my senses. The flowers sleep in the gray shadows. . .

STRAFOREL: (*Quietly and comically leads musicians*) Music!

PERCINET: I am trembling like a reed. What can be wrong with me. Ah, I shall soon see her again.

STRAFOREL: (*As musicians play softly, he gets carried away with romance*) Amoroso!

PERCINET: Our first evening meeting. I can scarcely believe it. The breeze sounds like the rustle of her gown . . . one can no longer see the flowers . . . but their scent grows sweeter. And this old tree with a star at its top. . . . Music . . . ah, there is music, too . . . Night has come . . . Oh, gentle night . . . with its twinkling lights . . . there and there . . . one by one they come in the deep blue sky . . . sparkling sapphire and diamond. . . . Oh, stars, I thought you dazzling until I met Sylvette. Now her eyes outshine you a thousand times . . . oh, poor poor little stars . . .

(*The chimes strike eight. SYLVETTE appears at Right*)

SYLVETTE: The chimes have struck eight. He must be waiting by the wall.

(*SYLVETTE starts toward wall. STRAFOREL whistles and motions to men who seize her. She struggles and calls*)

SYLVETTE: Help! Help! Save me!

PERCINET: Good heavens!

SYLVETTE: Percinet, help! They are carrying me away. I am being abducted!

PERCINET: Fear not! I am coming! (*Leaps to the top of the wall*) I will save you!

STRAFOREL: (*To the musicians who play fast and exciting music*) *Tremolo!*

PERCINET: (*With sword drawn attacks the men who hold SYLVETTE. They are quickly overcome and flee*) Take that! And that! And that! (*Only STRAFOREL stands in the way*) Ah! (*They stand, in formal position for dueling, then begins a fast and furious duel. SYLVETTE trembles and gasps as PERCINET is pushed backwards and almost stumbles. Then she cries with joy when PERCINET forces STRAFOREL back. They circle. STRAFOREL moves desperately and comically. Finally he is forced back to the bench. He jumps upon it, making a last stand. PERCINET gives one mighty thrust. STRA-FOREL groans, drops his sword, and clutches his heart*)

STRAFOREL: Oh! Oh, oh! I am mortally wounded! (*With many last gasps, he struggles, and then falls limp, draped over the wall*)

PERCINET: (*Rushes to SYLVETTE*) Sylvette. (*Kneels and takes her hand*)

PASQUINOT: (*Appears at Right*) What is going on?

SYLVETTE: My hero! You saved my life!

PASQUINOT: What? Bergamin's son — saved your life?

SYLVETTE: Oh, yes!

PASQUINOT: (*Loud and clearly*) I give you to him.

PERCINET and SYLVETTE: (*He rises. They both look at audience*) Heavens!

PASQUINOT: (*Calls, and BERGAMIN appears at Left immediately, as if waiting*) Bergamin! Your son is a hero. He has saved my daughter.

BERGAMIN: (*Hurrying to the wall and with his usual comic difficulty, climbs upon the bench*) Bravo! Bravo!

PASQUINOT: Let us forgive and forget — and make them happy.

BERGAMIN: My hate has left me!

PERCINET: Did you hear, Sylvette? We must be dreaming!

BERGAMIN: The hatred of our two families will end with this marriage. Let peace come with the demolishing of the wall!

PERCINET: Who would have believed my father would change so!

SYLVETTE: I told you everything would turn out happily.

(*The lovers stand facing each, in eternal happiness. PASQUINOT stands by them gazing on them with fond blessings. STRAFOREL rises from the "dead," and hands BERGAMIN a slip of paper*)

STRAFOREL: Psst! Psst!

BERGAMIN: Yes?

STRAFOREL: Your signature.

BERGAMIN: My signature? What is it?

STRAFOREL: It is my bill!

(*STRAFOREL falls "dead" on the wall again. Tableau.*)

THE END

Cyrano de Bergerac

by Edmond Rostand
Adapted by Aurand Harris

CAST

LIGNIERE
CHRISTIAN DE NEUVILLETTE
RAGUENEAU
LE BRET
ROXANE, *Madeleine Robin*
THE DUENNA
A SPECTATOR
FIRST CADET

SECOND CADET
COUNT DE GUICHE
VISCOUNT DE VALVERT
MONTFLEURY
CYRANO DE BERGERAC
THE MONK
MOTHER MARGUERITE
SISTER MARTHE

TIME: *1640–1655*

PLACE: *France*

SETTINGS: *Théâtre de Bourgogne, Roxane's garden, Battlefield, and the Ladies of the Cross convent.*

Cyrano de Bergerac

(*SCENE: The stage and auditorium of the Hôtel de Bourgogne, Paris, 1640. A raised platform is at the back, which serves as the stage. At the back of it, between two poles, hangs a painted curtain with the words: Théâtre de Bourgogne. There are stools at right and left for the audience. Entrances are made D R and D L. There is music which dims out as LIGNIERE, a poet, enters L, followed by CHRISTIAN, a handsome soldier*)

LIGNIERE: We are here before they have lighted the candles. My friend, I came to help you, but since the lady has not arrived at the theatre . . .

CHRISTIAN: You know everyone in Paris. You can tell me her name.

LIGNIERE: You are in love!

CHRISTIAN: Yes. But I am afraid to speak because I do not know the manners of the Court. I am a soldier from the north. She sits in that box — on the right — at each performance.

RAGUENEAU: (*He enters L, excited. He is a tradesman*) Sir, have you seen Monsieur de Cyrano?

LIGNIERE: This is Ragueneau, favorite baker of all Paris.

RAGUENEAU: You are certain Monsieur de Cyrano is not here? Oh, what a relief. Montfleury acts in the play today, and Cyrano has ordered him off the stage for a month.

CHRISTIAN: Who is this Cyrano?

LIGNIERE: A soldier who knows how to handle a sword. (*LE BRET enters R. He is a gentleman and a soldier*) His friend Le Bret can tell you more. Le Bret! Baron Christian de Neuvillette. (*CHRISTIAN and LE BRET bow to each other*) Monsieur de Neuvillette is new in Paris.

CHRISTIAN: I am joining the Guards tomorrow, a Cadet.

RAGUENEAU: Have you seen Monsieur de Cyrano?

LE BRET: No. And I am worried what violence he may do!

LIGNIERE: (*To CHRISTIAN*) Cyrano is an extraordinary man.

RAGUENEAU: A poet!

LE BRET: A scientist!

LIGNIERE: A swordsman!

RAGUENEAU: A musician!

LIGNIERE: And he has an unusual appearance!

RAGUENEAU: (*First looks about cautiously*) Yes . . . yes. What a nose! First you say, "No, it is impossible!" Then you say, "He will take it off."

LE BRET: But he keeps it on, and points his sword at anyone who looks at it. (*ROXANE, a beautiful, rich, young lady, enters at R, followed by her DUENNA. They sit. A SPECTATOR, FIRST CADET, and SECOND CADET enter at L and sit. All ad-lib*)

LIGNIERE: People are arriving. They have lighted the candles. The play will begin.

CHRISTIAN: (*Points out ROXANE*) There she is! Tell me her name.

LIGNIERE: Madeleine Robin, known as Roxane.

CHRISTIAN: Roxane . . .

LIGNIERE: She is sharp-witted, clever, a lover of poetry . . .

CHRISTIAN: (*COUNT DE GUICHE, an elegant nobleman, enters at R. He is followed by VALVERT, his friend. They speak to ROXANE*) And who is that man?

LIGNIERE: That, my friend, is no friend of mine. He is the powerful Count de Guiche. Unfortunately . . . for you . . . he is in love with Roxane. But . . . fortunately for you . . . she is not in love with him.

CHRISTIAN: I have seen her again. I know her name. I must leave now.

LIGNIERE: Wait. You are being watched.

CHRISTIAN: (*Looks at ROXANE who smiles at him*) She is smiling
. . . at me! (*She waves furtively. He bows slightly. There are three raps
from the stage*)

RAGUENEAU: The play begins. Montfleury will be the first to
appear. (*Three more raps from the stage. CHRISTIAN exits L. Theatre
music is heard. MONTFLEURY, an affected actor, dressed in a shepherd's costume, enters on the platform and bows*)

MONTFLEURY:
"Happy is the man who far from the pomp of courts
Dwells in solitary shade, self-imposed;
Where Zephyrs whisper . . ."

CYRANO: (*His voice is heard off stage*) Stop! What voice do I hear
croaking on the stage?

LE BRET: It is Cyrano!

RAGUENEAU: Cyrano is here!

MONTFLEURY: (*Frightened*) "Happy is the man who far from the
pomp of . . ."

CYRANO: (*Off*) I have ordered you off the stage!

MONTFLEURY: (*Shaking*) "Happy is the man who far . . ."

CYRANO: (*Enters at L. He is an exceptional man of many parts, one
being his extraordinary long nose*) Silence! Your braying insults a donkey! I will count to three—then use my sword! (*Raises sword*) One!

MONTFLEURY: But—

CYRANO: Two!

MONTFLEURY: I say—

CYRANO: Three!

MONTFLEURY: Adieu. (*Exits from platform quickly*)

LE BRET: This is madness! (*There is excited ad-libbing among the
SPECTATORS. ROXANE and the DUENNA exit R. CADETS cheer
and exit L. LIGNIERE exits L*)

CYRANO: Clear the hall! Close the theatre!

LE BRET: Cyrano, this time you have gone too far!

SPECTATOR: (*Approaches CYRANO*) Montfleury is protected by the Grand Duke.

CYRANO: (*Shows his sword*) My protector is in my hand. Are you looking at my nose?

SPECTATOR: (*Frightened*) No.

CYRANO: Do you see a pimple on it?

SPECTATOR: No.

CYRANO: Or a fly?

SPECTATOR: I am not looking at your nose.

CYRANO: Why? Do you find it a trifle big?

SPECTATOR: Oh, no. It is very small.

CYRANO: Small? My nose is ENORMOUS! It is a sign of courage, wit, and power! (*Raises his sword*)

SPECTATOR: Help! Guards! (*He runs*)

DE GUICHE: Someone should silence him.

VALVERT: I will put him in his place. (*Goes to CYRANO, speaks with superior disdain as becomes a fop*) I see your nose IS very BIG.

CYRANO: (*Nods*) Yes, it is very big. (*Pause*) Is that all? Your speech is as short as your wit. You could have said, How do you drink without dunking it in the cup? Or, I see you are fond of birds, and carry a perch for them to roost on. Or, What a sign for a perfume shop! Or as an officer: Forward and attack. Shoot your cannon!

VALVERT: Such arrogance from an insolent bumpkin!

CYRANO: (*Cries in mock pain*) Oh! My sword has fallen asleep. I must exercise it.

VALVERT: Then draw it. (*Draws sword*)

CYRANO: (*Draws sword*) This challenge I hope will be worth my time. A parry — a coupe — the victory is mine.

VALVERT: You, a poet!

CYRANO: (*Announces*) "Ballade of the Duel between Monsieur de Bergerac and a Fool"

VALVERT: What is that?

CYRANO: The title of the poem I will improvise as I fence you.
Be warned: At the end of verse two,
I shall finish the poem — and you!
Position!

VALVERT: On guard!

CYRANO: And the ballade begins! (*They duel. It is an amusing and exhilarating experience for CYRANO, and a desperate contest for VALVERT*)
My sword —
    Where shall I place?
    Beneath the lace . . .

                                        of your collar?

A THRUST

    Or make a placket . . .
    In your jacket . . .

                                        at your heart?

A COUPE

    Or a quick dash . . .
    Under your sash . . .

                                        into your belly!

A RIPOSTE!

End of verse one.

How, now —
    You give ground . . .
    Circle around . . .

                                        in disarray!

A GLIDE!

Your face pales . . .
Your breath fails . . .

in dismay!

A FEINT!

With skill, with wit — oh, for a rhyme with "arget"! —
(*Knocks VALVERT's sword to the floor*)

— 'Tis done!

I close for the kill — Hit the target!
(*Pierces VALVERT who cries in pain*)

— I've won!

End of verse two.

(*CYRANO stands in triumph. RAGUENEAU and SPECTATOR support VALVERT and help him off R*)

DE GUICHE: Quick! Call my carriage. Monsieur de Bergerac, I see that you, like Don Quixote, attack windmills. But remember, a windmill's arm is strong and can cast you down into the mud.

CYRANO: Or upward among the stars! (*DE GUICHE exits R*)

LE BRET: Have you gone mad? You have made another enemy. Why don't you make a friend of Count de Guiche?

CYRANO: My white plume will not bow to a fool.

LE BRET: Why did you stop the play? Why do you hate Montfleury?

CYRANO: He is a bad actor. And one day I saw him looking — lecherously — at a certain young lady.

LE BRET: (*With implications*) A young lady?

CYRANO: Yes. I am in love.

LE BRET: With whom?

CYRANO: It is amusing. I, with a nose which goes before me by a quarter of an hour, I am in love with the most beautiful woman in Paris.

LE BRET: It is . . . Roxane.

CYRANO: Of course. Roxane.

LE BRET: Then tell her! She admires your wit, your courage—

CYRANO: Look at me and tell me that she admires my nose.

THE DUENNA: (*Enters R*) Monsieur de Bergerac. (*Bows*) My lady wishes to see you privately.

CYRANO: Roxane!

THE DUENNA: (*Bows*) She has certain things to tell you. (*Exits R*)

CYRANO: (*In ecstasy*) Roxane! Roxane requests an audience with me!

LE BRET: Calm yourself.

CYRANO: How can I be calm? At this moment I have ten hearts! One hundred arms! I can conquer an army! I can slay a giant!

ROXANE: (*Enters R*) Cyrano.

CYRANO: (*He Bows. LE BRET exits L*) You wanted to see me?

ROXANE: First, let me look at you. You have neglected me of late. I used to see you every day.

CYRANO: Those were happy years . . . when we were young. You came to Bergerac every summer.

ROXANE: Then you used a bulrush for a sword.

CYRANO: And we ate plums before they were ripe.

ROXANE: Now we are grown up, and . . . and that is part of what I must tell you. I . . . I am in love.

CYRANO: Ah.

ROXANE: With someone who doesn't know it.

CYRANO: Ah!

ROXANE: And he has only shown his love from a distance.

CYRANO: Ah!

ROXANE: And he is a Cadet in your regiment.

CYRANO: Oh. His name?

ROXANE.: Christian de Neuvillette.

CYRANO: Christian . . . But why are you telling me this?

ROXANE: Because you and most of your Cadets are Gascons, and—you always pick a quarrel with a new Cadet who is not. (*CYRANO nods*) But if you were his friend—Oh, everyone fears you! You could—

CYRANO: I could protect your little Cadet.

ROXANE: Oh, I knew you would! You will be his friend? Never let him fight a duel?

CYRANO: For you . . . I will.

ROXANE: Now I know why I adore you! I must go.

CYRANO: I will call your carriage. (*They start to leave*)

ROXANE: Tell him to write to me—poems and beautiful letters. (*Lightly*) Oh, Cyrano, I love you. I love the whole world today! (*They exit R. FIRST CADET and SECOND CADET are heard off L. They chant as they enter, and are followed by LE BRET and CHRISTIAN*)

CADETS:
"We are the bold, the brave Gascon Cadets,
Who fight to win and win the fight!
We are the bold, the brave Gascon Cadets!"

FIRST CADET: We want Cyrano! Cyrano!

SECOND CADET: We will drink to Cyrano!

LE BRET: You have already!

SECOND CADET: (*To CHRISTIAN*) The best lesson — (*With superior contempt*) — a new Cadet — can learn is to hear the brave feats of Cyrano de Bergerac.

FIRST CADET: (*Tauntingly to CHRISTIAN*) A Cadet who is not a Gascon must be a coward.

CHRISTIAN: I am not a Gascon. I am not a coward.

FIRST CADET: Listen to the bragging northerner.

SECOND CADET: You must learn many things. If you value your life, never, in front of Cyrano, never mention the word — (*Taps his nose three times*)

CHRISTIAN: You mean nos —

SECOND CADET: Never speak the word! He has killed two men because they (*Imitates*) talked through their nose.

FIRST CADET: To use your handkerchief, can be your death!

CHRISTIAN: (*To LE BRET*) Monsieur, what should a new Cadet do when — (*Looks at others with brave defiance*) southerners — become too boastful?

LE BRET: Show them that a northerner has more courage than they.

CHRISTIAN: Thank you. (*CYRANO enters R*)

SECOND CADET: Cyrano! We are searching for you!

LE BRET: They are eager to hear of your adventure last night.

FIRST CADET: Ten against one! Tell us!

CYRANO: It was nothing.

FIRST CADET: Tell us!

CYRANO: Very well. Ten cut-throats had been hired to bludgeon my friend. The night was dark. I could not see beyond —

CHRISTIAN: Your nose. (*Silence. All look at CYRANO*)

CYRANO: What! Who is this man? You dare to —! (*Threateningly, starts toward CHRISTIAN*)

LE BRET: His name is Christian de Neuvil —

CYRANO: Christian! (*He is shocked, then controls himself*) As I was saying, for the sake of a friend I was —

CHRISTIAN: Sticking out your nose.

CYRANO: (*Struggling to control his anger*) Then — suddenly — I felt a sword slash —

CHRISTIAN: The tip of your nose.

CYRANO: (*More tense*) I drew my blade. We stood —

CHRISTIAN: Nose to nose!

CYRANO: (*In rage, starts toward CHRISTIAN*) By heaven I will . . . ! (*Stops, breathes heavily, continues*) I plunged, parried a thrust with —

CHRISTIAN: Your nose in the air!

CYRANO: (*Shouts*) Go! All of you! Out! I will be alone with this man!

FIRST CADET: (*The CADETS scurry in a quick exit at R. LE BRET exits with them*) He will slice him to slivers!

SECOND CADET: Nothing will be left. Not an ear.

FIRST CADET: Not a hair.

SECOND CADET: (*Whispers*) Not a nose!

CYRANO: Out! (*They are gone. CYRANO and CHRISTIAN face each other*) Embrace me!

CHRISTIAN: Sir?

CYRANO: You are a man of courage. I am pleased.

CHRISTIAN: Why?

CYRANO: I am like a brother to her — to Roxane.

CHRISTIAN: You? Her brother?

CYRANO: No, but almost.

CHRISTIAN: And she has told you . . . ?

CYRANO: Everything!

CHRISTIAN: (*Takes his hand*) How happy I am to meet you.

CYRANO: Roxane expects you to write her a letter.

CHRISTIAN: A letter? Then all is over. I am a simple soldier. I do not know how to speak or write of love.

CYRANO: It is easy.

CHRISTIAN: For you, but not for me. Oh, if only I could—

CYRANO: Ah, if only I had a handsome face. If only we were both ONE person. (*Looks at him*) Yes. Yes! (*Excited with the idea and challenge*) With your handsome looks and my eloquence of expression, we can win her!

CHRISTIAN: What do you mean?

CYRANO: I will tell you every day what to say, what to write—It is a challenge for any poet! You will be the one she sees. I, the one she hears.

CHRISTIAN: We will do it! My friend. (*They embrace*)

FIRST CADET: (*CADETS and LE BRET enter R, cautiously*) All is quiet.

SECOND CADET: I am afraid to look. (*They see CYRANO and CHRISTIAN embracing*)

FIRST CADET: What do I see!

LE BRET: Cyrano! (*CYRANO turns to them*)

SECOND CADET: Can it be he KNOWS what he is doing!

CYRANO: (*Draws sword*) Who dares say that word!

FIRST CADET: It is all right. He is still our fighting Cyrano!

(*Everyone laughs, CYRANO and SECOND CADET ad-lib, duel in mock combat, and exit L fencing. Others follow, shouting boisterously.*

There is no break between the scenes. Music is heard as stagehands quickly remove the curtain behind the platform and the stools, and put a low balustrade at the front on the platform. SCENE: ROXANE's garden. Evening. The actors enter as the scene shift is ending. Music stops. The DUENNA enters R, followed by ROXANE)

ROXANE: Do you see him?

THE DUENNA: No.

ROXANE: He is never late.

THE DUENNA: Shhh. Someone is coming.

ROXANE: Is it Christian?

THE DUENNA: No.

ROXANE: Oh. (*Turns to go*)

THE DUENNA: It is — Cyrano.

ROXANE: Cyrano. (*Returns*)

CYRANO: (*Enters L*) I have come, as usual, to inquire if Christian is still the perfect romantic lover.

ROXANE: Oh, more than perfect!

CYRANO: And his letters, his poems?

ROXANE: He writes better than he speaks. (*Quotes*) "The more you take of my heart, the more I have to give."

CYRANO: (*Nods*) As good as I could have written.

ROXANE: "If kisses could be written by my pen, you would read this letter with your lips."

CYRANO: I admit that is very good!

THE DUENNA: Quick! Count De Guiche is coming. (*To CYRANO*) Go inside. He must not find you here.

ROXANE: Hurry! He must not suspect that I am in love with Christian. (*CYRANO exits R*)

DE GUICHE: (*Enters L*) Mademoiselle. I have come to say goodby. I will command the Guards. We leave tonight.

ROXANE: The Guards! (*Aside*) Christian.

DE GUICHE: You tremble.

ROXANE: I am in despair at . . . at the news you tell.

DE GUICHE: Despair? (*Surprised, but hopeful*) You are concerned about me?

ROXANE: To know that he . . . the man I care for most . . . is being sent to war . . .

DE GUICHE: The man you care for most?

ROXANE: (*Controlling herself*) You are leaving? And Cyrano and the Cadets are leaving?

DE GUICHE: I have ordered them to the front line!

ROXANE: (*Sweetly, cunningly*) And that is the way you will get your revenge on Cyrano?

DE GUICHE: Let him show his bravery under fire!

ROXANE: But he loves danger. You are rewarding him. There is, however, a way you could make him suffer. Leave him behind . . . and all his Cadets. To punish Cyrano, take him *away* from danger.

DE GUICHE: Only a woman could have thought of such a masterly trick! Yes, I will keep him behind. (*Intimately*) You and I — we will be in league together. (*She smiles. He shows her envelopes*) These are the orders I will give. (*Takes out one envelope*) Except for this one. The Cadets will stay behind. (*Softly*) Oh, I cannot leave you, now that you have revealed your feelings. I will hide in the monastery near-by and tonight come to see you in secret.

ROXANE: You will be discovered, disgraced!

DE GUICHE: I will wear a disguise.

ROXANE: But the war?

DE GUICHE: I will go tomorrow.

ROXANE: (*With all her feminine persuasion*) Please, I beg you . . . go.

DE GUICHE: Yes. But I will return tonight. Goodby, Roxane. (*Kisses her hand*)

ROXANE: Goodby. (*DE GUICHE exits L*) Promise not to tell Cyrano. He would never forgive me if he knew I robbed him of his war. (*Calls*) Cyrano. Cyrano.

CYRANO: (*Enters R*) Has he gone?

ROXANE: (*Gaily*) Yes, gone. And all our troubles are gone. Excuse me. I must look my best when Christian arrives. (*She blows him a kiss and exits R, followed by THE DUENNA*)

CYRANO: (*Bows her off, then calls softly*) Christian. Christian. Are you there? (*CHRISTIAN enters L*) Come, there is no time to lose. Prepare your memory, while I tell you the words to say tonight.

CHRISTIAN: No. I am tired of saying your speeches — and shaking lest I forget the words. I thank you for helping me, but now that I know she loves me, I will speak for myself.

ROXANE: (*Enters R*) Christian?

CHRISTIAN: (*Suddenly frightened*) Cyrano! Do not leave me!

CYRANO: Speak for yourself. (*Exits L*)

ROXANE: Christian?

CHRISTIAN: Roxane!

ROXANE: Ah, it is you. The night is so dark, but I can hear your voice. What beautiful words will you say tonight? (*CHRISTIAN clears his throat*) I am listening.

CHRISTIAN: I love you.

ROXANE: Yes, speak to me of love.

CHRISTIAN: I love you.

ROXANE: Yes.

CHRISTIAN: I love you.

ROXANE: Enlarge on your theme. How much do you love me?

CHRISTIAN: I love you—so much.

ROXANE: Your tongue is tied tonight! Oh, let your heart overflow with dazzling words.

CHRISTIAN: I love you.

ROXANE: Again! (*Starts to leave*)

CHRISTIAN: No. I don't love you.

ROXANE: (*Stops*) That is better.

CHRISTIAN: I adore you!

ROXANE: (*Disappointed*) Oh.

CHRISTIAN: I love you. I adore you.

ROXANE: You repeat yourself. No. Until you have more to say—goodby. (*Exits R*)

CHRISTIAN: But—I love you.

CYRANO: (*Enters L*) I bow to you on your great success.

CHRISTIAN: Cyrano! Help me!

CYRANO: Speak for yourself.

CHRISTIAN: If I don't win her back I will die.

CYRANO: Look! She is at her window. (*Points to balcony*)

CHRISTIAN: I will die.

CYRANO: Don't shout.

CHRISTIAN: (*Whispers*) I will die.

CYRANO: It is dark . . . she cannot see you . . . Yes, we will repair the damage. You stand below . . . there. And I, in the shadow, will whisper what you are to say. Call to her.

CHRISTIAN: Roxane.

ROXANE: (*Appears on platform*) Who is there?

CHRISTIAN: Christian.

ROXANE: Have you thought of something beautiful to say?

CHRISTIAN: (*Repeats the words which CYRANO whispers to him*) Take my love . . . take my happiness . . . so it will be . . . your happiness.

ROXANE: That is better.

CHRISTIAN: (*Still repeating CYRANO's words*) Each time . . . I look upon you . . . a new virtue . . . in me . . . is born.

ROXANE: Much better. But you speak so haltingly.

CYRANO: (*Pulls CHRISTIAN into shadow and takes his place*) This is too difficult. Stand here.

ROXANE: Your words are strong, but they hesitate tonight.

CYRANO: (*Taking CHRISTIAN's place, speaks softly*) It—it is because—because of the darkness. My words must search and climb to find your ears.

ROXANE: I will come down. (*Turns*)

CYRANO: No!

ROXANE: Then you climb up to me.

CYRANO: No!

ROXANE: Why not?

CYRANO: This is a moment of magic . . . to talk to you unseen.

ROXANE: Your voice—it is different.

CYRANO: Because I am protected by the darkness and I dare to be myself. I have no fear of being laughed at.

ROXANE: Laughed at?

CYRANO: I have always hidden behind my wit. But now I can speak the true words that are in my heart. I love you. Roxane—Roxane your name rings in my heart like a bell. I ask only one thing—

CHRISTIAN: (*In the shadow, loudly*) A kiss!

ROXANE: What!

CYRANO: (*To CHRISTIAN*) A kiss? You are rushing too fast!

ROXANE: (*Pleased*) You asked for—

CYRANO: A kiss. Forgive me. I was too bold. So—the kiss—grant it not.

CHRISTIAN: Why not?

CYRANO: Quiet, Christian.

ROXANE: What are you saying?

CYRANO: I was saying . . . to my impetuous heart, "Quiet, Christian." (*Looks off L*) But someone is coming. Hide inside.

ROXANE: Oh! (*Exits off platform*)

THE MONK: (*A Capuchin MONK enters with lantern, L*) Excuse me, monsieur. I am looking for the house of Madame—Roxane—Robin.

CYRANO: (*Turns THE MONK around, starts him back off L*) My good Father, the way to her house is—straight ahead.

THE MONK: Straight ahead . . . thank you. I will pray for you in my prayers tonight. (*Exits L*)

CHRISTIAN: I must have one kiss.

CYRANO: No. (ROXANE *appears on balcony*) He is gone.

ROXANE: (*Eager*) Let us continue. We were talking about . . . about . . .

CYRANO: A kiss. After all what is a kiss? It is the seal of a tender promise. It is a secret whispered to listening lips.

ROXANE: Come! Climb up to the balcony so I may see your face.

CYRANO: (*To CHRISTIAN*) Climb up to her.

ROXANE: Give me that tender promise . . .

CYRANO: Climb!

ROXANE: That whispered secret . . .

CYRANO: Climb!

CHRISTIAN: (*On balcony, embraces her*) Ah, Roxane!

CYRANO: I, too, feel her kiss, because, as she is kissing his lips, she also, is kissing the words I spoke. (*Looks off*) Another intruder! It is the monk again. (*Takes a step forward, pretending he has just arrived, calls loudly*) Roxane!

ROXANE: Who is it?

CYRANO: Cyrano.

CHRISTIAN: (*Surprised*) Cyrano?

ROXANE: Wait. I am coming down. (*She exits from platform. CHRISTIAN follows*)

THE MONK: (*Enters L*) Monsieur. Monsieur, you are mistaken. This is Madeleine — Roxane — Robin's house.

CYRANO: You said, "Rolin."

ROXANE: (*Enters R, followed by CHRISTIAN*) What is it?

THE MONK: I have a letter to deliver, a holy message, I am sure, sent from a worthy lord.

ROXANE: It is from Count de Guiche. (*Aside, reads letter to herself*) "I am staying behind . . . at the monastery. I send you this by a simple-minded monk . . . etcetera . . ." Trickery! And using a father of the church. (*She beams with an idea*) The church! I will outwit Count de Guiche with his own trick. (*To THE MONK*) Good Father, the letter tells what you must do. (*THE MONK holds lantern up for her to read better. She pretends to read*) "This letter is delivered into your hands by a wise and saintly man of the church. He is to perform a ceremony of holy matrimony . . . in your house . . . without delay. You must marry Christian . . . secretly . . . and at once . . . etcetera . . ."

THE MONK: A ceremony of holy matrimony! The angels of heaven have blessed you. (*Holds lantern to CYRANO*) Are you the husband to be?

CHRISTIAN: No. I am!

THE MONK: Let us go within and begin the holy service. (*Exits R*)

ROXANE: Count de Guiche will be here soon. Delay him.

CYRANO: (*Nods*) Hurry!

ROXANE: (*To CHRISTIAN*) Come! (*They exit R*)

CYRANO: Detain the Count — yes. But how? He will be disguised. *I* will be disguised. (*Lays sword aside and pulls hat down*) I will shadow my face, change my voice, alter my walk — and I must do it quickly — because here he is. (*Quickly climbs to balcony*)

DE GUICHE: (*Enters L, wearing a mask and fumbling in the dark*) Where is that stupid monk? Where is the house? Where am I? Devil take this mask! (*CYRANO leaps, falling in front of DE GUICHE*) What? How? Who is this? Where did he fall from?

CYRANO: (*Sits up, speaks with an accent*) I fell from the moon!

DE GUICHE: The moon?

CYRANO: The moon!

DE GUICHE: No one can fall from the moon.

CYRANO: (*Stands, speaks forcefully*) I fell from the moon!

DE GUICHE: Very well, you fell out of the moon. (*Aside*) He is a madman.

CYRANO: I arrived by a thunderbolt. My eyes are full of stardust.

DE GUICHE: He is a lunatic.

CYRANO: (*Grabs DE GUICHE*) And I am drunk with milk!

DE GUICHE: Milk?

CYRANO: From the Milky Way.

DE GUICHE: Let me pass. I want—

CYRANO: You want to know how I got to the moon?

DE GUICHE: He is raving mad!

CYRANO: I have discovered four ways to fly. I can cover myself with bottles filled with morning dew, and when the sun draws up the dew, I am drawn up with it.

DE GUICHE: A madman, but a clever one.

CYRANO: And I can heat air in a chest, which will cause a great gale of wind that will sweep me upward.

DE GUICHE: That is two ways.

CYRANO: Or I can construct a steel grasshopper, moved by blasts of gunpowder, and ride it into the sky.

DE GUICHE: Three.

CYRANO: Finally, I can sit on an iron plate and fling a magnet into the air. The iron will follow the magnet, then I quickly throw the magnet again and again, until I reach the moon.

DE GUICHE: But which one did you choose?

CYRANO: (*Speaks in his natural voice*) I need not detain you any longer, Count de Guiche. The ceremony is over.

DE GUICHE: I know that voice! (*The DUENNA enters with candles. In the brightness, DE GUICHE sees CYRANO, who takes off his hat*) And that nose! Cyrano!

CYRANO: (*Bows*) They have just been married.

DE GUICHE: Who? (*ROXANE enters R, holding CHRISTIAN's arm*) Roxane! Christian! You are very clever madame, with your tricks. But you are not clever enough. For you must now tell your husband goodby. (*To CHRISTIAN*) Your regiment is leaving. Your orders are: Join it immediately!

ROXANE: Not the Cadets!

DE GUICHE: (*Gives envelope to CHRISTIAN*) Deliver this at once.

ROXANE: Oh, Christian!

DE GUICHE: Report at once!

CHRISTIAN: Roxane!

DE GUICHE: At once! (*CHRISTIAN salutes and exits L. DE GUICHE follows him*)

ROXANE: Christian! (*To CYRANO, who starts L*) Oh, promise me you will look after him.

CYRANO: I will try.

ROXANE: Promise you will keep him out of danger.

CYRANO: I'll do my best.

ROXANE: Promise that he will never be cold or hungry!

CYRANO: If I can.

ROXANE: Promise that he will write often!

CYRANO: Ah! That is one promise I can keep!

(*CYRANO exits L. ROXANE looks after him, then runs to R and exits. There is music as the stagehands remove the balustrade, and put a cutout silhouette of a cannon on the platform. Music dims out as gun fire is heard in the distance. LE BRET enters immediately at R, walking into the scene: The battlefield*)

LE BRET: More shooting! Devil take them! Can't they wait until the sun is up? (*More shots are heard*) And again! (*Looks off L*) Oh, it is Cyrano, creeping back through the lines.

VOICE: (*Off L*) Halt! Who goes there?

CYRANO: (*Off L*) Cyrano de Bergerac!

SECOND VOICE: (*Off L, closer*) Halt! Who goes there?

CYRANO: (*Off L*) Bergerac, you fool! (*He enters L*)

LE BRET: You are back again — and safe!

CYRANO: Shhh! You will wake the soldiers.

LE BRET: You are a madman! To face death! To risk your life every night to send a letter!

CYRANO: But I promised Roxane that he would write — often.

LE BRET: Go, get some sleep. (*Starts U R*) Where are you going now?

CYRANO: I am going to address another letter. (*LE BRET exits U R with a huff of disgust, as CHRISTIAN enters L*)

CHRISTIAN: Cyrano?

CYRANO: Yes.

CHRISTIAN: I can't sleep. They will attack within an hour.

CYRANO: It will be bloody.

CHRISTIAN: I keep thinking of Roxane. I want to tell her all that is in my heart . . . send her one last letter.

CYRANO: I understand. Here is your farewell letter. (*Gives him letter*)

CHRISTIAN: You have already written it?

CYRANO: I, too, wanted to tell her goodby. Oh, dying is unimportant. But not to see her — never to see her again — (*There is a distant clamor off R*)

VOICE: (*Off R*) Halt! Who goes there? (*There are shouts and gun shots*)

LE BRET: (*Enters U R*) What is it?

FIRST CADET: (*Enters, excited, D R*) Horses and a carriage!

DRIVER'S VOICE: (*Off R*) King's service! King's service!

LE BRET: King's service? Hats off! Beat the salute! (*Off, roll of the drum*) Fall in! (*All stand at attention*)

ROXANE: (*Enters D R*) Good morning.

LE BRET: You? King's service?

ROXANE: The King of Love!

CHRISTIAN: Roxane! Here . . . in the midst of the battle?

ROXANE: The siege has lasted too long! I had to see you. So I came through the enemy's line. And whenever my carriage was stopped, I smiled from the window —

LE BRET: But what purpose did you state?

ROXANE: I always answered, "I am going to see my lover." And every officer bowed and waved me on.

CHRISTIAN: Your lover?

ROXANE: Forgive me, but if I had said, "My husband," they would not have let me pass.

LE BRET: You must leave. It is too dangerous here.

CYRANO: You must go quickly! I will see to the carriage. (*Exits*)

LE BRET: In less than an hour —

ROXANE: The battle will start!

LE BRET: Yes.

ROXANE: I will stay by my husband.

LE BRET: Then grant us a favor. Give us courage. Honor us. Take my arm. We are weary and hungry, madame. Smile — and give us hope.

ROXANE: Yes. I will join you — soon. (*LA BRET exits*)

CHRISTIAN: Oh, Roxane! (*They embrace*) Tell me, why have you risked your life to come here?

ROXANE: I had to see you — because of your letters . . . each one was more beautiful than the last. So I came to beg your forgiveness. At first I only loved you because you were handsome.

CHRISTIAN: And now?

ROXANE: Now I love YOU, not for your looks, but — for your own self — which you revealed in every letter.

CHRISTIAN: (*Alarmed*) Oh, Roxane!

ROXANE: It is better now! It wasn't really love before. But now, if you were ugly, I would still love you.

CHRISTIAN: No . . . no!

ROXANE: What is the matter?

CHRISTIAN: I must go . . . I must tell . . . I must speak to someone. I am keeping you from the soldiers. Go. They need you. They are about to die. Let them see you smile. For me . . .

ROXANE: Dear Christian. (*She exits R*)

CHRISTIAN: (*Calls*) Cyrano. Cyrano!

CYRANO: (*Enters L*) What is it?

CHRISTIAN: She doesn't love me. It is you she loves! And you love her. It was in your letters. You must tell her.

CYRANO: No.

CHRISTIAN: Why?

CYRANO: Look at my face. My nose!

CHRISTIAN: She said she would love me even if I were ugly! It is you — the man who wrote the letters that she loves. You must tell her everything.

CYRANO: No.

CHRISTIAN: Our wedding was in secret. It can be broken. I will not go on deceiving her — that I — am you. I will walk to the end of the post. Tell her she must choose — choose one of us. She is coming. (*Calls*) Roxane. (*ROXANE enters R*) Cyrano has important news to tell you. (*He exits L*)

ROXANE: What is it?

CYRANO: What you told him, was it the truth?

ROXANE: Oh, yes. I would love him even if he were — were —

CYRANO: If he were ugly?

ROXANE: Yes! (*Shots are heard off*) They are shooting. The battle has started.

CYRANO: If he were grotesque?

ROXANE: Yes.

CYRANO: You would still love him.

ROXANE: Even more!

CYRANO: (*Aside*) Can it be that I . . . that she . . . Oh, Roxane, I must tell you . . . tell you everything.

LE BRET: (*Enters L*) Cyrano! Come at once.

CYRANO: Yes?

LE BRET: Shhh! (*Whispers to CYRANO*)

CYRANO: No!

ROXANE: What is it?

CYRANO: (*Deathly still*) All is over.

(*The battle has started. Gun fire is heard to the end of the scene*)

ROXANE: What is it? All the shooting—

CYRANO: It is finished. I can never tell her now.

ROXANE: What has happened? What . . . ? (*She sees two CADETS who enter L, supporting CHRISTIAN, as he staggers between them*) Christian! (*She rushes to him as they lay him on the ground*)

LE BRET: He was hit by the first shot of the battle. (*LE BRET and CADETS exit quietly*)

ROXANE: Christian.

CHRISTIAN: (*Raising his head*) Roxane . . .

ROXANE: Yes . . . yes. Lie still. I'll stop the bleeding. (*She goes to bucket, upstage, dips scarf into water*)

CYRANO: (*Kneeling, speaks softly to CHRISTIAN*) Christian . . . you must hear me. I told her everything.

CHRISTIAN: Who . . . who did she . . .

CYRANO: You. You. She will always love you.

CHRISTIAN: Roxane . . .

ROXANE: Yes . . . (*CHRISTIAN dies in her arms*) . . . yes. Is he . . . dead? (*CYRANO nods*) Here is a letter in his pocket . . . the last one . . . for me.

CYRANO: (*Quietly*) Roxane, you must go now. The battle will be fierce.

ROXANE: He is dead. (*Cries*) He was a perfect man.

CYRANO Yes.

ROXANE A poet.

CYRANO: Yes.

ROXANE: A noble and loving soul.

CYRANO: Yes.

ROXANE: Now he is dead. (*Buries her face in his cape*)

CYRANO: And I — I, too, have died. In him, she also mourns for me. (*Trumpets are heard over the battle sounds*) Two deaths have I to avenge: Christian's and — and my happiness lost forever! Sound the drums! Play the fifes! (*Drums roll. Fifes play. Background becomes red, as he exits shouting*)
"We are the bold, the brave Gascon Cadets,
Who fight to win and win the fight!
We are the bold, the brave — "

(*He is gone. Sound reaches a climax, then stops as lights dim quickly. ROXANE and CHRISTIAN exit. There is church music and lights come up again as stage hands remove cannon and put a church window at the front of the platform and a chair D L.*)

SCENE: *A garden in the convent of The Sisters of the Cross.*

TIME: *Fifteen years later. MOTHER MARGUERITE and SISTER MARTHE, an impulsive young nun, enter U L, walking into the scene*)

SISTER MARTHE: And I must also tell you that Sister Claire looked in the mirror twice to fix her headdress. (*MOTHER MARGUERITE shakes her head*) And Sister Marie stole a prune out of the tart this morning. I saw her!

MOTHER MARGUERITE: I will tell their sins to Monsieur Cyrano this evening.

SISTER MARTHE: (*Delighted*) Oh, yes! and he will tease them! He will say, (*Imitates him*) "Ah, young nuns are very vain and very greedy."

MOTHER MARGUERITE: (*Smiles*) And very good.

SISTER MARTHE: Is it true he has come to the convent every Saturday for fifteen years?

MOTHER MARGUERITE: Yes, ever since Madame Roxane came to live with us in our cloister.

SISTER MARTHE: He is so witty! And he likes the little cakes I make.

MOTHER MARGUERITE: And well he should. Last Saturday he had not eaten for two days.

SISTER MARTHE: Oh, Mother!

MOTHER MARGUERITE: Monsieur Cyrano is a poor and lonely man.

SISTER MARTHE: Does no one help him?

MOTHER MARGUERITE: He will take no help. He still wears his white plume with pride. He would be angry if he thought you pitied him. (*Looks off L*) We must go inside. Madame Roxane is coming into the park with a visitor.

SISTER MARTHE: It is Monsieur Le Bret. I wonder what they talk about?

MOTHER MARGUERITE: About their old friend Monsieur Cyrano, I imagine.

SISTER MARTHE: Yes. (*Delighted with the hope*) And, perhaps, of wicked worldly things. (*MOTHER MARGUERITE and SISTER MARTHE exit D R. LE BRET and ROXANE enter D L*)

LE BRET: I wanted to see you before Cyrano came.

ROXANE: How is he doing?

LE BRET: Badly. He still makes new enemies every day. He continues to speak, to write, to attack all that is false. He has few friends and lives in poverty. It is whispered by his enemies, "Cyrano will meet with a fatal accident — soon." I knew he would be out alone today, and that he would come here.

ROXANE: He comes every Saturday and tells me the news. I call him my Talking Gazette. His chair is always placed there, and I embroider while I wait. When the clock strikes, I don't even turn to look, because I know I will hear his cane, and he is here. (*SISTER MARTHE enters D R*) What is it?

SISTER MARTHE: Ragueneau is at the gate and wishes to see you, madame.

ROXANE: Let him come in. (*SISTER MARTHE exits D R*) Poor Ragueneau. He has come to tell us more of his troubles. I will leave him to you.

RAGUENEAU: (*Enters D R*) Ah, madame! Monsieur!

ROXANE: (*Pleasantly*) Excuse me. Tell Le Bret your trouble. I will be back soon. (*She exits L*)

RAGUENEAU: (*Breathless*) I am glad you are here. There is trouble. Cyrano!

LE BRET: What happened?

RAGUENEAU: He was coming out of his house. I hurried to join him, but at the corner, a lackey, from an upstairs window, dropped a heavy log—

LE BRET: The cowards!

RAGUENEAU: And hit him.

LE BRET: Is he alive?

RAGUENEAU: Barely. I fetched a doctor—he must not move—his head is wrapped in bandages—there is no one to tend him.

LE BRET: We will go. Quick, through the chapel. It is closer. (*They exit U R as ROXANE enters D L*)

ROXANE: Le Bret? Le Bret . . . ? Gone? And Ragueneau, too. Why would they leave so quickly? (*SISTER MARTHE enters with chair*) Ah, here is the chair for my old friend. Put it there in the usual place.

SISTER MARTHE: (*Places it D R*) It is our best chair . . . for Monsieur Cyrano.

ROXANE: Thank you. (*SISTER MARTHE exits D R*) He will be here soon. (*She sits D L with embroidery. Chimes strike*) Yes, the hour has struck. Strange . . . the chimes have finished but he is not here. He is going to be late for the first time. But he will come. He will come, I'm sure.

SISTER MARTHE: (*Enters D R*) Monsieur de Bergerac is here. (CYRANO *appears D R. SISTER MARTHE exits. He walks slowly, leaning on his cane. His hat is pulled down. He moves and talks with great effort*)

ROXANE: (*Continues to sew, not looking at him. She teases him pleasantly*) You are late for the very first time.

CYRANO: (*With difficulty he sits in chair. He speaks with great effort, trying to hide his pain with a forced cheerfulness*) I was detained by — by an unexpected visitor.

ROXANE: Who?

CYRANO: An old acquaintance.

ROXANE: You sent him away?

CYRANO: Yes, for a little while.

ROXANE: Good. It is time for my gazette. Tell me, what is happening in the world.

CYRANO: (*With great effort*) Saturday, the nineteenth, after eating eight helpings of grape preserves, the King became ill. (*In more pain*) On Wednesday, Madame Montglat said, "No," to Count de Fiesque. On Thursday, Madame Montglat said, "Yes," to Count de Fiesque. On — (*His head falls*)

ROXANE: (*Turns and sees him for the first time*) He has fainted! (*Rushes to him*) Cyrano!

CYRANO: (*Opens his eyes*) What is it? What . . . ? Oh! It is nothing. It is my old wound from the siege of Arras. It is gone.

ROXANE: You have your wound from that battle. And I have mine — here. (*Puts hand over her heart*) Where I keep his letter . . . stained with tears and blood. (*It begins to grow dark*)

CYRANO: His last letter. Once you said you would let me read it. I would like to read it now.

ROXANE: (*Takes it from small bag which hangs around her neck*) Here.

CYRANO: (*Reads*) "Farewell, Roxane. I feel that death is near. But my heart is still filled with untold love. Yet I must die. Never again will my eyes kiss your beauty . . ."

ROXANE: (*Puzzled*) How well you read his letter.

CYRANO: ". . . And my heart cries out . . ."

ROXANE: Your voice . . .

CYRANO: ". . . Farewell, goodby . . ."

ROXANE: Your voice is like . . .

CYRANO: ". . . My dearest, my treasure . . ."

ROXANE: I have heard it before . . .

CYRANO: ". . . my love."

ROXANE: Under my window . . .

CYRANO: "My heart shall never leave you. My love for you cannot be measured . . ."

ROXANE: It is dark! How can you read? (*He stops, alarmed that he has been caught, then lowers his head*) It was you. All the time — it was you! The letters — they were you. The voice in the dark was you. Oh, Cyrano, why didn't you tell me? Why didn't you say you loved me!

LE BRET: (*He and RAGUENEAU enter U R*) Here he is! I knew he would be. Cyrano! You fool!

CYRANO: Quiet. I have not finished my gazette. Today, Saturday, the twenty-sixth, Monsieur de Bergerac was murdered. (*Takes off hat, showing the bandages*)

ROXANE: What has happened to you?

CYRANO: It was my wish to be struck down by a sword in a worthy battle. But Fate has laughed at me again. I was struck down in an ambush, by a lackey with a log. I have failed in everything, even in death.

ROXANE: You must live! Live! (*Softly*) I love you.

CYRANO: No, Roxane. It is only in fairy tales, when Beauty says, "I love you," that the beast loses his ugliness. You see those words have no magic on me. I am the same. You will excuse me now. I must go. My moonbeam comes to take me away. (*ROXANE sinks before him, crying. He sits up*) You must always mourn for Christian because he truly loved you; and perhaps now you will mourn for me, who also loved you.

ROXANE: Oh, Cyrano . . .

CYRANO: (*Suddenly stands*) No! Not in a chair! I will meet my visitor standing — with my sword in hand. (*Draws sword*)

LE BRET: Cyrano!

ROXANE: Cyrano!

CYRANO: I see you now with your ugly skull without a nose. What! You dare look at MY nose! (*Lifts sword*) What is that you say? It is useless to fight. True, but I will always fight my old enemies — (*With a thrust of his sword*) Lies! . . . Prejudice! . . . Stupidity! . . . Vanity! I will fight . . . fight . . . fight . . . (*Duels wildly, then stops breathless*) You have robbed me of everything . . . the acclaim of glory . . . the sweetness of love! But there is one thing you cannot take. (*Forward with his sword*) It is . . . (*His sword falls. He staggers. LE BRET and RAGUENEAU catch him*)

ROXANE: (*Beside him*) What is it?

CYRANO: My . . . white . . . plume . . . (*He and his hand fall lifeless*)

CURTAIN

The Importance of Being Ernest
by Oscar Wilde
Adapted by Aurand Harris

Introduction

It has been noted that like Dr. Samuel Johnson, but without the aid of a Boswell, Oscar Wilde is a writer whose life is better known than most of his writings. The exception is *The Importance of Being Ernest*, his one play that deservedly has achieved classic status and continues to be produced. Wilde, fortunately for us, functioned as his own Boswell, including his best witticisms and epigrams in his writings.

Oscar Fingal O'Flahertie Wills Wilde was born in Dublin, Ireland, October 16, 1845, the second son of a prominent physician. He studied literature at Trinity College, Dublin, and entered Oxford University in 1874, where he won academic honors, and began to be known as an eccentric. Later in London he wrote romantic poetry and adopted a distinctive way of dressing — knee breeches, a velvet jacket, and carrying a sunflower or a lily. With studied frivolity in behavior and dress, he became heir to the dandyism of Beau Brummel. This, at first, did more than his poetry to make him famous.

His first plays were second-rate melodramas, modeled on the "well-made play" of the period. With *An Ideal Husband, Lady Windermer's Fan*, which were still essentially melodramas, he added occasional moments which anticipated Wilde's unique touch. Only in *The Importance of Being Ernest*, his last play, did he totally free himself from melodramatic plots and unconvincing moralizing, to write a masterpiece of high comedy.

With the success of *The Importance of Being Ernest*, Wilde became the toast of London. But on the gala opening night, 1895, the Marquis of Queensbury, father of Lord Alfred Douglas, a young poet and friend of Wilde's, created a public scene, accusing Wilde of improper behavior. Wilde sued for libel, lost, and was himself tried for immoral practices and found guilty. With Wilde's advocacy of the philosophy of "Art for art's sake"; his insistence that life's goal is the pursuit of pleasure; his exotic public posturing; and his written assaults upon commonplace values, it was no surprise that the conventional world would strike back at him, impugning his character and ideas. Four days after *The Importance of Being Ernest* opened, events began which brought about his disgrace, imprisonment and exile. Wilde, a broken man, died in Paris in 1900.

The Importance of Being Ernest is a celebration of wit. Max Beerbohm, reviewing a revival of the play in 1902, wrote, "The fun depends mainly on what the characters say, rather than on what they do. They speak a kind of beautiful nonsense . . . Throughout the dialogue is the horse-play of a distinguished intellect and a distinguished imagination — a horse-play among words and ideas, conducted with poetic dignity."

Wilde called *The Importance of Being Ernest* "A Trivial Comedy for Serious People," commenting that the first act is "ingenious," the second "beautiful," and the third "abominably clever." The play stylishly satirizes birth, romance, the institution of marriage, and death — all the things that society values as important.

CAST

JOHN WORTHING, J.P.
ALGERNON MONCRIEFF
REV. CANON CHASUBLE, D.D.
MERRIMAN, *Butler*
LANE, *Manservant*
LADY BRACKNELL
HON. GWENDOLEN FAIRFAX
CECILY CARDEW
MISS PRISM, *Governess*

SCENES: 1. *Algernon's flat in London*
          2. *A room in the Manor House, Woolton*

TIME: *1895*

The Importance of Being Ernest

SCENE 1: (ALGERNON'S flat in London. The sound of a piano is heard in the next room. LANE is arranging tea on the table. Music stops.)

ALGERNON: (*Enters.*) Did you hear what I was playing, Lane?

LANE: I didn't think it polite to listen, sir. (*Exits.*)

ALGERNON: I don't play accurately — anyone can play accurately — but I play with wonderful expression. Ah, I see you have got the cucumber sandwiches cut for Lady Brecknell. (*Tastes a sandwich. Bell rings.*) Who can that be — so early?

LANE: (*Enters.*) Mr. Ernest Worthing. (*Enters JACK. LANE exits.*)

ALGERNON: How are you, my dear Ernest? What brings you up to town?

JACK: Oh, pleasure, pleasure! Eating as usual I see, Algy!

ALGERNON: (*Stiffly.*) I believe it is customary in good society to take some slight refreshment at five o'clock.

JACK: Who is coming to tea?

ALGERNON: Oh, merely Aunt Augusta and Gwendolen.

JACK: How perfectly delightful!

ALGERNON: I am afraid Aunt Augusta won't quite approve of your being here. The way you flirt with Gwendolen is perfectly disgraceful. It is almost as bad as the way Gwendolen flirts with you.

JACK: I am in love with Gwendolen. I have come up to town expressively to propose to her.

ALGERNON: I thought you had come up for pleasure. I call that business. (*JACK starts to take a sandwich.*) Please don't touch the cucumber sandwiches. They are ordered specially for Aunt Augusta. (*He takes another one and eats it.*)

JACK: Well, you have been eating them all the time.

ALGERNON: That is quite different. She is my aunt. Have some bread and butter. The bread and butter is for Gwendolen.

JACK: (*Helps himself.*) And very good bread and butter it is too.

ALGERNON: Well, my dear fellow, you need not eat as if you were already married to her. You are not married to her, and I don't think you ever will be.

JACK: Why do you say that?

ALGERNON: Well, in the first place, girls never marry the men they flirt with. In the second place, I don't give my consent.

JACK: Your consent?

ALGERNON: My dear fellow, Gwendolen is my first cousin. And before I allow you to marry her, you will have to clear up the whole question of Cecily. (*Gets cigarette case.*)

JACK: Cecily? I don't know anyone of the name of Cecily.

ALGERNON: This is the cigarette case you left last time you dined here. But when I look at the inscription inside, I find that the thing isn't yours after all. This cigarette case is a present from someone of the name of Cecily, and you said you didn't know anyone of that name.

JACK: Well, if you want to know, Cecily happens to be my aunt.

ALGERNON: But why does she call herself little Cecily if she is your aunt? (*Reading.*) "From little Cecily with her fondest love."

JACK: My dear fellow, some aunts are tall, some aunts are not tall. That is a matter that surely an aunt may be allowed to decide for herself. For Heaven's sake give me back my cigarette case. (*Follows Algernon around the room.*)

ALGERNON: But why does your aunt call you her uncle? "From little Cecily, with her fondest love to her dear Uncle Jack." Besides, your name isn't Jack, it is Ernest.

JACK: It isn't Ernest; it's Jack.

ALGERNON: You have always said it was Ernest. You answer to the name of Ernest. You are the most earnest-looking person I ever saw. It's on your cards. Here is one of them. (*Takes card from case.*) "Mr. Ernest Mowthing. The Albany." I'll keep this as a proof that your name is Ernest. (*Puts card in his pocket.*)

JACK: My name is Ernest in town, and Jack in the country; and the cigarette case was given to me in the country.

ALGERNON: Yes, but that does not account for the fact that your small Aunt Cecily calls you her dear uncle. Come, old boy, you had much better have the thing out at once. I have always suspected you of being a secret Bunburyist; and I am quite sure of it now.

JACK: Bunburyist? What on earth do you mean by a Bunburyist?

ALGERNON: I'll reveal to you the meaning of the incomparable expression as soon as you inform me why you are Ernest in town and Jack in the country.

JACK: Old Mr. Thomas Cardew, who adopted me when I was a little boy, made me in his will guardian to his grand-daughter, Miss Cecily Cardew. Cecily, who addresses me as her uncle, lives at my place in the country under the charge of her admirable governess, Miss Prism.

ALGERNON: Where is that place in the country, by the way?

JACK: That is nothing to you, dear boy. You are not going to be invited.

ALGERNON: But why are you Ernest in town and Jack in the country?

JACK: When one is placed in the position of guardian, one has to adopt a very high moral tone. And as a high moral tone is hardly conducive to one's health or one's happiness, in order to get up to town I have always pretended to have a younger brother of the name of Ernest, who lives in the Albany, and gets into the most dreadful scrapes. That, my dear Algy, is the whole truth pure and simple.

ALGERNON: The truth is rarely pure and never simple. What you really are is a Bunburyist. You have invented a very useful younger brother called Ernest, in order that you may be able to come up to town as often as you like. I have invented an invaluable permanent invalid called Bunbury, in order that I may be able to go down into the country whenever I choose. If it wasn't for Bunbury's extraordinary bad health, I wouldn't be able to dine with you tonight, for I have been really engaged to Aunt Augusta for more than a week.

JACK: I haven't asked you to dine.

ALGERNON: I know. You are absurdly careless about sending out invitations. Besides, now that I know you to be a confirmed Bunburyist, I naturally want to talk to you about Bunburying.

JACK: I am not a Bunburyist at all. If Gwendolen accepts me, I am going to kill my brother. Cecily is a little too much interested in him.

ALGERNON: (*Bells are heard.*) Ah! that must be Aunt Augusta. Now if I get her out of the way for ten minutes, so that you can have an opportunity for proposing to Gwendolen, may I dine with you tonight?

LANE: (*Enters.*) Lady Bracknell and Miss Fairfax.

LADY BRACKNELL: (*She and GWENDOLEN enter.*) Good afternoon, dear Algernon, I hope you are behaving very well.

ALGERNON: I am feeling very well, Aunt Augusta.

LADY BRACKNELL: That is not quite the same thing. In fact the two things rarely go together. (*Nods to Jack with icy coolness.*)

ALGERNON: (*To Gwendolen.*) Dear me, you are smart!

GWENDOLEN: I am always smart. Am I not, Mr. Worthing?

JACK: You are quite perfect, Miss Fairfax.

LADY BRACKNELL: I am sorry if we are late, Algernon, but I was obliged to call on dear Lady Harbury. I hadn't been there since her poor husband's death. I never saw a woman so altered; she looks quite twenty years younger. And now I'll have a cup of tea and one of those nice cucumber sandwiches you promised me.

ALGERNON: Good heavens! Lane! Why are there no cucumber sandwiches?

LANE: (*Gravely.*) There were no cucumbers in the market this morning, sir.

ALGERNON: No cucumbers!

LANE: No, sir. Not even for ready money.

ALGERNON: That will do, Lane, thank you.

LANE: Thank you, sir. (*Exits.*)

LADY BRACKNELL: It really makes no matter, Algernon. I had some crumpets with Lady Harbury, who seems to me to be living entirely for pleasure now.

ALGERNON: I hear her hair has turned quite gold from grief. (*Serves tea to Lady Bracknell.*) I am afraid, Aunt Augusta, I shall have to give up the pleasure of dining with you tonight. I have just had a telegram to say that poor Bunbury is very ill again.

LADY BRACKNELL: This Mr. Bunbury seems to suffer from curiously bad health.

ALGERNON: Yes, poor Bunbury is a dreadful invalid.

LADY BRACKNELL: Well, I think it is high time that Mr. Bunbury made up his mind whether he was going to live or to die. This shilly-shallying with the question is absurd. I should be much obliged if you would ask Mr. Bunbury to be kind enough not to have a relapse on Saturday, for I rely on you to arrange my music for my last reception.

ALGERNON: Ah yes. We will run over the program now, if you will kindly come into the next room for a moment.

LADY BRACKNELL: Thank you, Algernon. Gwendolen, you will accompany me. (*LADY BRACKNELL and ALGERNON exit. GWEN-DOLEN remains behind.*)

JACK: Charming day it has been, Miss Fairfax.

GWENDOLEN: Pray don't talk about the weather, Mr. Worthing. Whenever people talk about the weather, I always feel certain that they mean something else.

JACK: I do mean something else.

GWENDOLEN: I thought so. In fact, I am never wrong.

JACK: (*Nervously.*) Miss Fairfax, ever since I met you I have admired you more than any girl . . . I have ever met since . . . I met you.

GWENDOLEN: Yes, I am quite well aware of the fact. For me you have always had an irresistible fascination. We live, as I hope you know, Mr. Worthing, in an age of ideals. And my ideal has always been to love someone of the name of Ernest. The moment Algernon first mentioned that he had a friend called Ernest, I knew I was destined to love you.

JACK: You mean to say that you couldn't love me if my name wasn't Ernest?

GWENDOLEN: It is a divine name. It produces vibrations.

JACK: I can think of lots nicer names. Jack, for instance, is a charming name.

GWENDOLEN: Jack? It produces absolutely no vibrations. The only safe name is Ernest.

JACK: Gwendolen, I must get christened at once—I mean we must get married at once.

GWENDOLEN: Married? But you haven't proposed to me yet. And I think it only fair to tell you beforehand that I am fully determined to accept you.

JACK: (*On his knees.*) Gwendolen, will you marry me?

GWENDOLEN: Of course, I will, darling. How long you have been about it.

LACY BRACKNELL: (*Enters.*) Mr. Worthing! Rise, sir, from this semirecumbent posture. It is most indecorous.

GWENDOLEN: Mamma! Mr. Worthing has not quite finished yet.

LADY BRACKNELL: Finished what, may I ask?

GWENDOLEN: I am engaged to Mr. Worthing. (*They rise together.*)

LADY BRACKNELL: Pardon me, you are not engaged to any one. When you do become engaged, I will inform you. And now I have a few questions to put to you, Mr. Worthing. While I am making these inquiries, you, Gwendolen, will wait for me below in the carriage.

GWENDOLEN: Mamma!

LADY BRACKNELL: In the carriage, Gwendolen! (*GWENDOLEN blows kisses to Jack as she goes to door.*) Gwendolen, the carriage!

GWENDOLEN: Yes, mamma. (*Exits.*)

LADY BRACKNELL: (*Sits, takes out note-book.*) You can take a seat, Mr. Worthing.

JACK: Thank you, Lady Bracknell. I prefer standing.

LADY BRACKNELL: Do you smoke?

JACK: Yes, I must admit I smoke.

LADY BRACKNELL: I am glad to hear it. A man should always have an occupation. Are your parents living?

JACK: I have lost both my parents.

LADY BRACKNELL: To lose one parent, Mr. Worthing, may be regarded as a misfortune; to lose both looks like carelessness. Who was your father?

JACK: I am afraid I really don't know. It would be nearer the truth to say that my parents seem to have lost me. I—I was found.

LADY BRACKNELL: Found!

JACK: The late Mr. Thomas Cardew, an old gentleman of a very charitable disposition, found me, and gave me the name of Worthing, because he happened to have a first class ticket for Worthing in his pocket at the time. Worthing is a place in Sussex. It is a seaside resort.

LADY BRACKNELL: Where did the charitable gentleman who had a first class ticket for this seaside resort find you?

JACK: (*Gravely.*) In a hand-bag.

LADY BRACKNELL: A hand-bag?

JACK: (*Very seriously.*) Yes, Lady Bracknell. I was in a hand-bag — a somewhat large, black leather hand-bag, with handles to it — an ordinary hand-bag in fact.

LADY BRACKNELL: In what locality did this Mr. Cardew come across this ordinary hand-bag?

JACK: In the cloak-room at Victoria Station. It was given to him in mistake for his own.

LADY BRACKNELL: The cloak-room at Victoria Station?

JACK: Yes. The Brighton line.

LADY BRACKNELL: The line is immaterial. Mr. Worthing, I confess I am bewildered by what you have just told me. To be born, or at any rate bred, in a hand-bag, whether it had handles or not, seems to me to display a contempt for ordinary decencies.

JACK: May I ask you then what you would advise me to do?

LADY BRACKNELL: I would strongly advise you, Mr. Worthing, to try to acquire some relations.

JACK: I can produce the hand-bag at any moment.

LADY BRACKNELL: Sir, you can hardly imagine that I would allow my only daughter to marry into a cloak-room, and form an alliance with a parcel. Good morning, Mr. Worthing! (*She sweeps out in majestic indignation.*)

JACK: Good morning! (*From the other room, ALGERNON starts playing the Wedding March on the piano.*) For goodness' sake don't play that ghastly tune, Algy!

ALGERNON: (*Music stops. He enters.*) Didn't it go off all right, old boy? You don't mean to say Gwendolen refused you?

JACK: Oh, Gwendolen is right as a trivet. But her mother is perfectly unbearable.

ALGERNON: Did you tell Gwendolen the truth about your being Ernest in town and Jack in the country?

JACK: Before the end of the week I shall have got rid of Ernest. I will say he died in Paris of apoplexy.

ALGERNON: Apoplexy is hereditary. You had much better say a severe chill.

JACK: Very well then. My poor brother Ernest is carried off suddenly by a severe chill. That gets rid of him.

ALGERNON: But I thought you said that . . . Miss Cardew was a little too interested in your poor brother Ernest. Won't she feel his loss a good deal?

JACK: Cecily is not a silly romantic girl. She has got a capital appetite, goes for long walks, and pays no attention at all to her lessons.

ALGERNON: I would rather like to see Cecily.

JACK: I will take very good care you never do.

LANE: (*Enters.*) Miss Fairfax.

GWENDOLEN: (*She enters. LANE exits.*) Algy, kindly turn your back. I have something very particular to say to Mr. Worthing.

JACK: My own darling!

GWENDOLEN: Ernest, we may never be married. From the expression on mamma's face, I fear we never shall. But although she may prevent us from becoming man and wife, and I may marry someone else, and marry often, nothing can alter my eternal devotion to you. Your town address at the Albany I have. What is your address in the country?

JACK: The Manor House, Woolton, Hertfordshire. (*ALGERNON, who has been listening, smiles, and writes the address on his shirt-cuff.*)

GWENDOLEN: (*Repeats.*) The Manor House, Woolton, Hertford-shire. I will communicate with you daily. Algy, you may turn around now. You may also ring the bell.

JACK: You will let me see you to your carriage, my own darling?

GWENDOLEN: Certainly.

JACK: (*To LANE, who enters.*) I will see Miss Fairfax out. (*They exit.*)

LANE: Yes, sir.

ALGERNON: Tomorrow, Lane, I am going Bunburying.

LANE: Yes, sir.

ALGERNON: I shall probably not be back till Monday. You can pack all the Bunbury suits.

LANE: Yes, sir.

ALGERNON: (*Reads.*) The Manor House, Woolton, Hertfordshire. (*ALGERNON exits. Music. LANE and MERRIMAN, another butler, move a few pieces of furniture, etc., setting the next scene.*)

SCENE 2: (*A room in the Manor House. LANE and MERRIMAN exit, as MISS PRISM enters.*)

PRISM: Cecily, Cecily! Come. (*CECILY enters.*) It is time for intellectual pleasures. Your German grammar is on the table. We will repeat yesterday's lesson.

CECILY: But I don't like German. It isn't at all a becoming language. I know perfectly well that I look quite plain after my German lesson.

PRISM: Child, you know how anxious your guardian is that you should improve yourself in every way.

CECILY: Dear Uncle Jack is so very serious! Sometimes he is so serious that I think he cannot be quite well.

PRISM: You must remember his constant anxiety about his unfortunate brother — Ernest.

CECILY: I wish Uncle Jack would allow his unfortunate young brother — Ernest — to come down here sometimes. I am sure you would be a good influence on him. (*Begins to write in her diary.*)

PRISM: I do not think that even I could produce any effect on a character so irretrievably weak and vacillating. Indeed, I am not in favour of this modern mania for turning bad people into good people at a moment's notice. As a man sows so let him reap. Put away your diary, Cecily. Memory, my dear child, is the diary that we all carry about with us.

CECILY: I believe that memory is responsible for nearly all the three-volume novels we read.

PRISM: Do not speak slightingly of the three-volume novel. I wrote one myself in earlier days.

CECILY: Did you really, Miss Prism? And was your novel published?

PRISM: Alas! no. The manuscript unfortunately was abandoned. I used the word in the sense of lost or mislaid.

CECILY: Oh, I see Dr. Chasuble coming up through the garden.

PRISM: Dr. Chasuble! This is indeed a pleasure.

CHASUBLE: (*Enters.*) And how are we this morning? Miss Prism, you are, I trust, well?

CECILY: Miss Prism has just been complaining of a slight headache. I think it would do her so much good to have a short walk with you in the park, Dr. Chasuble.

PRISM: Cecily, I have not mentioned anything about a headache.

CECILY: No, dear Miss Prism, I know that, but I felt instinctively that you had a headache.

CHASUBLE: I hope, Cecily, you are not being inattentive in your studies. Were I fortunate enough to be Miss Prism's pupil, I would hang upon her lips. (*PRISM reacts.*) I spoke metaphorically.

PRISM: Dear Doctor, I find I have a headache after all; and a walk might do it good.

CHASUBLE: With pleasure, Miss Prism, with pleasure.

PRISM: Cecily, you will read your Political Economy in my absence. The chapter on the Fall of the Rupee you may omit. It is somewhat too sensational. (*She and CHASUBLE exit.*)

CECILY: (*Throws books.*) Horrid Political Economy! Horrid Geography! Horrid German!

MERRIMAN: (*Enters.*) Mr. Ernest Worthing has just driven over from the station. He has brought his luggage with him.

CECILY: (*Takes card and reads.*) "Mr. Ernest Worthing, The Albany." Uncle Jack's brother! Ask Mr. Ernest Worthing to come here.

MERRIMAN: Yes, Miss. (*Exits.*)

CECILY: I have never met any really wicked person before. I feel rather frightened. I am so afraid he will look just like everyone else. (*ALGERNON, very debonair, enters.*) He does!

ALGERNON: You are my little cousin Cecily, I am sure.

CECILY: And you are Uncle Jack's brother, Cousin Ernest — my wicked cousin Ernest.

ALGERNON: Oh! I am not really wicked at all, Cousin Cecily.

CECILY: If you are not, then you have certainly been deceiving us all in a very inexcusable manner.

ALGERNON: Of course I have been rather reckless.

CECILY: I am glad to hear it. I am sure it must have been very pleasant. Although I don't think you should be so proud of that.

ALGERNON: I'm not. That is why I want you to reform me. You might make that your mission.

CECILY: I'm afraid I've no time, this afternoon.

ALGERNON: Being with you, I feel better already.

CECILY: You are looking a little worse.

ALGERNON: That is because I am hungry.

CECILY: How thoughtless of me. I should have remembered that when one is going to lead an entirely new life, one requires regular and wholesome meals. Won't you come into the dining room?

ALGERNON: You are the prettiest girl I ever saw.

CECILY: Miss Prism says that all good looks are a snare.

ALGERNON: They are a snare that every sensible man would like to be caught in.

CECILY: Oh, I don't think I would care to catch a sensible man. I shouldn't know what to talk to him about. (*They exit. MISS PRISM and DR. CHASUBLE enter.*)

PRISM: You are too much alone, dear Dr. Chasuble. You should get married. A misanthrope I can understand — a womanthrope, never! You do not seem to realize that by persistently remaining single, a man converts himself into a permanent public temptation.

CHASUBLE: But is a man not equally attractive when married?

PRISM: No married man is ever attractive except to his wife.

CHASUBLE: And often, I've been told, not even to her. (*JACK enters, slowly. He is dressed in deepest mourning.*)

PRISM: Mr. Worthing!

CHASUBLE: Mr. Worthing?

JACK: (*Shakes Prism's hand in tragic manner.*) I have returned sooner than I expected.

CHASUBLE: Dear Mr. Worthing, I trust this garb of woe does not betoken some terrible calamity?

JACK: My brother.

CHASUBLE: Still leading his life of pleasure?

JACK: Dead.

CHASUBLE: Your brother Ernest dead?

JACK: Quite dead.

PRISM: What a lesson for him! I trust he will profit by it.

JACK: Poor Ernest! He had many faults; but it is a sad, sad blow.

CHASUBLE: You were with him at the end?

JACK: No. He died in Paris. A severe chill.

PRISM: As a man sows, so shall he reap.

CHASUBLE: Charity, dear Miss Prism, charity! None of us are perfect. I myself am peculiarly susceptible to draughts. You would no doubt wish me to make some allusion to this tragic affliction in next Sunday's sermon. (*JACK nods and shakes CHASUBLE'S hand tragically.*) The text can be adapted to almost any occasion, from celebrations to christenings.

JACK: Christenings? The fact is, dear Doctor, I would like to be christened myself this afternoon.

CHASUBLE: But surely you have been christened already?

JACK: I don't remember anything about it.

CHASUBLE: At what hour would you wish the ceremony performed?

JACK: Oh, I might trot around about five.

CECILY: (*Enters.*) Uncle Jack! Oh, I am pleased to see you. But what horrid clothes you have got on. (*JACK kisses her brow in a melancholy manner.*) What is the matter, Uncle Jack? You look as if you had a toothache, and I have got such a surprise for you. Who do you think is in the dining-room? Your brother!

JACK: Who?

CECILY: Your brother Ernest.

JACK: What nonsense! I haven't got a brother.

CECILY: Oh, don't say that. However badly he may have behaved he is still your brother. I'll tell him to come out. (*Exits.*)

CHASUBLE: These are very joyful tidings.

JACK: My brother is in the dining-room? (*CECILY and JACK enter.*) Good heavens!

ALGERNON: Brother John, I have come down from town to tell you that I am very sorry for all the trouble I have given you, and that I intend to lead a better life in the future. (*Offers his hand, which JACK does not shake.*)

CECILY: Uncle Jack, you are not going to refuse your brother's hand?

JACK: Nothing will induce me to take his hand.

CECILY: Uncle Jack, there is some good in everyone. Ernest has just been telling me about his poor invalid friend Mr. Bunbury.

JACK: Bunbury! I won't have him talking to you about Bunbury or anything else.

CECILY: Uncle Jack, if you don't shake hands with Ernest, I will never forgive you.

JACK: Never forgive me?

CECILY: Never, never, never!

JACK: Well, this is the last time I shall ever do it. (*Shakes hand.*)

CHASUBLE: It's pleasant, is it not, to see so perfect a reconciliation? I think we might leave the two brothers together.

PRISM: Cecily, you will come with us.

CHASUBLE: You have done a beautiful action today, dear child.

CECILY: I feel very happy. (*PRISM, CHASUBLE and CECILY exit.*)

JACK: You young scoundrel, Algy, you must get out of this place as soon as possible.

MERRIMAN: (*Enters.*) I have put Mr. Ernest's things in the room next to yours, sir.

JACK: What?

ALGERNON: I am afraid I can't stay more than a week this time.

JACK: Merriman, order the dog-cart at once. Mr. Ernest has been suddenly called back to town.

MERRIMAN: Yes, sir. (*Exits.*)

ALGERNON: What a fearful liar you are, Jack. No one has called me.

JACK: Your duty as a gentleman calls you back.

ALGERNON: Cecily is a darling.

JACK: You are not to talk of Miss Cardew like that. I don't like it.

ALGERNON: Well, I don't like your clothes. You look perfectly ridiculous. It is perfectly childish to be in deep mourning for a man who is actually staying for a whole week with you.

JACK: You are certainly not staying with me for a whole week.

ALGERNON: I certainly won't leave you so long as you are in mourning. It would be most unfriendly.

JACK: Well, will you go if I change my clothes?

ALGERNON: Yes, if you are not too long. I never saw anybody take so long to dress, and with such little results.

JACK: (*In triumph.*) This Bunburying, as you call it, has not been a great success for you. Goodbye. (*Exits.*)

ALGERNON: I think it has been a great success. I'm in love with Cecily and that is everything.

CECILY: (*Enters.*) I thought you were with Uncle Jack.

ALGERNON: He's going to send me away.

CECILY: Then have we got to part?

ALGERNON: But before we do, I hope I shall not offend you if I state that you seem to me to be the visible personification of absolute perfection.

CECILY: Thank you. If you will allow me, I will copy your remarks into my diary. (*Starts to write.*) Pray, Ernest, do not stop. I delight in taking down dictation. I have reached "absolute perfection."

ALGERNON: (*Taken aback.*) Ahem! Ahem!

CECILY: Oh, don't cough, Ernest. When one is dictating one should speak fluently. Besides, I don't know how to spell a cough.

ALGERNON: (*Speaking rapidly.*) Cecily, ever since I first looked upon your wonderful and incomparable beauty, I have dared to love you wildly. Will you marry me?

CECILY: You silly boy! Of course. We have been engaged for the last three months.

ALGERNON: For the last three months?

CECILY: Ever since dear Uncle Jack first confessed that he had a younger brother who was very wicked, I fell in love with you. Besides, of course, there is the question of your name. You must not laugh at me, but it had always been a girlish dream of mine to love someone whose name was Ernest.

ALGERNON: You mean you could not love me if I had some other name?

CECILY: But what name?

ALGERNON: Oh, any name you like — Algernon — for instance.

CECILY: I might respect you. I might admire your character, but I fear that I should not be able to give you my undivided attention. Besides, Ernest is your name.

ALGERNON: Ahem! Your Rector here is, I suppose, thoroughly experienced in the practice of all rites of the Church?

CECILY: Oh yes, Dr. Chasuble has never written a single book, so you can imagine how much he knows.

ALGERNON: I must see him at once on a most important christening—I mean on most important business. I shan't be away more than half an hour.

CECILY: Couldn't you make it twenty minutes?

ALGERNON: I'll be back in no time. (*Kisses her and rushes out.*)

CECILY: What an impetuous boy he is! I must enter his proposal in my diary.

MERRIMAN: (*Enters.*) A Miss Fairfax has just called to see Mr. Worthing.

CECILY: Pray ask the lady to come in here. And you can bring tea.

MERRIMAN: Yes, Miss. (*Exits.*)

CECILY: Miss Fairfax. I suppose one of the many good elderly women who are associated with Uncle Jack in some of his philanthropic work in London.

MERRIMAN: (*Enters.*) Miss Fairfax. (*GWENDOLEN enters. MERRIMAN exits.*)

CECILY: Pray let me introduce myself. My name is Cecily Cardew.

GWENDOLEN: Cecily Cardew? (*They shake hands.*) What a very sweet name. I like you already. My first impressions are never wrong.

CECILY: How nice of you to like me so much. Pray sit down.

GWENDOLEN: (*Stands.*) I may call you Cecily, may I not?

CECILY: With pleasure!

GWENDOLEN: And you will always call me Gwendolen, won't you?

CECILY: If you wish.

GWENDOLEN: Then that is all quite settled, is it not?

CECILY: I hope so. (*A pause. They both sit down together.*)

GWENDOLEN: My mamma, whose views on education are remarkably strict, has brought me up to be extremely short-sighted; so do you mind my looking at you through my glasses? (*Examines Cecily through a lorgnette.*)

CECILY: Not at all. I am very fond of being looked at.

GWENDOLEN: You are here on a short visit, I suppose.

CECILY: Oh no. I live here.

GWENDOLEN: Really? Your mother no doubt resides here also?

CECILY: Oh no. I have no mother, nor, in fact, any relations. My dear guardian, with the assistance of Miss Prism, has the arduous task of looking after me.

GWENDOLEN: Your guardian?

CECILY: Yes. I am Mr. Worthing's ward.

GWENDOLEN: Ernest never mentioned to me he had a ward.

CECILY: I beg your pardon, Gwendolen, did you say Ernest?

GWENDOLEN: Yes.

CECILY: Oh, but it is not Mr. Ernest Worthing who is my guardian. It is his brother.

GWENDOLEN: Ernest never mentioned to me that he had a brother. You are quite, quite sure that it is not Mr. Ernest Worthing who is your guardian?

CECILY: Quite sure. In fact, I am going to be his.

GWENDOLEN: I beg your pardon?

CECILY: Mr. Ernest Worthing and I are engaged to be married.

GWENDOLEN: I think there must be some slight error. Mr. Ernest Worthing is engaged to me.

CECILY: I am afraid you must be under some misconception. Ernest proposed to me exactly ten minutes ago. (*Shows diary.*)

GWENDOLEN: It is very curious for he asked me to be his wife yesterday afternoon at 5:30. I am sorry, dear Cecily, but I am afraid I have the prior claim.

CECILY: I feel bound to point out that since Ernest proposed to you he clearly has changed his mind.

MERRIMAN: (*Enters with tea tray.*) Shall I lay tea here as usual, Miss?

CECILY: Yes, as usual. (*Both girls restrain their emotions.*)

GWENDOLEN: Are there many interesting walks in the vicinity, Miss Cardew?

CECILY: Oh, yes. From the top of the hill one can see five counties.

GWENDOLEN: I don't think I should like that; I hate crowds.

CECILY: (*Sweetly.*) I suppose that is why you live in town?

GWENDOLEN: Quite a well-kept garden you have, Miss Cardew. I had no idea there were any flowers in the country.

CECILY: Oh, flowers are as common here, Miss Fairfax, as people are in London. May I offer you some tea? Sugar?

GWENDOLEN: No, thank you. Sugar is not fashionable any more.

CECILY: (*Puts four lumps of sugar into the cup.*) Cake or bread and butter?

GWENDOLEN: Bread and butter, please. Cake is rarely seen at the best houses.

CECILY: (*Puts large slice of cake on plate.*) Hand that to Miss Fairfax. (*MERRIMAN does so, and exits. GWENDOLEN sips tea, puts cup down at once, holds up cake. Rises in indignation.*)

GWENDOLEN: You have filled my tea with lumps of sugar; and though I asked for bread and butter, you have given me cake. I warn you, Miss Cardew, you may go too far.

CECILY: (*Rises.*) To save my poor, innocent trusting boy there are no lengths to which I would not go. (*JACK enters.*)

GWENDOLEN: Ernest! My own Ernest!

JACK: Gwendolen! Darling! (*Offers to kiss her.*)

GWENDOLEN: (*Draws back.*) A moment! May I ask if you are engaged to be married to this young lady?

JACK: (*Laughs.*) To dear little Cecily! Of course not.

GWENDOLEN: Thank you. You may. (*Offers her cheek.*)

CECILY: (*Sweetly.*) I knew there must be some misunderstanding, Miss Fairfax. The gentleman whose arm is at present around your waist is my guardian, Mr. John Worthing. This is Uncle Jack.

GWENDOLEN: Jack! Oh! (*ALGERNON enters.*)

CECILY: Here is Ernest.

ALGERNON: (*Goes to Cecily.*) My own love! (*Offers to kiss her.*)

CECILY: A moment, Ernest! May I ask you — are you engaged to be married to this young lady?

ALGERNON: Good heavens! Gwendolen! Of course I'm not engaged to Gwendolen.

CECILY: Thank you. (*Offers her cheek.*) You may. (*He kisses her.*)

GWENDOLEN: I felt there was some slight error, Miss Cardew. The gentleman who is now embracing you is my cousin, Mr. Algernon Moncrieff.

CECILY: (*Breaking away.*) Algernon Moncrieff! Oh! (*Girls move together.*) Are you called Algernon?

ALGERNON: I cannot deny it.

GWENDOLEN: Is your name really John?

JACK: Yes. It has been for years.

CECILY: A gross deception has been practised on both of us.

GWENDOLEN: It is quite clear, Cecily, that neither of us is engaged to be married to anyone.

CECILY: Mr. Moncrieff, kindly answer me the following question. Why did you pretend to be my guardian's brother?

ALGERNON: In order that I might have an opportunity of meeting you.

GWENDOLEN: Mr. Worthing, what explanation can you offer to me for pretending to have a brother? Was it in order that you might have an opportunity of coming up to town to see me?

JACK: Can you doubt it, Miss Fairfax?

GWENDOLEN: (*To Cecily.*) Their explanations appear to be quite satisfactory.

CECILY: I am more than content.

GWENDOLEN: But there are principles at stake that one cannot surrender. Which of us should tell them?

CECILY: Could we not both speak at the same time?

GWENDOLEN: An excellent idea! I nearly always speak at the same time as other people. Will you take the time from me? (*She beats time with uplifted finger. They both speak together.*) Your Christian names are still an insuperable barrier. That is all.

JACK and ALGERNON: (*Together.*) Our Christian names! Is that all? But we are going to be christened this afternoon.

GWENDOLEN: (*To Jack.*) For my sake you are prepared to do this terrible thing?

CECILY: (*To Algernon.*) To please me you are ready to face this fearful ordeal?

JACK: We are. (*Clasps hands with Algernon.*)

GWENDOLEN: (*To Jack.*) Darling!

ALGERNON: (*To Cecily.*) Darling! (*They fall into each other's arms.*)

MERRIMAN: (*Enters.*) Lady Bracknell.

JACK: Good heavens!

LADY BRACKNELL: (*Enters. MERRIMAN exits.*) Gwendolen! What does this mean?

GWENDOLEN: Merely that I am engaged to be married to Mr. Worthing, mamma.

LADY BRACKNELL: Come here. Sit down. Sit down immediately. Hesitation of any kind is a sign of mental decay in the young, of physical weakness in the old. (*To Jack.*) Apprised, sir, of my daughter's sudden flight by her trusty maid, I followed her at once by a luggage train. You will clearly understand that all communication between yourself and my daughter must cease immediately from this moment! And now as regards Algernon! Algernon!

ALGERNON: Yes, Aunt Augusta.

LADY BRACKNELL: May I ask if it is in this house that your invalid friend Mr. Bunbury resides.

ALGERNON: Oh, no. In fact, Bunbury is dead. The doctors found out that Bunbury could not live — so Bunbury died.

LADY BRACKNELL: He seems to have had great confidence in the opinion of his physicians. I am glad, however, that he made up his mind at the last to some definite course of action. Now may I ask, Mr. Worthing, who is that young person whose hand my nephew Algernon is now holding in what seems to me a peculiarly unnecessary manner?

JACK: That lady is Miss Cecily Cardew, my ward.

ALGERNON: I am engaged to be married to Cecily, Aunt Augusta.

LADY BRACKNELL: I beg your pardon?

CECILY: Mr. Moncrieff and I are engaged to be married, Lady Bracknell.

LADY BRACKNELL: I do not know whether there is anything peculiarly exciting in the air of this particular part of Hertfordshire, but the number of engagements that go on seem to me considerably above the proper average. I think some preliminary inquiry on my part would not be out of place. Mr. Worthing, is Miss Cardew at all connected with any of the larger railway stations in London?

JACK: Miss Cardew is the grand-daughter of the late Mr. Thomas Cardew of 149 Belgrave Square.

LADY BRACKNELL: That sounds not unsatisfactory.

JACK: I have also in my possession certificates of Miss Cardew's birth, baptism, whooping cough, registration, vaccination, confirmation, and the measles; both the German and the English variety.

LADY BRACKNELL: Ah, a life crowded with incident. Has Miss Cardew any little fortune?

JACK: About a hundred and thirty thousand pounds in the Funds.

LADY BRACKNELL: Ah. Miss Cardew seems to me a most attractive young lady, now that I look at her. Come over here, dear. Pretty child! Your dress is sadly simple, and your hair seems about as Nature might have left it. But we can soon alter all that. Well, I suppose I must give my consent.

JACK: I beg your pardon for interrupting, but this engagement is quite out of the question. I am Miss Cardew's guardian, and she cannot marry without my consent.

LADY BRACKNELL: On what grounds do you object?

JACK: My dear Lady Bracknell, the matter is entirely in your own hands. The moment you consent to my marriage with Gwendolen, I will most gladly allow your nephew to form an alliance with my ward.

LADY BRACKNELL: You must be quite aware that what you propose is out of the question!

CHASUBLE: (*Enters.*) I am happy to say everything is quite ready for the christenings.

LADY BRACKNELL: The christenings? Is not that somewhat premature?

CHASUBLE: Both these gentlemen have expressed a desire for immediate baptism. Miss Prism and I have been waiting in the church.

LADY BRACKNELL: Miss Prism! Did I hear you mention a Miss Prism? Is this Miss Prism a female of repellent aspect, remotely connected with education?

CHASUBLE: She is the most cultivated of ladies, and the very picture of respectability.

LADY BRACKNELL: It is obviously the same person. I must see her at once. Let her be sent for.

CHASUBLE: She approaches; she is nigh.

PRISM: (*Enters.*) Dear Doctor Chasuble, I was worried what was detaining you.

LADY BRACKNELL: Prism! (*PRISM reacts.*) Come here, Prism! Prism, where is that baby? Twenty-eight years ago, Prism, you left Lord Bracknell's house in charge of a perambulator that contained a baby of the male sex. You never returned. A few weeks later, the perambulator, containing a manuscript of a three-volume novel, was found. But the baby was not there. Prism! Where is that baby?

PRISM: Lady Bracknell, I do not know. I only wish I did. The facts are these. On the morning you mention, I prepared to take the baby out in its perambulator. I had also with me a somewhat old, but capacious hand-bag, in which I had intended to place the manuscript of a work of fiction that I had written. In a moment of mental abstraction, I deposited the manuscript in the bassinette and placed the baby in the hand-bag.

JACK: But where did you deposit the hand-bag?

PRISM: Do not ask me, Mr. Worthing.

JACK: Miss Prism, this is a matter of no small importance to me. Where did you deposit the hand-bag that contained that infant?

PRISM: I left it in the cloak-room of one of the larger railway stations in London.

JACK: What railway station?

PRISM: Victoria. The Brighton line.

JACK: I must retire to the next room for a moment. Gwendolen, wait here for me. (*Exits.*)

CHASUBLE: What do you think this means, Lady Bracknell?

LADY BRACKNELL: I dare not even suspect, Dr. Chasuble. I need hardly tell you that in families of high position strange coincidences are not supposed to occur.

JACK: (*Enters, with hand-bag.*) Is this the hand-bag, Miss Prism? The happiness of more than one life depends on your answer.

PRISM: (*Calmly.*) It seems to be mine. Yes, here is the injury it received through the upsetting of a Gower Street omnibus in younger days. And here, on the lock, are my initials. The bag is undoubtedly mine. I am delighted to have it restored to me. It has been a great inconvenience being without it all these years.

JACK: Miss Prism, more is restored to you than this hand-bag. I was the baby you placed in it.

PRISM: You?

JACK: Yes. Mother!

PRISM: Mr. Worthing, I am unmarried! (*Points to Lady Bracknell.*) There is the lady who can tell you who you really are.

JACK: Lady Bracknell, I hate to seem inquisitive, but would you kindly inform me who I am?

LADY BRACKNELL: I am afraid that the news I have to give you will not altogether please you. You are the son of my poor sister, Mrs. Moncrieff, and consequently Algernon's elder brother.

JACK: Algy's elder brother! Then I have a brother after all.

GWENDOLEN: But what is your Christian name, now that you have become someone else?

JACK: Aunt Augusta, at the time when Miss Prism left me in the hand-bag, had I been christened already? (*She nods.*) What name was I given? Let me know the worst.

LADY BRACKNELL: Being the eldest son you were naturally christened after your father.

JACK: Yes, but what was my father's Christian name?

LADY BRACKNELL: I cannot at the present moment recall what the General's Christian name was. But I have no doubt he had one. He was eccentric, I admit. But only in later years.

JACK: Algy! Can you recollect what our father's Christian name was?

ALGERNON: My dear boy, we were never even on speaking terms. He died before I was a year old.

JACK: His name would appear in the Army List of the period. Yes! The Army Lists of the last forty years are here. These delightful records should have been my constant study. (*Rushes and gets books.*) M. Generals . . . Mallam, Maxbohm, Magley—what ghastly names they have—Moncrieff! Lieutenant, 1840, Captain, Lieutenant-Colonel, Colonel, General 1869. Christian names, Ernest John. (*Speaks calmly.*) I always told you, Gwendolen, my name was Ernest. Well, it is Ernest after all. I mean it naturally is Ernest.

GWENDOLEN: My own Ernest! I felt from the first that you could have no other name!

JACK: Gwendolen, it is a terrible thing for a man to find out suddenly that all his life he has been speaking nothing but the truth.

CHASUBLE: (*To Prism.*) Laetitia! (*Embraces her.*)

PRISM: Frederick! At last!

ALGERNON: Cecily! (*Embraces her.*) At last!

JACK: Gwendolen! (*Embraces her.*) At last!

LADY BRACKNELL: My nephew, you seem to be displaying signs of triviality.

JACK: On the contrary, Aunt Augusta, I've now realized for the first time in my life the vital importance of Being Ernest.

CURTAIN

Introduction

Candida, which George Bernard Shaw called "An Extraordinary Ordinary Play," was initially a limited success, although it soon became one of his most enduringly popular plays. One of Shaw's rare character comedies, it also retains his predilection for comedies of ideas which increases its stageworthiness today.

George Bernard Shaw, the great iconoclast, was born in Ireland in 1856. He claimed he learned little in the various schools he attended but gained an early knowledge of music from his mother who was a singer. At age twenty, he followed her to London where he began writing music criticism for the *Star* and the *World*. Later he branched out into dramatic criticism for the *Saturday Review*. In his reviews, he irritated the theatrical establishment by ridiculing popular melodramas, comedies and poorly translated continental plays. He paved the way for the new drama of the twentieth century by praising Ibsen whose work was then being attacked as offensive.

In addition to criticism, Shaw developed an interest in social and political reform and incorporated his ideas in five unsuccessful novels. As he became more deeply involved with the Fabian Society, he turned to writing plays in which he could voice his political ideas, taking as his model the "new drama" of Ibsen. His first play, *Widower's House*, presented in 1892 as a private production, launched his long career as the foremost British dramatist of his time. Of *Widower's House*, he wrote, "I had not achieved a success, but I provoked an uproar; and the sensation was so agreeable that I resolved to try again."

The result was *Arms and the Man*, 1894. It was one of four plays — which also eventually included *Candida* — which he labeled *Plays Pleasant*. Shaw intentionally disregarded the techniques utilized in current "well-made plays." He introduced to the stage such political and social topics as prostitution, war, health, economics and the position of women in society. His plays had little of what was then considered "action," but they presented clash of ideas sprinkled with wit.

Shaw, who might have easily become a successful actor, directed many of the first productions of his early plays. He was in the vanguard of making plays publishable by providing colorful stage directions and writing long stimulating essays as prefaces.

He began writing *Candida* on October 2, 1894, and completed it on December 7, 1894. It is one of Shaw's best structured scripts with social issues subordinated to fully-realized characters. He said he based the character of Morell on three Christian Socialist clergymen he knew. He claimed he had no model for Candida and said he borrowed her name from Candida Bartolucci, an Italian lady he never met. He denied that the young poet was based on himself, as a critic claimed, insisting the inspiration came from reading DeQuincey's account of his adolescence and *Confessions*. *Candida* is an especially good example of Shaw's early commitment to the proposition that conflict in drama can arise from ideas and beliefs just as effectively as from physical action or emotional passion. *Candida* sets the pattern for future Shaw plays with its mockery of conventional Victorian domesticity and its liberation of the young poet to carry out life's nobler purpose.

When he died at age ninety-four, he had written over fifty plays and referred to himself as a "writing machine." However he regarded himself — and Shaw was a great self-publicist — he changed the British stage, restored ideas to world theatre and became one of the most influential figures in modern dramatic literature. As has been said, "Mr. George Bernard Shaw is a writer of comedy with a tragic cry in his soul."

REVEREND JAMES MORELL
MISS PROSERPINE GARNETT, *Prossy*
REVEREND ALEXANDER MILL, *Lexy*
MRS. JAMES MORELL, *Candida*
EUGENE MARCHBANKS

TIME: *A day in October, 1894.*

SCENE: *The drawing room, St. Dominic's Parsonage, London.*

Candida

(*SCENE: The drawing room of St. Dominic's Parsonage, London, 1894. There is a large window at back, in front of which is a long table, littered with pamphlets, letters, and the like. A chair is at the end of the table. This is where REVEREND MORELL does his work. On a smaller table is a typewriter. This is where his typist does her work. On the right wall is a fireplace with a chair and sofa near it. A door leading to the dining area is by the fireplace. A larger doorway is on the opposite side, leading to the front hall and stairs. There are bookshelves, bric-à-brac, but nothing useless or pretentious in the room, money being too scarce in the house of an East End parson to be wasted on snobbish trimmings.*

The REVEREND JAMES MORELL sits in his chair at the end of the table. He is a vigorous, genial, popular man of forty, robust and good-looking, full of energy, with pleasant, hearty, considerate manners, and a sound unaffected voice, which he uses with the clear athletic articulation of a practised orator, and with a wide range and perfect command of expression.

The typist, MISS PROSERPINE GARNETT, is a brisk little woman about thirty, neatly but cheaply dressed, notably pert and quick of speech and not very civil in her manner. She is clattering away busily at her machine whilst MORELL opens the last of his morning's letters. He reads its content with a comic groan of despair.)

PROSERPINE: Another lecture?

MORELL: Yes. The Hoxton Freedom Group wants me to address them on SUNDAY morning. (*Hands her letter*) Tell them to come to church if they want to hear me on Sunday.
(*As they continue to work, their proceedings are enlivened by the entrance of the REVEREND ALEXANDER MILL, a young graduate of Oxford who is giving the East End of London the benefit of his*

University training. He is a conceitedly well-intentioned, enthusiastic immature novice. MORELL looks up indulgently)

MORELL: Well, Lexy? Late again, as usual.

LEXY: I'm afraid so.

PROSERPINE: You have all the work to do this afternoon.

LEXY: Is she in earnest, Morell?

MORELL: Yes. My wife's coming up for two days.

LEXY: But if the children had scarlatina, do you think it wise—

MORELL: Scarlatina! Rubbish! It was German measles. I brought it into the house myself from the Pycroft Street School. A parson is like a doctor, my boy; he must face infection as a soldier must face bullets. Catch the measles if you can, Lexy: my wife will nurse you; and what a piece of luck that will be for you! Eh?

LEXY: *(Smiles uneasily)* It's so hard to understand you about Mrs. Morell—

MORELL: Ah, my boy, get married to a good woman; and then you'll understand. That's a foretaste of what will be best in the Kingdom of Heaven. Yes. Get a wife like my Candida! *(Exits R, with some papers)*

LEXY: What a thorough loving soul he is!

PROSERPINE: Oh, a man ought to be able to be fond of his wife without making a fool of himself about her. Candida here, and Candida there! It's enough to drive anyone out of their senses to hear a woman raved about in that absurd manner merely because she's got good hair and a tolerable figure.

LEXY: I had no idea you had any feeling against Mrs. Morell.

PROSERPINE: I have no feeling against her. She's very nice, very good-hearted. I'm very fond of her. Now, about your work. Here's a list for the afternoon *(LEXY starts to leave at L)*

MORELL: *(Rushes in from R)* Is that a carriage I hear?

LEXY: *(Exiting at L)* It's a cab stopping in front. It's Mrs. Morell.

MORELL: Candida here already! (*Crosses to doorway*)

CANDIDA: (*Enters L*) Yes, James. I'm here. I'm home.

(*She is a woman of thirty-three, with the double charm of youth and motherhood. Her ways are those of a woman who has found that she can always manage people by engaging their affection, and who does so frankly and instinctively without the smallest scruple; but her courage, largeness of mind and dignity of character ennobles her cunningness*)

MORELL: Candida! My—my darling! I intended to meet you at the train. Oh! (*He embraces her with penitent emotion*) My poor love.

CANDIDA: There! There! There! I wasn't alone. Eugene has been down with us; and we traveled together.

MORELL: (*Pleased*) Eugene!

CANDIDA: Yes. He's struggling with my luggage, poor boy. Go out, dear, at once, or he'll pay for the cab, and I don't want that.

(*MORELL rushes out at L*)

PROSERPINE: Welcome home, Mrs. Morell.

CANDIDA: I didn't see you, Miss Garnett. It's good to be back, even for just a few days.

PROSERPINE: I'll tell Maria you have arrived.

CANDIDA: (*Looking out window*) Poor Eugene. He's so shy.

PROSERPINE: He can't be too poor. His uncle is an earl.

CANDIDA: Oh, he's a dear boy. We are very fond of him. (*PROSER-PINE nods and exits R*) Come in, Eugene. (*MARCHBANKS enters at L. He is a strange, shy youth of eighteen, with a shrinking manner that shows the painful sensitiveness of very swift and acute apprehensiveness in youth, before the character has grown to its full strength*) Why so sad? And why were you so melancholy in the cab?

MARCHBANKS: I was wondering how much I ought to give the cab-man. But it's all right. He beamed all over when Morell gave him two shillings. I was on the point of offering him ten.

(*MORELL enters L*)

CANDIDA: Oh, James, dear, he was going to give the cabman ten shillings!

MORELL: Never mind, Marchbanks. The overpaying instinct is a generous one.

MARCHBANKS: No: cowardice, incompetence. Mrs. Morell's quite right.

CANDIDA: Of course she is. (*Takes up handbag*) And now I must leave you to James for the present. I suppose you are too much of a poet to know the state a woman finds her house in when she's been away for three weeks. Now hang my cloak across my arm. (*He does*) Now my hat. Now open the door for me. (*He does*) Thank you.

(*She exits L*)

MORELL: You'll stay to dinner.

MARCHBANKS: I mustn't. I mean I can't.

MORELL: You mean you won't.

MARCHBANKS: No: I should like to, indeed. Thank you very much. But—but—the truth is, Mrs. Morell told me not to. She said she didn't think you'd ask me to stay, but that I was to remember, if you did, that you didn't really want me to.

MORELL: (*With affectionate seriousness*) My dear lad, in a happy marriage like ours, there is something very sacred in the return of the wife to her home. (*EUGENE reacts with a horror-stricken expression*) Candida thought I would rather not have you here; but she was wrong. I'm very fond of you, my boy, and I should like you to see for yourself what a happy thing it is to be married as I am.

MARCHBANKS: Happy! Your marriage! You believe that!

MORELL: (*Buoyantly*) I know it, my lad.

MARCHBANKS: (*Wildly*) No: it isn't true. I'll force it into the light.

MORELL: Force what?

MARCHBANKS: There is something that must be settled between us. You think yourself stronger than I am; but I shall stagger you if you have a heart in your breast.

MORELL: (*Powerfully confident*) Stagger me, my boy. Out with it.

MARCHBANKS: First—

MORELL: First?

MARCHBANKS: I love your wife.

MORELL: (*Amazed, then bursts into laughter*) Why, my dear child, of course you do. Everybody loves her: they can't help it.

MARCHBANKS: You dare say that of her! You think that way of the love she inspires! It is an insult to her.

MORELL: (*Also angry*) Take care. I am being patient. I hope to remain patient. Don't force me to show you the indulgence I should show to a child. Be a man.

MARCHBANKS: Oh, let us put aside all that cant. It horrifies me when I think of the doses, the sermons, she has had to endure all these years with you. You! You, who have not one thought—one sense—in common with her.

MORELL: (*Philosophically*) She seems to bear it pretty well. (*Seriously*) My boy, you are making a fool of yourself. It is easy to shake a man's faith in himself. To take advantage of that, to break a man's spirit is devil's work.

MARCHBANKS: I told you I should stagger you.

MORELL: (*They confront one another threateningly for a moment. Then MORELL recovers his dignity*) Eugene, listen to me. Some day I hope and trust you will be a happy married man like me. (*MORELL controls himself at EUGENE'S reaction, and continues with great artistic beauty of delivery*) You can be one of the makers of the Kingdom of Heaven on earth; and—who knows?—you may be a master builder where I am only a humble journey-man.

MARCHBANKS: Is it always like this for her? Preach! Preach! Preach!

MORELL: (*Stung*) Marchbanks: you make it hard for me to control myself. My talent is like yours, the gift of finding words for divine truth.

MARCHBANKS: It's the gift of gab, nothing more and nothing less. Oh, it's an old story: you'll find it in the Bible. I imagine King David, in his fits of enthusiasm, was very like you. "But his wife despised him in her heart."

MORELL: Leave my house. Do you hear? (*Advances on him threateningly*)

MARCHBANKS: (*Shrinks back*) Let me alone. Don't touch me. (*MORELL grabs him powerfully by the lapel of his coat*) Stop, Morell. Let me go!

MORELL: (*With slow emphatic scorn*) You little sniveling cowardly whelp. (*Releases him*) Go, before you frighten yourself into a fit.

MARCHBANKS: (*Relieved by the withdrawal of MORELL'S hand*) I'm not afraid of you. It's you who are afraid of me.

MORELL: (*Quietly, as he stands over him*) It looks like it, doesn't it?

MARCHBANKS: You are driving me out of the house because you daren't let her choose between your ideas and mine. Send me away. Tell her how you were strong and manly, and shook me as a terrier shakes a rat. If you keep back one word of truth from her, then you will know to the end of your days that she really belongs to me and not to you. Goodbye, Mr. Clergyman. (*As he turns to door, CANDIDA enters at L*)

CANDIDA: Are you going, Eugene? (*Looks observantly at him*) Well, dear me, just look at you. You are a poet, certainly. Look at him, James! Look at his collar! Look at his tie! Look at his hair! One would think somebody had been throttling you. Here! Stand still! (*She tidies him up*) There! Now you look so nice that I think you'd better stay for dinner after all, though I told you you mustn't. (*She puts a final touch to the bow tie. He kisses her hand*) Don't be silly.

MARCHBANKS: I want to stay, of course; unless the reverend gentleman, your husband, has anything to advance to the contrary.

CANDIDA: Shall he stay, James, if he promises to be a good boy and help me to lay the table?

MORELL: (*Shortly*) Oh yes, certainly: he had better stay. (*Starts off L*)

CANDIDA: I'll call you when it's time to help me. (*Holds out her hands to MARCHBANKS. He holds them. She exits at R*)

MARCHBANKS: (*Holds his hands which have touched hers to his heart*) I am the happiest of mortals.

MORELL: So was I — an hour ago. (*He exits L*)

MARCHBANKS: (*Alone, repeats her name*) Candida . . . Candida . . . (*Sees typewriter, pecks out her name with one finger*) C — a — n — d — (*Hits wrong key and suddenly the carriage shoots across with a bang. Worried, he starts turning knobs and wheels*)

PROSERPINE: (*Enters R*) What are you doing with my typewriter, Mr. Marchbanks?

MARCHBANKS: I'm very sorry, I only turned a little wheel. It gave a sort of click.

PROSERPINE: (*Fixes typewriter*) I suppose you thought it was a sort of barrel-organ. Nothing to do but turn the handle, and it would write a poem for you straight off, eh?

MARCHBANKS: (*Seriously*) I suppose a machine could be made to write a poem — a love letter.

PROSERPINE: How would I know?

MARCHBANKS: I thought clever people, like you, always had to have love affairs to keep them from going mad.

PROSERPINE: (*Outraged*) Mr. Marchbanks!

MARCHBANKS: Perhaps I shouldn't have alluded to your love affairs.

PROSERPINE: I haven't any love affairs.

MARCHBANKS: Really! Then you are shy, like me.

Candida

by George Bernard Shaw
Adapted by Aurand Harris

NOTICE

This book is offered for sale at the price quoted only on the under-standing that, if any additional copies of the whole or any part are necessary for its production, such additional copies will be purchased. The attention of all purchasers is directed to the following: This work is protected under the copyright laws of the United States of America, in the British Empire, including the Dominion of Canada, and all other countries adhering to the Universal Copyright Convention. Violations of the Copyright Law are punishable by fine or imprisonment, or both. The copying or duplication of this work or any part of this work, by hand or by any process, is an infringement of the copyright and will be vigorously prosecuted.

Permission for an amateur stage performance of this play may be obtained upon payment of a royalty fee of Fifteen ($15.00) Dollars for the first performance and Ten ($10.00) Dollars for each subsequent performance in advance. This fee must be paid for each performance whether for charity or gain, or whether admission is charged or not. Since performance of this play without the payment of the royalty fee renders anybody participating liable to severe penalties imposed by the law, anybody acting in this play should be sure, before doing so, that the royalty fee has been paid. Professional rights, reading rights, radio broadcasting, television and all mechanical rights, etc. are strictly reserved. Royalty fee should be paid directly to BAKER'S PLAYS, Boston, Mass. 02111.

Whenever the play is produced, the author's name must be carried in all publicity, advertising and programs. Also, the following notice must appear on all printed programs: "Produced by special arrangement with Baker's Plays, Boston, MA."

PROSERPINE: Certainly I am not shy.

MARCHBANKS: (*Secretly*) You must be: that is the reason there are so few love affairs in the world. We all go about longing for love: but we dare not utter our longing; we are too shy. (*Very earnestly*) Oh, Miss Garnett, I am just like you. (*Mysteriously*) I go about in search of love. But when I try to ask for it, this horrible shyness strangles me. (*Whispers*) It must be asked for: it is like a ghost; it cannot speak unless it is first spoken to. (*Usual voice, with deep melancholy*) All the love in the world is longing to speak; only it dare not, because it is shy! shy! shy! That is the world's tragedy.

PROSERPINE: You must stop talking like this, Mr. Marchbanks. It is not proper.

MARCHBANKS: (*Hopelessly*) Nothing that's worth saying is proper.

PROSERPINE: Then hold your tongue.

MARCHBANKS: But does that stop the cry of your heart?

PROSERPINE: It's no business of yours whether my heart cries or not. But I have a mind to tell you, for all that.

MARCHBANKS: I know. And so you haven't the courage to tell him?

PROSERPINE: Him? Who?

MARCHBANKS: The man you love. It might be anybody. The young curate, perhaps.

PROSERPINE: Mr. Mill! I'd rather have you than him.

MARCHBANKS: No, really: I'm very sorry; but you mustn't think of that. I—

PROSERPINE: (*Testily*) Oh, don't be frightened: it's not you. It's not any one particular person.

MARCHBANKS: I know. You feel that you could love anybody that offered—

PROSERPINE: (*Exasperated*) Anybody that offered! No, I do not. What do you take me for?

MARCHBANKS: It's no use. You won't make me real answers: only those things that everybody says.

PROSERPINE: Well, if you want original conversation, wait until Mr. Morell comes. He'll talk to you. Oh, you needn't make wry faces over him. He can talk better than you. (*With temper*) Yes! He'd talk your little head off.

MARCHBANKS: (*Suddenly enlightened*) Ah! I understand now. Your secret. Tell me: is it really and truly possible for a woman to love him? I must know. I can see nothing in him but words, sermons, preaching! You can't love that.

PROSERPINE: I simply don't know what you're talking about.

MARCHBANKS: You do. You lie.

PROSERPINE: Oh!

MARCHBANKS: Is it possible for a woman to love him?

PROSERPINE: (*Looks him straight in the face*) Yes. (*He turns away with a gasp*) Whatever is the matter with you?

CANDIDA: (*Is heard as she enters, carrying an oil reading lamp*) If you stay with us, Eugene, I think I will hand over the cleaning of the lamps to you. (*Rescued, PROSERPINE makes a quiet exit L*)

MARCHBANKS: You have soiled your hands! Yes, I will stay on one condition: that you hand over all the rough and dirty work to me.

CANDIDA: That is very gallant; but I think I should like to see how you do it first. (*Goes to door at L and calls*)

MARCHBANKS: Your beautiful fingers dabbling in paraffin oil!

CANDIDA: James . . . ? James, where are you?

MORELL: (*Off*) Coming, dear.

CANDIDA: You have not been looking after the house properly.

MORELL: (*Entering*) What have I done — or not done — my love?

CANDIDA: My own particular pet scrubbing brush has been used for blacking your shoes.

MARCHBANKS: (*Gives a wail of horror*) You, scrubbing with a brush.

CANDIDA: What is it, Eugene? Are you ill?

MARCHBANKS: Soiling your hands with a scrubbing brush.

CANDIDA: Never mind. Wouldn't you like to present me with a nice new one, with an ivory back inlaid with mother-of-pearl?

MARCHBANKS: (*Soft and musically*) No, not a scrubbing brush, but a boat to sail away in, far from here, where the marble floors are washed by the rain and dried by the sun; where the lamps are stars and don't need to be filled with paraffin oil every day.

MORELL: (*Harshly*) And where there is nothing to do but to be idle, selfish, and useless.

MARCHBANKS: (*Firing up*) Yes, to be idle, selfish, and useless: that is, to be beautiful and free and happy. Hasn't every man desired that for the woman he loves? That's my deal: what's yours? Sermons and scrubbing brushes!

CANDIDA: (*Quietly*) He cleans the boots, Eugene. You will clean them tomorrow for saying that about him.

PROSERPINE: (*Enters L, with telegram, gives it to MORELL who reads it*) A telegram. It's reply paid. The boy's waiting. (*To CANDIDA*) Maria is ready for you now in the kitchen, Mrs. Morell. The onions have come.

MARCHBANKS: (*Convulsively*) Onions!

CANDIDA: Yes, onions: nasty little red onions. And you shall help me slice them. To the kitchen.

MARCHBANKS: With all my heart! (*Runs off R*)

MORELL: (*Gives telegram to PROSERPINE*) Send an answer. Tell them. "No." I will not attend the meeting tonight. (*PROSERPINE nods and exits L*)

CANDIDA: Come here, dear. Let me look at you. My boy is not looking well. Has he been overworking? Must you go out every night lecturing and talking? Of course what you say is all very true, but it does no good. The truth is, James dear, they come because you preach so splendidly. Why, it's as good as going to a play for them. And the women: why do you think they are so enthusiastic?

MORELL: (*Shocked*) Candida!

CANDIDA: Oh, I know. You think it's your sermons. They are all in love with you. And you are in love with preaching because you do it so beautifully.

MORELL: Candida: what dreadful cynicism! Or—can it be—are you jealous?

CANDIDA: Yes, I feel a little jealous sometimes. Not jealous of any of them. Jealous for somebody else, who is not loved as he ought to be.

MORELL: Me?

CANDIDA: YOU! Why, you're spoiled with love. No: I mean Eugene.

MORELL: Eugene!

CANDIDA: It seems unfair that all the love should go to you. Someone should give some to him.

MORELL: You know that I have perfect confidence in you, Candida, of your goodness, of your purity.

CANDIDA: Oh, you are a clergyman, James, a thorough clergyman!

MORELL: So Eugene says.

CANDIDA: Eugene is always right. He's a wonderful boy. I have grown fonder and fonder of him. Do you know, James, that though he has not the least suspicion of it himself, he is ready to fall madly in love with me?

MORELL: Oh, he has no suspicion of it himself, has he?

CANDIDA: Not a bit. Some day he will know, and he will know that I must have known. I wonder what he will think of me then.

MORELL: No evil, I hope.

CANDIDA: That will depend on what happens to him. If he learns love from a good woman, then it will be all right: he will forgive me. But suppose he learns it from a bad woman, as so many men do, will he forgive me for not teaching him myself? For abandoning him for the sake of my goodness and purity, as you call it? Ah, James, how little you understand me. I would give them both to poor Eugene if there were nothing else to restrain me. But there is: put your trust in my love for you, James; for if that went, I should care very little for your sermons.

MORELL: His words!

CANDIDA: Whose words?

MORELL: Eugene's.

CANDIDA: (*Delighted*) He is always right. He understands me; and you, darling, you understand nothing. (*Laughs and kisses him*)

MORELL: (*He recoils as if stabbed*) How can you bear to do that when —

CANDIDA: (*Amazed*) My dear, what's the matter?

MORELL: Don't touch me.

CANDIDA: James!!

MARCHBANKS: (*Enters R*) Is anything the matter?

MORELL: (*With great constraint*) Nothing but this: that either you were right, or Candida is mad.

CANDIDA: (*Relieved and laughing*) Oh, you're only shocked. Is that all? (*Gaily*) This comes of James teaching me to think for myself, and never to hold back out of fear of what other people may think of me. It works beautifully as long as I think the same things as he does. But now! because I have just thought something different look at him! Just look!

MARCHBANKS: No, you are being cruel, and I hate cruelty. It is a horrible thing to see one person make another suffer.

CANDIDA: Poor boy. Have I been cruel? Did I make it slice nasty little red onions!

MARCHBANKS: Oh, stop, stop: I don't mean myself. You have tortured him frightfully. I can feel his pain.

CANDIDA: *I?* torture James? What nonsense!

LEXY: (*Enters L, anxious and important*) I've just come from the Guild of St. Matthew. They are in the greatest consternation about your telegram. They've taken the large hall in Mare Street and spent a lot of money on posters, and your telegram said you couldn't come.

CANDIDA: Couldn't come! But why, James?

MORELL: (*Almost fiercely*) Because I don't choose. May I not have one night at home with my wife, and my friends?

CANDIDA: (*They are all amazed at this outburst*) Oh, do go, James. We'll all go! We'll all sit on the platform.

MARCHBANKS: (*Terrified*) No! Everyone will stare at us.

CANDIDA: They'll be too busy looking at James to notice you.

MORELL: (*Looks at CANDIDA and then at MARCHBANKS*)

MORELL: Tell the Guild of St. Matthew that I am coming. And you are coming, Lexy, I suppose?

LEXY: Certainly.

CANDIDA: We're all coming, James.

MORELL: No. You are not coming; and Eugene is not coming. You will stay here and entertain him — to celebrate your return home.

CANDIDA: But, James —

MORELL: (*Authoritatively*) I insist. You do not want to come; and he does not want to come. Oh, don't concern yourselves: there will be plenty who will want to hear me. And — I should be afraid to let myself go before Eugene. He is so critical of preaching and sermons. He knows I am afraid of him. He told me so. Well, I shall show him how much afraid I am by leaving him here in your custody.

MARCHBANKS: That is brave. That is beautiful.

CANDIDA: But — but — Is anything the matter, James? I can't understand —

MORELL: (*Taking her tenderly in his arms and kissing her on the forehead*) Ah, I thought it was *I* who couldn't understand, dear.

(*The lights dim down and out, marking a passing of several hours. When the lights dim up, CANDIDA and MARCHBANKS are sitting by the fire. He is in a small chair, reading aloud. A pile of manuscripts are on the carpet beside him. CANDIDA is in the easy chair. The poker, a light brass one, is upright in her hand. Leaning back and looking intently at the point of it, she is in a waking dream, miles from her surroundings and completely oblivious of EUGENE*)

MARCHBANKS: (*Breaking off in his reading*) Every poet that ever lived has put that thought into a sonnet. (*Looks at her*) Haven't you been listening? (*No response*) Mrs. Morell!

CANDIDA: Eh?

MARCHBANKS: Haven't you been listening?

CANDIDA: (*With a guilty excess of politeness*) Oh, yes. I'm longing to hear what happens to the angel.

MARCHBANKS: I finished the poem about the angel quarter of an hour ago.

CANDIDA: I'm so sorry, Eugene. I think the poker must have hypnotized me.

MARCHBANKS: It made me horribly uneasy.

CANDIDA: (*She puts it down*) Why didn't you tell me? (*He picks up another manuscript*) No, no more poems, please. You've been reading to me ever since James went out. I want to talk. I want to be amused. Don't you want to?

MARCHBANKS: (*Half in terror, half enraptured*) Yes.

CANDIDA: Then come along. (*She moves her chair back to make room*)

MARCHBANKS: (*He timidly stretches himself on the hearth-rug, face upwards, and throws back his head across her knees, looking up at her*) Oh, I've been so miserable all the evening, because I was doing right. Now I'm doing wrong; and I'm happy. There is only one word I want to speak.

CANDIDA: What one is that?

MARCHBANKS: (*Softly*) Candida, Candida, Candida, Candida, Candida.

CANDIDA: And what have you to say to Candida?

MARCHBANKS: Nothing but to repeat your name a thousand times. Every time it is a prayer to you. I feel I have come into Heaven, where want is unknown.

MORELL: (*He enters L, halts on the threshold, and takes in the scene at a glance*) I hope I didn't disturb you.

CANDIDA: (*Starts up, but without the smallest embarrassment, laughing at herself. EUGENE, capsized by her sudden movement, recovers himself without rising, and sits on the rug hugging his ankles, also quite unembarrassed*) Oh, James, how you startled me! I was so taken up with Eugene that I didn't hear your latchkey. How did the meeting go off? Did you speak well?

MORELL: I have never spoken better in my life.

CANDIDA: Good! And where are the others?

MORELL: I believe they are having supper somewhere.

CANDIDA: Oh, in that case, Maria may go to bed. I'll tell her.

  (*Exits R*)

MORELL: (*Looking sternly down at MARCHBANKS*) Well?

MARCHBANKS: (*Impishly humorous*) Well?

MORELL: Have you anything to tell me?

MARCHBANKS: Only that I have been making a fool of myself here in private whilst you have been making a fool of yourself in public. (*Eagerly scrambling up*) But don't be afraid. I swore not to say a word in your absence that I would not have said in your presence.

MORELL: Did you keep your oath?

MARCHBANKS: It kept itself until a few minutes ago. Up to that moment I went on desperately reading to her my poems. I was standing outside the gate of Heaven, and refusing to go in. Oh, you can't think how heroic it was, and how uncomfortable! Then—

MORELL: Then?

MARCHBANKS: Then she couldn't bear being read to any longer.

MORELL: And you approached the gate of Heaven at last?

MARCHBANKS: Yes.

MORELL: Well? (*Fiercely*) Speak, man: have you no feeling for me?

MARCHBANKS: (*Softly and musically*) Then she became an angel; and there was a flaming sword that turned every way, so that I couldn't go in; for I saw that the gate was really the gate of Hell.

MORELL: (*Triumphantly*) She repulsed you!

MARCHBANKS: No, she offered me her wings, the wreath of stars on her head, the lilies in her hand, the crescent moon beneath her feet—

MORELL: (*Seizing him*) Out with the truth, man: my wife is my wife: I want no more of your poetic fripperies.

MARCHBANKS: (*Without fear or resistance*) Catch me by the shirt collar, Morell: she will arrange it for me as she did before. I shall feel her hands touch me.

MORELL: You young imp!

MARCHBANKS: I am not afraid now. I disliked you before. But I saw today—when she tortured you—that you love her. Since then I have been your friend. You may strangle me if you like.

MORELL: (*Releasing him*) Eugene, if you have a spark of human feeling left in you—will you tell me what has happened during my absence?

MARCHBANKS: What happened! Why, the flaming sword— (*MORELL stamps with impatience*)—Well, in plain prose, I loved her so exquisitely that I wanted nothing more than the happiness of being in such love. And before I had time to come down from the highest summits, you came in.

MORELL: So it is still unsettled. Still the misery of doubt.

MARCHBANKS: Misery! I am the happiest of men. I desire nothing now but her happiness. Oh, Morell, let us both give her up. Why should she have to choose between a wretched little nervous disease like me, and a pig-headed parson like you? Let us go on a pilgrimage, you to the east and I to the west, in search of a worthy lover for her: some beautiful archangel with purple wings—

MORELL: Some fiddlestick! Oh, if she is mad enough to leave me for you, who will protect her? Who will help her?

MARCHBANKS: She does not ask those silly questions. It is she who wants somebody to protect, to help. Some grown up man who has become as a little child again. Don't you see, I am the man, Morell: I am the man. Send for her and let her choose between— (*He stops as if petrified when he sees* CANDIDA *enter*)

CANDIDA: (*Enters R*) What on earth are you at, Eugene?

MARCHBANKS: James and I are having a preaching match; and he is getting the worst of it.

CANDIDA: (*Sees* MORELL *is distressed, she hurries to him, greatly vexed*) You have been annoying him. I won't have it. Do you hear, Eugene, I won't have it.

MARCHBANKS: Oh, you are not angry with me, are you?

CANDIDA: Yes, I am: very angry.

MORELL: Gently, Candida, gently. I am able to take care of myself.

CANDIDA: Yes, dear, of course you are. But you mustn't be annoyed and made miserable. (*To* EUGENE) Now are you sorry for what you did?

MARCHBANKS: (*Earnestly*) Yes. Heartbroken.

CANDIDA: Then off to bed like a good boy.

MARCHBANKS: (*To* MORELL) Oh, I can't go now, Morell. I must be here when she—Tell her.

CANDIDA: Tell her what?

MORELL: (*Slowly*) I—I meant to prepare your mind carefully for this.

CANDIDA: Yes, dear, I am sure you did.

MORELL: Well — er —

CANDIDA: Well?

MORELL: Eugene declares that you are in love with him.

MARCHBANKS: No, no, no, no, never. I did not, Mrs. Morell: it's not true. I said I loved you. I said I understood you, and that he couldn't.

MORELL: And he said that you despised me in your heart.

CANDIDA: Did you say that?

MARCHBANKS: (*Terrified*) No, no, no! I — I — (*Desperately*) It was David's wife.

MORELL: He has claimed that you belong to him and not to me; and, rightly or wrongly, I have come to fear that it may be true. We have agreed — he and I — that you shall choose between us now. I await your decision.

CANDIDA: Oh! I am to choose am I? I suppose it is quite settled that I must belong to one or the other.

MORELL: (*Firmly*) Quite.

MARCHBANKS: (*Anxiously*) Morell, you don't understand. She means that she belongs to herself.

CANDIDA: I mean that, and a good deal more, Master Eugene, as you will both find out presently. And pray, my lords and masters, what have you to offer for my choice? I am up for auction, it seems. What do you bid, James?

MORELL: (*With proud humility*) I have nothing to offer you but my strength for your defence, my honesty for your surety, my ability and industry for your livelihood, and my authority and position for your dignity. That is all it becomes a man to offer to a woman.

CANDIDA: And you, Eugene? What do you offer?

MARCHBANKS: My weakness. My desolation. My heart's need.

CANDIDA: That's a good bid, Eugene. Now I know how to make my choice. (*She pauses and looks curiously from one to the other*)

MORELL: (*Appeals from the depths of his anguish*) Candida!

MARCHBANKS: Coward!

CANDIDA: I give myself to the weaker of the two. (*EUGENE divines her meaning at once: his face whitens like steel in a furnace*)

MORELL: (*Bowing his head with the calm of collapse*) I accept your sentence, Candida.

CANDIDA: Do you understand, Eugene?

MARCHBANKS: Yes. I have lost. He cannot bear the burden.

MORELL: (*Incredulously*) Do you mean me, Candida?

CANDIDA: (*Smiles*) Let us talk like three friends. You have told me, Eugene, how nobody has cared for you since your old nurse died; how miserable you were at Eton, always lonely and misunderstood.

MARCHBANKS: I had my books. I had Nature. And at last I met you.

CANDIDA: Now I want you to look at this other boy here! Spoiled from his cradle. Ask James' mother and his sisters what it cost to save James the trouble of doing anything but be strong and clever and happy. Ask me what it costs to be James' mother and sisters and wife and mother to his children all in one. I build a castle of comfort and love for him. And when he thought I might go away with you, his only anxiety was — what should become of me! And to tempt me to stay he offered me his strength for my defence! his industry for my livelihood! his dignity for my position! his — ah, I am mixing up your beautiful cadences and spoiling them, am I not, darling?

MORELL: (*Embraces her*) It's all true, every word. You are my wife, my mother, my sisters, you are the sum of all loving care to me.

CANDIDA: (*Smiles, to EUGENE*) Am I your mother and sisters to you, Eugene?

MARCHBANKS: (*In disgust*) Ah, never. Out, then, into the night with me!

CANDIDA: You are not going like that, Eugene?

MARCHBANKS: (*With the ring of a man's voice*) I know the hour when it strikes. I am impatient to do what must be done.

MORELL: Candida, don't let him do anything rash.

CANDIDA: Oh, there is no fear. He has learnt to live without happiness.

MARCHBANKS: I no longer desire happiness. Life is nobler than that. Parson James, I give you my happiness with both hands. I love you because you have filled the heart of the woman I loved. Goodbye.

CANDIDA: One last word. How old are you, Eugene?

MARCHBANKS: As old as the world now. This morning I was eighteen.

CANDIDA.: Eighteen! Will you, for my sake, make a little poem out of the two sentences I am going to say to you? And will you promise to repeat it to yourself whenever you think of me?

MARCHBANKS: Say the sentences.

CANDIDA: When I am thirty, she will be forty-five. When I am sixty, she will be seventy-five.

MARCHBANKS: In a hundred years, we shall be the same age. But I have a better secret than that in my heart. Let me go now. The night outside grows impatient.

CANDIDA: Goodbye. (*She takes his face in her hands; and as he divines her intention and falls on his knees, she kisses his forehead. Then he flies out into the night. She turns to MORELL, holding out her arms to him*) Ah, James! (*They embrace. But they do not know the secret in the poet's heart*)

THE END

A Toby Show
by Aurand Harris

Introduction

A *Toby Show* is a pastiche of a type of entertainment popular in a colorful era in American drama that began in the early years of the twentieth century and began a precipitous decline after the Great Depression. Before the development of radio, talking pictures, and television, troupes of traveling actors brought live entertainment into rural areas of the country—especially the mid-west and South. Playing in local opera houses and in tents, these repertoire companies performed three-act plays—a different bill each night of the week—supplemented by vaudeville between acts as well as orchestra or band. From this branch of the entertainment business—there were four hundred traveling companies at one time—emerged a truly American folk character named Toby.

Toby was a red-headed, freckle-faced country comedian, a country bumpkin who outsmarted the city slicker. Just as Harlequin in European drama became the stellar attraction in *Commedia dell' arte's* company of stock characters, Toby developed into the chief attraction of the rural Toby troupes. The plays they presented may have utilized familiar plots and drawn their stock characters in poster colors, but they entertained unsophisticated audiences and in many ways approximated America's version of the *Commedia dell'arte*. A *Toby Show* is a re-creation of a classic form, now extinct, in a period of early American theatre.

It is impossible to document Toby's birth anymore than Paul Bunyan's or any other folk hero's. Some authorities try to link him to Greek or Shakespearean comedies; others, to the New England rube or the "silly kid" roles in early commercial plays. Whatever his origin, Toby finally emerged from the mists of mythology and moved into the theatrical spotlight somewhere in Louisiana, sometime in 1911 when Fred Wilson, the red-headed, freckled, leading comic on Murphy's Comedians appeared one night as Toby Haxton in *Clouds and Sunshine* and the next, as Toby Thompkins in *Out of the Fold*. On the third evening, his character was called another name, but the audience dubbed him Toby. The name stuck and Toby was on its way to being born.

For many years Toby shows were only an arm of the repertoire theatre. Eventually, plays starring him filled the production schedule. It is estimated that in 1916 there were two hundred comedians calling themselves Toby — each a star in his territory.

Fittingly, *A Toby Show* retells the Cinderella story, one of the rep playwright's favorite plots, skillfully injecting Toby into the familiar story as a variation of the fairy godmother just as the "country playwrights" once did.

The play is a celebration of Toby. A SHOW starring TOBY, who, with his crown of red hair, was once King of the tent repertoire theatre in rural America.

TOBY
CINDY
MRS. VANUNDERSQUIRE
SOPHIA
MAUDERINA
BURTOCK
COLONEL

TIME: *A summer day, 1915*

SCENE: *The parlor of the Van Undersquire mansion.*

A Toby Show

(*After a short overture by a small orchestra at the right side of the stage — traditionally a march and a popular song of the day, i.e. "O Susannah!" — the house lights dim as the footlights come up, and Toby steps out in front of the curtains lighted with a follow spot. His entrance music is "Turkey in the Straw." Toby is a likeable, fun-loving, country rube comic with red freckles, red wig, and country clothes. He talks, jokes, and laughs freely with the audience.*)

TOBY: Howdy, folks. Glad to see you. (*To front row.*) Glad you got here early and got a front row seat. (*To back row.*) And howdy do to you, way back there. Lady, will you please remove — (*Grins.*) Will all the ladies, and gentlemen, too, please remove their hats. No hats, no smoking, and if the baby cries, please take it out. (*Lively.*) Today Toby comes to town! If you don't know Toby, I'll tell you who he is. He's a country fellow. Some folks call him a hayseed, but you can bet your bottom dollar he can outsmart any city slicker. He's got red hair on his head and red freckles on his nose. And he's about as high as a chicken sitting on a roosting-pole. (*Measures his own height with his hand.*) Proudly I present America's own favorite, funny fellow — Toby! (*Spotlight moves to side of proscenium arch. No one enters. Spotlight moves back to Toby, who grins and waves.*) He's standing right in front of you. Yup, I'm Toby! You're dang tootin' I'm Toby. And we're going to give you a humdinger of a rip-snorting Toby Show! (*Closer.*) In this play, you're going to see, there is a girl who has a step-mother — Oh, hoity-toity! (*Poses comically and wiggles hips.*) And she makes the girl do all the work while her own two daughters primp and get ready for a party. And at the ball that night there's a Prince who — I ain't going to tell no more. I have to lickity-split now, because I'm on my way to this swell-elegant house. I've come to the big city — all dressed up in my best bib and tucker — to get me a job. And here it is. (*Takes newspaper clipping from pocket.*) "Rich lady wants handyman for light work." I'm handy and a man and the lighter the work the better! (*Laughs.*) This is the place where it's all going to happen. Pull the curtains and let the show begin!

(*Music for the opening of the curtain. SCENE: elegant drawing room, 1915. Ornate double doorway, D.R. Smaller doorway D.L. Three open French doors, or open archways, at back, elevated on a one-step platform. Terrace exterior backing. Ornate fireplace with large portrait above it on left wall. Ornate mirror with console table beneath on the right wall. Sofa with table behind it at R. Chair by fireplace at L. Toby is awed by the grandness.*)

TOBY: Take a look at that. Swell-elegant! I'll bet she's so rich she has four cars, one to drive in each direction. (*Laughs. Telephone rings.*) Something is ringing. Cowbell! Church bell? Fire bell! Oh, it's one of them new tel-E-phones. (*Rings.*)

CINDY: (*Off.*) I'm coming. I'm coming. Just a minute. I'm coming.

TOBY: (*By proscenium arch.*) Somebody's coming. (*Rings. CINDY enters L, running and carrying a dress. She is young, pretty, and is dressed plainly. Although she is treated like a servant, she is always vital, cheerful, and sometimes spunky. She speaks into the telephone.*)

CINDY: Hello. The VanUndersquire residence. Who is calling, please? The Society editor of the *News*! She'll be here. She's coming. She's here. Mrs. VanUndersquire. (*MRS. VANUNDERSQUIRE enters L. She is elegantly dressed, haughty, commanding, and comically affected in her speech and manner.*)

TOBY: Hoity-TOITY! I'll bet she's so rich she has a different dentist for every tooth! (*Laughs.*)

MRS. V.: (*Stands, holding the telephone.*) Mrs. VanUndersquire? Yes, Mrs. VanUndersquire is speaking.

TOBY: It's Mrs. VanUnderSKIRT.

MRS. V.: Oh, the society editor! Yes, I am giving a dance tonight — a masquerade ball — in honor of his Royal Highness Prince Burtock. (*Laughs affectedly.*) He's a real live prince. (*To Cindy.*) Hurry and finish my dress. (*Into telephone.*) His mother was a friend of my late second husband. She married a Balkan prince, and now her son — no throne of course — is honoring us with a visit. (*To Cindy.*) Hang the lanterns in the garden, get the chairs for the orchestra, and, (*CINDY starts to R, then L, drops dress.*) My dress! Oh, you nitwit! (*Into telephone.*) No, no, not you — not you! (*Glares at Cindy.*) My stepdaughter.

CINDY: I can't do everything at once.

MRS. V.: Well, someone do something!

TOBY: Hold the horses! I'm a-coming! (*Exits at side.*)

MRS. V.: Yes, the Prince is young, handsome, and very rich. I haven't seen him, but he is arriving today. We are expecting him at any minute, expecting the bell to ring at any moment. (*Doorbell rings.*) Oh, the bell! He's here. The prince is here! (*To Cindy.*) Put on the apron and cap. (*Points to them on table.*)

CINDY: Apron and cap?

MRS. V: The maid's apron and cap.

CINDY: But I'm not the maid.

MRS. V.: You will be the maid while the Prince is here. The cap — the apron — ON! (*Doorbell rings. CINDY gets apron and cap.*) He's waiting. You half-wit! (*Into telephone.*) No, no, no, not you!

TOBY: (*Enters R, and shouts happily.*) Howdy, folks. The door was open and here I am!

MRS. V.: (*Freezes, her back to Toby.*) He's here. (*Puts telephone down, CINDY freezes, cap over eyes. MRS. V. regains her composure, turns slowly and speaks with great affection, and curtsies.*) How do you do. I am Lizzenna — (*Swallows.*) — Lizzenna Smythers VanUndersquire.

TOBY: (*Shakes her hand vigorously.*) Howdy do. Glad to meet you, Lizzie.

MRS. V.: (*Gasps in astonishment.*) We have been waiting — to see your countenance.

TOBY: See my what? (*Alarmed.*) Is it showing?

MRS. V.: We are honored that you will inhabit our unostentatious domicile.

TOBY: You want to trade that big word for two little ones?

MRS. V.: (*Surprised, then laughs with forced affectation.*) Oh-oh-oh, What a royal sense of humor. You do understand English?

TOBY: Sure. If you can speak it.

MRS. V.: I shall call my daughters. (*To Cindy.*) Tell Sophia and Mauderina to come at once. Hurry. (*CINDY exits R.*) If I may take the liberty, I have something to whisper in your ear.

TOBY: (*Quickly cleans out ear with finger and tilts head.*) Let her whisp.

MRS. V.: My daughters in YOUR presence may be a bit shy— overcome with modesty.

TOBY: Aw, shucks, fetch 'em in. My sister, she's modest, too. Yessirree. My sister is so modest that she blindfolds herself when she takes a bath. (*Laughs. MRS. V. is startled, then affectedly joins the laughing. They build the laughing, each topping the other. CINDY enters R.*)

CINDY: The girls are ready. (*CINDY exits R.*)

MRS. V.: Entrez-vous. (*SOPHIA enters R and stands. She is comically overdressed, imitates her mother's affectation.*) May I present my older daughter, Sophia.

TOBY: Howdy do. Glad to meet you, Soffee. (*Shakes hands vigorously.*)

SOPHIA: (*She ALWAYS speaks musically, up and down the scales, holding certain notes with melodic tremors.*) How do you do. How do you do.

TOBY: Listen at her talk. She sounds prettier than the church organ.

MRS. V.: Sophia is precociously musical.

SOPHIA: (*Speaking very very musically.*) Be at home here—now, please do-oo-oo-oo. How do you do. How do you do.

TOBY: (*Imitates her comically, with the same musical rhythm and notes.*) I'm at home when I hear a cow—moo-oo-oo-oo. (*Laughs.*)

MRS. V.: And now may I present my second daughter. (*Waves.*) Entrez-vous-hoo. (*MAUDERINA enters R, and stands. She is also comi-*

cally overdressed, but the two daughters look nothing alike. She is also comically affected.) My younger daughter, Mauderina.

TOBY: Howdy do. Glad to meet you, Maud. (*Shakes hands vigorously.*)

MAUDERINA: (*She ALWAYS speaks in verse, stressing clearly and loudly each rhyming word.*) A welcome BOUQUET of words we SAY, and wish you MAY enjoy your STAY.

TOBY: Listen at her talk! Fancy words that rhyme like a book.

MRS. V.: Mauderina is lyrical, versical and poetical. Come, girls. Show him to the garden and do take a peep at my gazebo.

TOBY: Peep? (*Aside.*) I'll take a goldarn good look.

SOPHIA: A summer house is a place for a rendezvous. (*SOPHIA exits L.*)

TOBY: For who?

MAUDERINA: Turtle doves FLY—BY—and bill and COO.

(*MAUDERINA exits L.*)

TOBY: They do? (*Looks after girls and shouts.*) Hot diggitty-dog! Hold the horses! I am a-coming! (*Makes a fast funny exit, stops, waves.*) Tootle-doo. (*Exits. CINDY enters R. There is a loud sound offstage of a flying machine.*)

CINDY: What is that? It sounds like a machine in the air. (*Runs to French doors at back. Points in air, excitedly.*) It is. It's a flying machine. He's circling around.

MRS. V.: Tell him to fly away.

CINDY: (*Motions.*) Go away. He's waving back. (*Waves.*) Hello.

MRS. V.: Tell him to GO AWAY.

CINDY: Go away. Away. He's coming back.

MRS. V.: I will tell him to leave. (*MRS. V. goes to French doors.*) Go away! Away! And stay away! (*Sounds dim out quickly.*) There. (*Romantically*) Tonight — in the moonlight, the Prince will dance with Sophia and Mauderina.

CINDY: I hope he will ask me to dance.

MRS. V.: You to dance?

CINDY: I like to dance.

MRS. V.: You are plain with no beauty or proper clothes.

CINDY: But I —

MRS. V.: You will stay in the kitchen. (*Points. CINDY starts.*) You and the Prince. (*Laughs.*) For you it is pots and pans.

   (*MRS. V. exits R.*)

CINDY: Pots and pans . . . apron and cap . . . press her dress . . . (*Angrily throws dress on chair, then with spunk puts her chin up.*) If my real mother were here . . . (*Looks at portrait over mantel.*) If my father . . . if you were still alive . . . I'd go to the ball. I would wear . . . (*Grabs the dress.*) . . . a beautiful dress. (*Holds dress up in front of her.*) and the Prince would look right at ME. I'd be — a razzle-dazzle. (*Sings and dances a fast fox-trot. Stops and then pantomimes talking to Prince.*) Oh, I would be charmed to dance, your highness — if you can tango. (*She sings and does a funny tango. BURTOCK enters at back at French doors. He is young, handsome, and a Prince. He wears coveralls, helmet with goggles which are pushed up. His face is smeared with dirt and there is a small cut on his forehead. CINDY ends her dance, curtsies and smiles at imaginary partner.*) Thank you, your highness. You dance very well.

BURTOCK: So do you.

CINDY: (*Does a double take.*) What? Who? (*Sees Burtock.*) Where did you come from?

BURTOCK: I — I fell out of the sky. (*Takes off helmet and comes into room.*)

CINDY: It's you! In the aeroplane!

BURTOCK: (*Nods and smiles.*) Yes.

CINDY: You're bleeding!

BURTOCK: I bounced a little as I landed on the drive.

CINDY: I'm very good at first aid. Hold still. (*Wipes his face with apron.*)

BURTOCK: It's nothing.

CINDY: You can't bleed to death. Besides your face is dirty. (*Wipes it vigorously.*)

BURTOCK: (*Face to face. He smiles.*) Your face is—very pretty.

CINDY: (*Resigned, states facts cheerfully.*) No. I am plain and have no beauty. The Prince will never dance with me.

BURTOCK: The Prince?

CINDY: Tonight.

BURTOCK: I think he would.

CINDY: I'll be in the kitchen. Miss Pots and Pans, that's me.

BURTOCK: You are expecting a Prince?

CINDY: He just arrived. The Prince is in the garden.

BURTOCK: (*To audience.*) He is?

CINDY: But he—he isn't like my prince.

BURTOCK: Your prince?

CINDY: My prince is dressed in shining armour and he will come riding on his white horse to rescue me.

BURTOCK: That's quite a prince.

CINDY: When you're an orphan you make things up—use your imagination.

BURTOCK: Are you an orphan? I am, too.

CINDY: No mother? No father?

BURTOCK: Just a grandfather.

CINDY: Just a step mother.

BURTOCK: Then that makes us — well, we're a-a-a-a-a —

CINDY: Yes, we are! We're both a-a-a-a — Shake!

BURTOCK: Shake! (*They shake hands. MRS. V. is heard singing loudly off R.*)

CINDY: Here she comes. You have to go! She TOLD you to go away.

(*MRS. V. enters singing loudly and comically.*)

MRS. V.: "Here comes the bride. Here comes Sophia — or Mauderina — " (*Sees Cindy.*) You still here! Off to the kitchen! and who — who is this?

BURTOCK: I am — (*MRS. V. looks him over with her lorgnette.*)

MRS. V.: I can see. You are the new handyman.

BURTOCK: I —

MRS. V.: Never mind your name. You look strong — if untidy. Take him to the kitchen.

BURTOCK: But —

MRS. V.: Both of you — out, out, out!

CINDY: Come on. I'll wash your face. (*She starts to pull him toward the kitchen.*)

BURTOCK: (*Amused, smiles to audience.*) All right. (*Doorbell rings.*)

MRS. V.: The doorbell! Answer the door. (*CINDY holding Burtock's arm starts R.*) No, no, take him out. (*CINDY starts L.*) Hang the lanterns. Dump the garbage! (*Doorbell rings.*) I'm coming. (*Hurries Cindy off.*) Out! Out! Out! (*CINDY and BURTOCK exit L. COLONEL enters R. He is a comic old man — "G-string Man" — with a white beard and he is hard of hearing. He uses a cane. MRS. V. turns and sees him.*) Who are you?

COLONEL: (*Speaks in a funny squeaky voice — it sounds like a G-string of the violin.*) I know who I am. Who are you?

MRS. V.: I am Lizzenna Smythers VanUndersquire.

COLONEL: Eh?

MRS. V.: (*Louder.*) I am Lizzenna Smythers VanUndersquire.

COLONEL: I am pleased to meet you. Mrs. VanUnderWATER.

MRS. V.: Undersquire. Squire!

COLONEL: Fire? Fire!

MRS. V.: No, no!

COLONEL: Please don't shout. You will frighten Ulysses. (*To imaginary dog to whom he speaks throughout the play.*) Quiet, Ulysses. That's a good boy — good boy. We have found the right house — Mrs. Van UnderSHIRT. (*Pets imaginary dog.*)

MRS. V.: Ulysses? You mean, there is a dog in my house?

COLONEL: Eh?

MRS. V.: A dog! Dog! DOG!

COLONEL: Three dogs? No just one. Ulysses. Happy, happy boy. That's right, wag your tail, waggy waggy.

MRS. V.: Dogs, I do not perMIT.

COLONEL: Eh?

MRS. V.: Do not perMIT.

COLONEL: Sit? Thank you. (*COLONEL sits.*)

MRS. V.: You do not underSTAND.

COLONEL: Stand? (*COLONEL stands. MRS. V. draws herself up to full height.*)

MRS. V.: I am Mrs. VanUndersquire and I do not —

COLONEL: I AM pleased to meet you, Mrs. VanUnderGROUND.

MRS. V.: Take your dog out, out, out! (*There are three loud long dog barks. She gasps.*)

COLONEL: Good boy. (*Pets dog.*) Now that Ulysses has said hello, I will tell you why I am here. I am here because of my grandson, Prince Burtock.

MRS. V.: Prince Burtock! Your grandson!

COLONEL: It was a long march, but I made it . . . made it . . . made it. (*He goes to sleep standing up.*)

MRS. V.: You are here because — (*COLONEL snores and whistles.*) He's gone to sleep standing up! Colonel, wake up! (*Stomps her feet. There are long and loud dog barks. She jumps.*) Oh! Oh! Oh!

COLONEL: (*Opens his eyes and points.*) You stepped on Ulysses' paw.

MRS. V.: (*Looks about confused.*) Oh, excuse me. Excuse me, Ulysses.

COLONEL: My grandson, Prince Burtock — is here for a special reason. He is to choose a wife. His mother, my daughter, married a foreign title —

MRS. V.: Yes, I know.

COLONEL: And when she died she left a will.

MRS. V.: A will?

COLONEL: The Prince to inherit his fortune must marry . . . must marry . . . (*Goes to sleep. Snores loudly.*)

MRS. V.: Yes, marry . . . marry? (*COLONEL snores and whistles.*) Oh, he's snoring again. Colonel, wake up. Oh, Ulysses, Ulysses, where are you? (*Whistles and gives a heavy stomp. There is a loud and long barking of a dog.*)

COLONEL: (*Points.*) You stepped on Ulysses' tail. The Prince, to inherit his fortune, must marry a daughter of his mother's friend, Mr. Charles VanUndersquire.

MRS. V.: Yes, I am MRS. Van Undersquire.

COLONEL: I am glad to meet you, Mrs. VanUnderTAKER.

MRS. V.: I have two daughters.

COLONEL: Eh?

MRS. V.: Daughters. I have TWO.

COLONEL: A FEW? No, he can only marry one. I am here to see that he marries and inherits his fortune.

MRS. V.: And I will see that you are victorious!

COLONEL: (*Salutes.*) Good soldier.

MRS. V.: The Prince is already here.

COLONEL: Here?

MRS. V.: In the gazebo.

COLONEL: Come on a zebra?

MRS. V.: No, no. He — look. Oh, he is hidden by the SHRUB.

COLONEL: In the bathTUB.

MRS. V.: He is with my two daughters.

COLONEL: Three of them — in the bathTUB.

MRS. V.: In the garden!

COLONEL: He got here first. Oh, shooty-tooty. In the war I was first . . . first . . . (*COLONEL sleeps, snores and whistles.*)

MRS. V.: (*Elated.*) The Prince must marry a VanUndersquire daughter. (*MRS. V. talks to portrait on wall.*) Oh, Mr. VanUndersquire, how fortunate that I made you adopt my two daughters. Now one of them will be a Princess. I must alert them. (*Goes to L, waves, calls sweetly.*) Sophia . . . Mauderina. Of course there is his daughter, Cindy. But the

Prince would never look at her. And — (*Scheming.*) — she is dressed like a servant, and I will keep her in the kitchen. (*SOPHIA enters L.*)

SOPHIA: Yes, Ma-maw. (*MAUDERINA enters L.*)

MAUDERINA: My NAME. I CAME.

MRS. V.: I have just learned from his grandfather — (*Points. GIRLS look. COLONEL snores and whistles.*) why the Prince is here. He is to pick a bride. (*GIRLS giggle.*) And the bride must be you — (*MAUDERINA giggles.*) or you. (*SOPHIA giggles.*) You must charm the Prince with your wit and beauty. (*GIRLS react.*) Sparkle in conversation. Walk with grace. (*MRS. V. demonstrates.*) And — remember — in time of trouble — a lady can always faint. (*She faints on sofa. Loud and long dog barks are heard.*)

COLONEL: (*Opens eyes and points.*) You are sitting on top of Ulysses. (*Angry dog barks are heard. MRS. V. screams, jumps up, runs, as if dog is snapping at her heels. Girls scream and run.*)

MRS. V.: OH! Oh! Help! Help! (*TOBY rushes in L.*)

TOBY: Whoa! Hold the horses! (*To audience, enjoying the confusion, laughs.*) Listen at the chickens cackling in the hen house.

MRS. V.: (*Controlling herself.*) Oh, thank heavens you are here. You have arrived just in time.

TOBY: In time for what?

MRS. V.: There is someone here to see you.

TOBY: To see me?

MRS. V.: Colonel, he is here.

COLONEL: Eh?

MRS. V.: Happy surprise! (*TOBY and COLONEL look at each blankly.*)

TOBY: Who's he?

COLONEL: Who is he?

MRS. V.: Your grandson.

COLONEL: My grandson? No.

MRS. V.: No.

COLONEL: He's not even my grandDAUGHTER.

MRS. V.: Not the Prince? Then who are you?

TOBY: Toby.

MRS. V.: Toby?

TOBY: Your new hired man.

MRS. V.: A servant? A servant! Oh, oh, oh! I am going to faint. (*She sways and gasps like a chicken cackling.*) Cluck . . . cluck . . . cluck . . . cluck . . . (*SOPHIA and MAUDERINA also cackle in hysteria.*)

COLONEL: Don't sit on Ulysses! (*Dog barks.*)

TOBY: (*Enjoying it.*) Cackle! Cackle! The chicks are clucking again!

(*CINDY and BURTOCK enter.*)

CINDY: What's going on?

BURTOCK: What has happened? (*All noise stops. MRS. V. looks at Burtock.*)

MRS. V.: You—you? (*She points to Toby.*) If he is Toby, then who— (*She points to Burtock.*) are you?

BURTOCK: I am—

COLONEL: Burtock!

BURTOCK: Grandfather!

CINDY: The Prince! In the kitchen, washing dishes! No! (*CINDY exits.*)

BURTOCK: Cindy! (*BURTOCK exits after her.*)

MRS. V.: The Prince! In the kitchen! DUMPING GARBAGE!! Oh, oh, oh! (*She sways and starts to faint, clucking. GIRLS squeal.*)

TOBY: The old hen is cackling again! (*MRS. V. faints in his arms. He is surprised.*) Whoa! (*TOBY laughs.*) Pull the curtains before she lays an egg! (*He laughs. Dog barks. GIRLS squeal. Quick curtain. Orchestra plays fast curtain music, "Turkey in the Straw." TOBY appears in front of the main curtain, lighted by a follow spot.*) Well, that was sure a whooping, mixed up, dingeroo! (*Laughs.*) And there's l−o−t−s MORE to come. Now you're going to see the second act of our Toby Show. The actors are all ready and waiting. Mrs. Hoity-toity−you ought to see her! She's all dolled up in a highfaluting hat. All right! We're going to begin. So get your feet in the stirrup and hang on to the saddle. Ready, set, let'er go! (*Curtain music as curtain opens. Scene: the same. A round table with a fancy cover of ruffles, lace, etc., and a tea service is at center, and a chair is by it.*) There's the table all set for the tea party. And here comes Mrs. VanUnderPAY. (*MRS. V. enters R, humming. She wears an elaborate hat.*)

MRS. V.: Toby!

TOBY: Yes ma'm.

MRS. V.: Come inside. Come inside. Are your feet dirty?

TOBY: Yes ma'm. But I've got my shoes on. (*Laughs and steps into "scene." MRS. V. looking down at him through lorgnette.*)

MRS. V.: Now that I know you are the handyman − and I have to have one for tonight − I must ask you a few questions. Have you any physical disabilities?

TOBY: Well, I couldn't see much until I was fourteen, then I got a haircut. (*TOBY laughs, enjoying the interview more and more, while MRS. V. becomes more exasperated.*)

MRS. V.: Oh, I do believe you are next door to a simpleton.

TOBY: Oh. Then I'll move away from you.

MRS. V.: YOU are not smart enough to talk to a half-wit.

TOBY: All right. I'll send you a letter! (*Laughs.*)

SOPHIA: (*Off, calls.*) Ma-maw. Ma-maw.

MRS. V.: (*Looks off R, cries with joy.*) It's Sophia! All dressed for tea.

(*SOPHIA enters R, wearing elaborate comic hat.*)

SOPHIA: I am ready, Ma-maw . . . Ma-maw.

MRS. V.: Oh my dear, you look beautiful. (*To Toby.*) Tell me, she is beautiful, is she not?

TOBY: Yes, she is not.

MRS. V.: (*Looks off R, cries with joy.*) And Mauderina. Come in, my dear. (*MAUDERINA enters R, also wearing a comic hat.*)

MAUDERINA: Mirror, mirror on the WALL, Tell me THAT my HAT is fairest of them ALL.

MRS. V.: It is enchanting, exquisite. Each of you will be the apple of his eye.

TOBY: Yup, the Apple Sisters, Cora 'n' Seedy.

MRS. V.: (*Sternly to Toby.*) And you — Off to the kitchen!

TOBY: Food! (*Starts eagerly.*) Yes ma'm. (*Stops.*) And if you don't mind, I'll have a ham sandwich.

MRS. V.: (*Waves him out.*) With pleasure!

TOBY: Oh, no. with mustard! (*TOBY laughs and exits L.*)

MRS. V.: Footsteps. The Prince! Ready, girls. Radiate. (*They smile.*) Scintillate. (*They pose hands.*) And gravitate. (*All curtsy low. Loud dog barks are heard. COLONEL enters R, running and holding imaginary leash which pulls him forcefully.*)

COLONEL: Stop, Ulysses. Stop, Ulysses. Ulysses, stop. He is chasing a rat! (*There is loud confusion. All speak at once. MRS. V. holds skirt and hops in a circle.*)

MRS. V.: A rat! E-e-ek!

SOPHIA: A rat! Hel-l-lp! (*Her voice goes up the scales as she goes up on footstool.*)

MAUDERINA: A rat! Where's the cat! (*COLONEL stops by Mrs. V. All is suddenly quiet.*)

COLONEL: No, Ulysses. She is not a rat. (*Dog barks questioningly.*) She is Mrs. VanUnderWEAR. (*Dog barks and there is bedlam again. GIRLS squeal. COLONEL is pulled about.*) Stop, Ulysses. (*BURTOCK enters at back. COLONEL, at back stops. All noise stops.*) Burtock!

MRS. V.: The Prince!

SOPHIA: The Prince!

MAUDERINA: The Prince!

MRS. V.: Radiate . . . Scintillate — Gravitate. (*MRS. V. and GIRLS quickly take positions smile and curtsy.*) Sophia and Mauderina will entertain us with a bit of artistic diversion. Mauderina will recite and declaim a favorite poem.

BURTOCK: She is one — one of the daughters that I have to marry?

COLONEL: Eh?

BURTOCK: To marry — according to the will.

COLONEL: The Battle of Bunker Hill! (*They continue talking.*)

MRS. V.: (*Confidentially to Mauderina.*) He is whispering — about you. Look! Cupid's arrow has pierced his heart. (*BURTOCK looks at Mauderina and then at audience horrified.*) Sophia will entertain with a vocal rendition of her favorite song.

BURTOCK: She is the other one? The other daughter?

COLONEL: Eh?

BURTOCK: I have to choose between those two?

COLONEL: You do.

BURTOCK: No. (*They argue.*)

MRS. V.: The Prince is growing more and more — enamoured. (*BUR-TOCK looks at girls, then at audience.*)

BURTOCK: I am APPALLED.

MRS. V.: (*Elated with her eavesdropping.*) ENTHRALLED! Oh, he has been smitten, bitten by the love bug.

COLONEL: You must announce your bride at the ball tonight.

BURTOCK: Neither one! (*Looks.*) Never! (*Looks.*) Ever!

COLONEL: Then it is goodbye to all your money.

BURTOCK: No.

COLONEL: Goodbye to your aeroplane.

BURTOCK: (*Weaker.*) No.

COLONEL: Yes. (*BURTOCK opens his mouth to speak but nothing comes out. He walks to girls, mouth open wider in a gasp. He can only gulp and stammer, and exits quickly at back.*)

COLONEL: Tonight the Prince will choose his bride.

MRS. V.: It will be an announcement ball.

COLONEL: A victory ball! Forward march! (*He exits.*)

MRS. V.: Now hurry! Dress in your finest and look your prettiest for the ball. (*SOPHIA goes R.*)

SOPHIA: I will be the one he chooses. (*SOPHIA exits R.*)

MAUDERINA: You will SEE. He will choose ME. (*MAUDERINA exits R.*)

MRS. V.: Oh, tonight will be a royal occasion! I must sparkle and shine. Yes, I will wear all my jewels. I'll get them from the safe. (*Looks at portrait.*) Mr. VanUndersquire, tonight there will be a royal proposal. The only question is, which daughter will be the bride. (*Looks around cautiously.*) Good. There is no one about to spy. (*The picture above the fireplace is hinged on one side. She swings the picture away from the wall, revealing a small wall safe; works dial lock and opens door of safe.*) Turn to six, back to four, and . . . I will wear the diamonds tonight. The diamonds which were Cindy's mother's, but which now are mine. (*Takes out and opens deposit box.*) Now let me see . . . Oh, all these papers . . . marriage certificate — birth certificates . . . (*Looks around, holds up blue legal paper, speaks confidentially.*) The will! Mr. VanUndersquire's last will — which I must keep a secret. No one — no one must ever read it. (*Off R, an ornate screen moves slowly through the doorway into the room. She sees it, gasps, and drops all the papers.*) What . . . who is it? (*TOBY is behind the screen and moving it. He peeks around the side.*)

TOBY: Me. Toby.

MRS. V.: Oh. Put the screen on the terrace for the musicians. (*She picks up papers, but overlooks the blue one which is left on floor.*)

TOBY: Yes ma'm. (*Leaves screen. Comes to her.*)

MRS. V.: Tonight you have a special duty. Now listen carefully. You must keep your eye on Cindy! (*He nods.*) Do not let her speak to anyone. (*He nods.*) Especially NOT to the Prince. (*TOBY starts to nod, then shakes head.*) She is to say not — a — word! (*TOBY gives his head a shake on each word. MRS. V. puts box back in safe and swings picture back in place.*) Quick, be about your work. Take away the tea table. Tidy up the room. And — remember your special duty. Nothing can stop my plans. Nothing WILL stop my plans. I will triumph tonight! (*MRS. V. exits R.*)

TOBY: Whoa now. Hold the horses. Keep my eye on Cindy. Don't let Cindy speak to nobody. Nothing will stop what plans? Something is going on here that ain't right. I may be from the country but I know right from wrong. And I'm beginning to smell a rotten apple in the barrel. A fish in the fruit dish! A skunk in the woodpile! (*TOBY points after Mrs. V. CINDY enters L.*)

CINDY: What are you shouting about?

TOBY: Monkey-business! And it's about you.

CINDY: Me?

TOBY: I'm going to do a little detectin'. How long have you been working here? (*CINDY picks up pink napkin from floor.*)

CINDY: I don't work here. I live here.

(*CINDY hands him napkin. TOBY puts napkin into pants pocket.*)

TOBY: How long have you been living here? (*CINDY picks up blue paper.*)

CINDY: I was born here. (*CINDY hands him blue paper.*)

TOBY: Born here! (*TOBY puts paper into pants pocket.*)

CINDY: It's my father's house. (*CINDY points to portrait.*) That's his picture.

TOBY: Is he—was he your Pa? Then who is she—(*TOBY wiggles and imitates Mrs. V.*) Mrs. Hoity-toity!

CINDY: (*Laughs.*) She is my stepmother.

TOBY: And she's got two daughters. She makes YOU stay in the kitchen—Ding-dang it! I keep thinking I've heard this before.

CINDY: Heard what before?

TOBY: Like—like in a story. (*Beams with his discovery.*) Yup, that's it! It's just like a story I read. And at the ball the Prince will—YOU have to go to the ball tonight.

CINDY: Oh, no.

TOBY: OH, YES! You're dang tootin' she HAS to go. And you HAVE to dance with the Prince.

CINDY: Dance with the Prince! (*Defeated.*) No. She'd see me.

TOBY: It's a dress-up masquerade, ain't it?

CINDY: I could wear a mask. YES! (*Depressed*) No. My voice.

TOBY: Don't talk. Yup, that's it. That's my orders! Don't talk to nobody. You are to say—(*Repeats business of shaking head.*) not—a—word.

CINDY: I wouldn't stay long.

TOBY: That's right! Just like the story. (*Impresses the fact.*) Yessirree, you HAVE to leave before the clock strikes twelve.

CINDY: Yes! NO!

TOBY: Now what?

CINDY: I don't have a dress — a beautiful dress.

TOBY: Now that's a twisteroo! How in the heck — in the story — did she get a dress!

CINDY: I have the shoes! My mother's wedding slippers.

TOBY: I got to get her a dress. Where there's a will there's a way — even if you don't know the way. You have to take the bull by the horns . . . put your shoulder to the wheel — you have to milk the cow to fill the bucket. (*TOBY sees tea table, points, yells with an idea.*) Whoa! Hold the horses! What's your favorite color?

CINDY: Pink.

TOBY: I've got the saddle on the right horse! Get behind that screen and start undressing.

CINDY: Undressing!

TOBY: SO you can start putting on your pink party dress. (*CINDY goes to screen.*)

CINDY: What party dress?

TOBY: The one I'm going to make, like in the story.

CINDY: What are you doing?

TOBY: I'm waving my magic wand. Scoot! (*She goes behind screen. TOBY, beside tea table, waves hand over it and sings a square-dance call.*) Dos-à-dos. Your partner to the right. Here's your dress. For tonight! (*With a flourish, he pulls off the lace, ruffled, circular pink tea tablecloth. Holds it around his waist — a perfect skirt. He twists and sings: Tune, "She'll Be Comin' Round the Mountain.*") "Oh, she'll be wearin' lace and ruffles at the ball, She'll be wearin' lace and ruffles at the ball . . ." Put it on! (*Tosses skirt over the screen. Thinks and points at his own body.*) She's got shoes, and a skirt — waist! She needs a waist. Waist. Waist. (*Looks about room, grins when he sees long beautiful silk table runner on table behind sofa.*) AH, a waist! (*Waves hand over runner.*) Dos-à-dos, Sashay to the fiddle; And hope to heck it fits around

around the middle. (*Pulls off runner, wraps it around his chest like a bodice. Sings.*) "Oh, she'll be wearin' a sash and bow at the ball, She'll be wearin' a sash and bow at the ball . . . !" Put it on. (*Tosses it over the screen. Feels his shoulders.*) Sleeves. Sleeves . . . Sleeves? Sleeves? (*Grins and points at two pillows on sofa, puffy like large puffed sleeves.*) Sleeves! (*Waves hand over pillows.*) Dos-à-dos Promenade, go, Two puff sleeves at your el-bow. (*Pulls out pillows from ornate casing. Sings.*) "She'll be wearin' sleeves that puff-puff, She'll be wearin' sleeves that puff-puff, She'll be wearing sleeves that puff-puff at the ball." Put 'em on! (*Throws them over the screen.*) How do you look?

CINDY: (*Shouts.*) I—I need—the dress needs—something around the neck.

TOBY: Around the neck. Something around the neck. Dog collar? Horse collar? Cow bell?

CINDY: I know! The dress needs—a ruffle of flowers!

TOBY: A ruffle of flowers! A ruffle of flowers? (*TOBY looks around.*) A ruffle of flowers? Flowers! Flowers! I've found a garden of them! (*Rips off a ruffle of artificial flowers which edge the lampshade. Holds it to his neck. Sings.*) "She'll be decked and dolled with flowers at the ball, She'll be decked and dolled with flowers at the ball . . ." Put 'em on! (*Throws it over screen.*) Now, how do you look?

CINDY: (*Shouts, excited and loud.*) OH! OH, quick! it's falling! I need a pin!

TOBY: A pin?

CINDY: (*In panic.*) A big one! A safety pin! QUICK!

TOBY: Hold everything! (*Frantically feels himself, takes big safety pin which fastens his only and one suspender on his pants.*) A pin . . . a pin . . . a big pin . . . Ah! (*Sings.*) "She'll be pinned UP tight and right, She'll be pinned UP tight and right . . ." Take it. (*Hands her pin. Her hand reaches for it.*) "She'll be pinned UP tight and right at the ball." (*Gives a pull to keep his pants up.*)

CINDY: I think—I think I am all ready.

TOBY: If you're ready, we're ready. Get set. One—out of the shed! Two—straight ahead! Three—knock us dead! (*CINDY floats out from around the screen, a vision of loveliness in her lace, ruffles, and puffs and flowers. She has put on a beautiful dress, which has the same material and trimmings which Toby collected. Her mob cap is gone and her hair hangs loose and shining. TOBY gives a loud whoop and continues it until she completes a circle, showing off her dress.*) Hoo-oo-oo-oo! You look like a princess!

CINDY: Do I?

TOBY: All you need is a crown. A crown . . . a crown . . . (*To audience.*) Anybody got a crown? A gold crown? Silver crown? (*Looks around room.*) A crown . . . a crown . . . (*Points at ornate birdcage by plants.*) A crown! (*Takes off the top ornament of the cage, which makes a perfect crown. Puts it on her head. Sings.*) "She'll be wearing a golden crown, She'll be wearing a golden crown, She'll be wearing a golden crown at the ball."

CINDY: Am I a — razzle-dazzle?

TOBY: You're a whiz-dinger! A ripsnorting whooper-dooper! (*TOBY pulls up pants.*)

CINDY: And I'll dance . . . yes, I'll dance with the Prince . . .

TOBY: (*Like a square dance caller.*) Oh, swing your partner . . . (*They start to square dance.*) Bow to your corners all, Bow to your partners all; To the left go around the hall. Dos-à-dos your corner. Back to back around you go. Dos-à-dos your partner. Go around, heel and toe. (*CINDY stops. His pants start to fall. CINDY sees them and points.*)

CINDY: Stop! Look!

TOBY: Whoa! Hold the horses! (*His pants fall, showing his bright red long underwear. He desperately tries to pull them up. They fall again. Orchestra plays loud music: "She'll Be Comin' Round the Mountain" for fast curtain. TOBY appears in front of the main curtain, lighted by a follow spot. He is fastening up the one suspender to his trousers. He laughs.*) Well, that was a hustle and a tustle! But we got her dressed. Yessirree! even if I got UNdressed. (*Laughs.*) But everything's all hitched up again, hitched up tight and right and out of sight! (*Laughs.*) And there's L-O-T-S MORE to come! If you've got a wooden nickel you can bet that in the last act of our play, the fiddles will be playing and the dressed-up folks a-dancing. And we're going to see IF Cindy gets the Prince, and — and IF I don't stop talking we'll never get to the party. So button on your dancing shoes and we'll cut a caper.

(*Ballroom music begins. TOBY exits at side. Curtains open. Scene: the same. At the back, the terrace is a fairyland of colored lanterns and masked couples dancing in colorful costumes. Music continues during the following scene of pantomime. TOBY enters from L, turns on a light. Stage is bright for the rest of the act. He motions for CINDY to enter. She enters L, beautiful in her princess costume and carries a half-mask. They stop at C. TOBY smiles and nods to assure her the moment is right for her entrance. He motions for her to go ahead. She nods, starts to back but stops, suddenly frightened. He motions for her to go ahead. She shakes her head and turns to go back L. He grabs her hand and turns her around, motions for her to go to the ball. She goes to back, ready to make her entrance at the ball. He stops her. He mimes zipping his lips and puts finger in front of his mouth signaling her not to talk. She nods, puts finger to her lips and starts again. He stops her. He holds up ten fingers, and then two more (twelve o'clock) then with two fingers running reminds her when she must leave. She nods, puts mask on, and runs off at back at L. BURTOCK who is dressed like a handsome fairytale prince and wearing a half-mask enters from R at back with MAUDERINA who is dressed in elegant gypsy costume and wearing a half-mask. They stop dancing.*)

PRINCE: Shall we? It is quieter in here. (*They move down. TOBY is hiding by proscenium arch.*)

TOBY: It's the Prince and all dressed up like—like a prince!

(*MAUDERINA sits.*)

BURTOCK: You are . . . you are?

MAUDERINA: Guess. Guess.

BURTOCK: Mauderina? (*MAUDERINA pushes up her half-mask.*)

MAUDERINA: Yes! Yes! And WHO are YOU? (*BURTOCK raises his half-mask.*) The Prince. I KNEW.

BURTOCK: I have something I must say. I—I—there is a question I must ask. The question is—(*BURTOCK kneels.*) Will you be my—(*BURTOCK swallows.*)

TOBY: Hold the horses! She's the wrong one.

BURTOCK: I, Prince Burtock, ask you — if you will — to be — to be — my — (*Turns away with distressed look.*) I cannot do it.

MAUDERINA: Continue your ADDRESS. My answer will be . . .

BURTOCK: My question is: (*Holds out hand.*) Can you read my palm? A gypsy fortune teller should read it well.

MAUDERINA: I thought the question would BE, "Will you marry ME?"

BURTOCK: Shall we dance? (*They dance off at back.*)

TOBY: Jumping jack-rabbits and leaping lizards, that was a close one! He can't ask her to jump the broomstick. He has to ask — Oh, oh! (*Shakes his head, dizzy.*) Out again, in again, gone again — he's here again! (*Quickly runs to side proscenium. BURTOCK enters at back with SOPHIA, who is dressed in an elegant native Swiss costume. They stop at C.*)

SOPHIA: O-o-o-o! We are all alone.

TOBY: It's Soffee, braying like a donkey.

BURTOCK: I have something I must say — something to ask you.

SOPHIA: Me-e-e-e?

BURTOCK: Yes, you-oo-oo. You!

TOBY: He's going to do it again.

BURTOCK: You are — Sophia? (*SOPHIA raises mask.*)

SOPHIA: How did you know? (*BURTOCK raises mask.*)

BURTOCK: I am Burtock.

SOPHIA: Oh, your highness. (*BURTOCK kneels.*)

BURTOCK: I must ask you — ask you — will you — will you be — will you be — (*BURTOCK swallows.*)

TOBY: Hold the horses! You're barking up the wrong tree!

BURTOCK: Will you be — (*BURTOCK makes a painful face and painful sound.*) U-u-ugh. I cannot do it.

SOPHIA: Be-be-c-d-e-f-g-h-I — will.

BURTOCK: My question is: Dressed like a Swiss Miss, can you yodel?

SOPHIA: Yodel? I thought he would propose! (*SOPHIA suddenly starts to yodel loudly.*) Yodel-lay-hitteos-who, etc.

BURTOCK: Shall we dance? (*They dance off R.*)

TOBY: (*Imitates yodel.*) Yodel-lay-etc. He flew that coop just in time! (*TOBY looks off L.*) Oh, oh, somebody else was listening at the keyhole. It's Mrs. VanMESSEDUP all DRESSEDUP like the Queen of Hearts, and the Colonel, looking like Napoleon. (*MRS. V. and the COLONEL peek in at the doorway at L, then enter. She is dressed in an elegant Queen of Hearts costume with much sparkling jewelry. He is dressed like Napoleon.*)

MRS. V.: The Prince was talking to each girl.

COLONEL: Eh?

MRS. V.: Talking, I'm sure, of wedding bells, rice and mating.

COLONEL: Ice skating?

MRS. V.: Is he trumping up to elope?

COLONEL: Jumping a rope?

MRS. V.: If we only knew — knew that he did propose.

COLONEL: If he blew his nose!

MRS. V.: No! If he did propose!

COLONEL: Without any clothes!

MRS. V.: Oh, Colonel, our victory is won.

COLONEL: Victory!

MRS. V.: Toby! Toby! (*TOBY steps into scene.*)

TOBY: Yes ma'm.

MRS. V.: That was quick. Tell the orchestra — where are your white gloves? (*TOBY holds up hands, looks at them.*)

COLONEL: The victory waltz! Shall we dance! (*COLONEL turns and steps into TOBY'S arms. They dance off R, COLONEL singing. TOBY is surprised, then laughs and dances wildly. SOPHIA runs in from back.*)

SOPHIA: Ma-maw! Oh Ma-maw, Ma-maw! A new girl has arrived.

MRS. V.: A new girl?

SOPHIA: A princess, and — and she is so beautiful. (*MAUDERINA runs in at back.*)

MAUDERINA: Oh, Ma-maw. YOU, YOU, YOU, Must DO, DO, DO — Something! A new girl in a pink GOWN, With a golden CROWN —

MRS. V.: Who? Who is she?

SOPHIA: We don't know. No one knows.

MAUDERINA: She BORES US. He IGNORES US.

MRS. V.: The Prince may dance with her, but the Prince will marry you — or you! COME, GIRLS! We must find the Colonel. March. (*GIRLS exit R.*) This is War! (*MRS. V. exits R. CINDY, wearing half-mask, enters from back with BURTOCK.*)

BURTOCK: Shall we rest this dance? (*She nods.*) You dance beautifully. (*She nods.*) But you don't speak. (*She shakes her head.*) You only smile. Shall we take off our masks? (*He raises his. She shakes head.*) You can talk? (*She nods.*) Then why don't you? Are you playing a game? (*She is surprised. He smiles.*) Ah, you are. Well, I can play that game, too. You don't talk. I don't talk. When you speak, I will speak. (*He takes an independent stance. She is confused. She motions wildly with her hands. He looks at her and smiles. She sits on sofa. He sits. She stands. He stands. She sits, stands, sits. He quickly follows her, doing the same, ending with them both standing. She laughs. He laughs. He bows and offers his arm. Music starts. She rises and steps into his arms. Pause. He gives a big wink to the audience. They dance off at back. TOBY enters L, and recites romantically.*)

TOBY: Roses are red, Violets are blue; He wrote on her slate, "I (*spells*) l−o−v−e you!" Yessirree! Those two are heading straight for the hitching post! Things are sure happening fast! It's got me all tuckered out! (*Takes pink napkin from pocket and wipes forehead.*) Where did I get this napkin? And a lot more things are going to happen before the clock strikes twelve. (*Takes out blue paper will and fans himself.*) Where did I get this piece of paper? And what the heck is it? (*Reads.*) "The last will of Charles VanUndersquire!" That's Cindy's Pa. This is his will! "I hereby do give this house to my only daughter, Lucinda . . . !" To Cindy! This is her house. It's not Mrs. VanUnderSTAIRS'. "And I do give all the family jewels, a diamond necklace, a ruby . . ." All the jewelry Mrs. VanUnderNEATH is wearing belongs to Cindy! Well, I'll be hornswoggled! It's enough to get your dander up − and mine's getting up pretty high! She sure is Mrs. VanUnderHANDED. She may have HIGHfaluting ways, but the truth is − she is a LOW-down, sneaking, stealing, no-count horse thief! (*Waves will.*) Stealing this house, stealing Cindy's jewels, making Cindy do the work! Right's right, and wrong's wrong, and this wrong I'm a-going to make right! Right? You're darn tootin' that's right! (*CINDY runs in from back carrying mask.*)

CINDY: Oh, Toby, it's a wonderful party. It's the best night of my life. (*CINDY sits, kicks off shoes, wiggles toes.*)

TOBY: And you can bet your life that YOUR life is going to get better. Where'd he go?

CINDY: To get two glasses of punch.

TOBY: Punch or lunch. Here he comes.

CINDY: Isn't he wonderful.

TOBY: Yup, she's found her knight in shining armor. (*BURTOCK enters at back and comes to Cindy, as TOBY goes to proscenium, outside of set. CINDY quickly puts on her mask. BURTOCK gives one cup to Cindy. They hold cups for toast, then sip. BURTOCK takes cups and puts them on table.*) Now you watch. In about a minute the clock is going to start striking twelve. And when it does things are going to start popping like popcorn in a skillet. (*Twelve slow, loud strikes of a clock are heard. CINDY freezes, looks about in panic.*)

BURTOCK: What is it? What's wrong? It is just the clock striking − striking twelve. (*CINDY starts to R.*) Where are you going? (*He blocks *her way. She runs to back. He blocks her. She runs to L.*) Why — why are you running away? Stop! (*He grabs her. She struggles, pushes him away, and he comically falls into chair, and she runs L, exits.*) Wait! Wait! (*He quickly starts after her, but is stopped by COLONEL who enters L.*)

COLONEL: Burtock!

BURTOCK: Out of my way! (*They dodge side to side.*)

COLONEL: Eh?

BURTOCK: Out of my way!

COLONEL: Play croquet? (*BURTOCK takes COLONEL under his arms, lifts him and puts him aside.*)

BURTOCK: Step aside! Aside! (*BURTOCK exits.*)

COLONEL: Bride! Bride! Picked your bride! He has picked his bride! Ah, his fortune is saved. I will call the family. Oh, we will sing a wedding song, and the wedding bells with ring . . . (*He pulls with right hand an imaginary bell rope.*)

TOBY: (*Loud and funny.*) Ding — dong. (*COLONEL, pleased, pulls rope with other hand.*) Dong — ding! (*COLONEL, elated, pulls rope with fast short movements, as he exits R. TOBY enjoys it all.*) Ding-dong-ding-dong-ding-dong. (*Laughs. BURTOCK rushes in L.*)

BURTOCK: She's gone. Not a trace of her — nothing. (*TOBY points to slippers.*)

TOBY: (*Whispers.*) Her slipper . . . her slipper. (*TOBY creeps to them.*)

BURTOCK: She disappeared — like that. But where? Where? Where? (*TOBY puts slipper at left of BURTOCK who ignores it.*) Where IS she? And who — who is she? (*BURTOCK turns to R. TOBY cautiously puts slipper at R by BURTOCK.*) How can I find her if I don't know — who! I don't know her name. I don't have a clue. I don't have — (*TOBY throws the slipper in front of BURTOCK. He sees it. Smiles at audience.*) Her slipper! Her golden slipper. (*Picks it up.*) Is there a name inside, an initial? Let me see. (*He goes to back, holds shoe up to light.*

CINDY runs in from L, without her mask. TOBY, at R, sees her and motions her to leave. She does not see him, but searches for her shoes. She sees one, picks it up. BURTOCK sees her, comes D.C., stands by her. She looks up, sees Burtock standing by her. CINDY covers her face, runs off L with shoe.)

CINDY: Oh — oh — OH!

BURTOCK: Cindy. Of course, the princess is Cindy! (*COLONEL enters R, followed by MRS. V., SOPHIA and MAUDERINA. They stop in single line, each facing front.*)

COLONEL: Forward march. Hep, hep, hep, hep . . . Burtock, we are here.

MRS. V.: Here.

SOPHIA: Here.

MAUDERINA: Here. (*TOBY has joined the end of the line.*)

TOBY: Here. (*They turn and look at him. There is loud dog barking. TOBY turns and pets imaginary dog in line beside him.*)

COLONEL: We are waiting for you to name your bride. Have you chosen, have you selected, have you —

BURTOCK: I HAVE! (*MRS. V. and DAUGHTERS break the line and exclaim with eager anticipation.*)

COLONEL: Which one?

BURTOCK: The one whose foot will fit this golden slipper.

COLONEL: Dipper? Put her foot in a dipper? (*MRS. V. grabs slipper.*)

MRS. V.: Girls! Put it on! (*They pull at slipper.*)

SOPHIA: Let me!

MAUDERINA: I — I — I will TRY — TRY — TRY.

MRS. V.: Girls! The oldest first. Sophia, put it on! (*SOPHIA sits. All watch as she comically with grunts, struggles to put it on.*)

SOPHIA: Uh! OOO! Ugh! Ow! (*TOBY acting as referee, kneels and takes shoe.*)

TOBY: Her foot's too long, longer than a horse trough! (*Laughs.*) Next! (*MAUDERINA grabs slipper, struggles and grunts comically to put it on.*)

MAUDERINA: O-o-o-o! Hu-hu-uh-uh! Aw!

TOBY: Her foot's wide, wider than a barn door. (*Laughs.*) Next girl!

MRS. V.: There is no other.

BURTOCK: Yes, there is. She is in the kitchen. Toby — call Cindy.

TOBY: You're darn tootin' I'll call. I'm the best hog-caller in the county. (*Crosses, comically gives a prize-winning hog call, ending with a loud "Cindy." CINDY runs in L, wearing maid's dress and cap.*)

CINDY: Did someone call?

BURTOCK: It is your turn to try on the slipper.

TOBY: Sit. (*CINDY sits.*)

SOPHIA: It won't fit HER foot.

MAUDERINA: Never, NEVER, Ever, EVER. (*PRINCE kneels and dramatically puts slipper on Cindy's foot.*)

TOBY: It fits!

BURTOCK: Cindy, will you . . . ?

COLONEL: No, NO! She's the maid. You will lose your fortune!

BURTOCK: Yes, I will lose a fortune, but I will gain a princess. Cindy, will you marry me?

CINDY: Yes!

COLONEL: NO! You must marry a daughter of Mr. Van — VanUndersquire!

TOBY: Hold the horses! Lightning has just struck twice! Prince, you got the right bride AND your fortune. Cindy is Mr. VanUndersquire's REAL daughter.

MRS. V.: Out! Out! Out! You are discharged. You meddling country bumpkin, you uncouth hayseed, you—

TOBY: And one more thing!

MRS. V.: Out! Out of my house!

TOBY: Your house? (*TOBY takes blue paper will from pocket.*) I happen to have in my hand—

MRS. V.: What is that?

TOBY: The last will of Mr. Van—

MRS. V.: Give it to me. Thief! (*She grabs for it, but TOBY hands it to BURTOCK who reads it.*)

TOBY: No, I ain't no thief. The thief is—Mrs. VanUnderCLOTHES!

MRS. V.: Oh!

TOBY: You stole this house. You stole them jewels. Everything belongs to Cindy. It's all writ there—in the will.

BURTOCK: It is true, Cindy. You are your father's only legal heir.

MRS. V.: Out! Out! Out!

TOBY: No ma'm. You got the cart hitched to the wrong horse. This time it's you and your mangey brood that's going out—out—out. (*To Sophia.*) YOU—to the kitchen—and wash the dishes. Start galloping! (*SOPHIA comically gasps, cries, and runs off L.*) YOU—to the kitchen—and scrub the floor. Start trotting! (*MAUDERINA comically gasps, cries, and runs off L.*) And you—(*MRS. V. draws herself up haughtily.*) YOU—DUMP THE GARBAGE! (*He points to kitchen. MRS. V. does not move. TOBY shouts.*) Ulysses! Ulysses! (*He whistles for dog. Dog barks are heard.*) Sick-em, Ulysses. Go get her. Sick'em, Ulysses. (*Loud dog barks continue.*) (*MRS. V. suddenly yells, runs toward doorway at L, grabs back of dress, shakes hips, as if attacked by dog.*)

MRS. V.: Help! Help! Oh! Oh! Oh! Oh! (*She runs off, with dog barking.*)

COLONEL: (*To center.*) Victory! Come, Ulysses. Forward march. Hep, (*Dog bark.*) hep, (*Bark.*) hep, (*Bark.*) . . . (*COLONEL marches off R.*)

BURTOCK: (*To center.*) It's waiting. Your white horse is waiting. (*CINDY runs to him.*) I'll start the propeller. (*Offers his arm to Cindy. She takes it and they run to back. They stop. CINDY waves to Toby. They exit.*)

TOBY: Off they fly — to live happy as the dickens! And me, I'm going back to the farm and the chickens. (*Orchestra starts playing "Turkey in the Straw!" TOBY dances.*) "Turkey in the straw, haw, haw, haw; Turkey in the Hay, hay, hay, hay. We gotta go and you gotta go, 'Cause this is the end of our Toby Show." (*Main curtain closes. He is in front of it in follow spot. Music continues. He waves and shouts, "Goodbye." Curtain calls. TOBY takes his place in the center of the cast line. ALL bow for a final time. TOBY steps forward and takes a bow alone. Curtains close behind him, in follow spot, he waves and calls "Goodbye," and exits at side.*)

THE END

AURAND HARRIS is eminently qualified to adapt this series of classic dramas for use in the contemporary educational theatre programs of the English speaking world.

Author of fifty published plays, some of which have been translated into ten languages, and produced in more than twenty countries, Mr. Harris is the recipient of more than fifteen playwriting awards and honors, and a Creative Writing Fellowship from the National Endowment for the Arts.

He is the Co-editor of two popular anthologies, PLAYS CHILDREN LOVE (Doubleday) and PLAYS CHILDREN LOVE, VOLUME 2, (St. Martin's Press). His published works for stage is the subject of a major anthology and critical analysis by Dr. Lowell Swortzell of New York University.

Aurand Harris was the second American playwright (Arthur Miller was the first) to be invited to China, 1987, to stage one of his plays, for the Children's Art Theatre of Shanghai. His RAGS TO RICHES opened the Chinese Children's Theatre to Western culture.

Harris is a celebrated teacher both of playwriting and children. He has lectured widely and taught at leading universities, among them Columbia Teacher's College; New York University; the University of Kansas; the University of Texas, Austin; Indiana University — Purdue University in Indianapolis; the University of Hawaii; California State University — Northridge, etc.